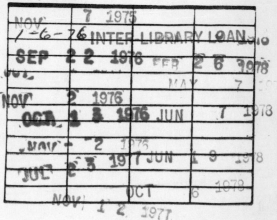

The Sun
Never
Sets
on
IBM

The Sun Never Sets on

IBM

Nancy Foy

William Morrow & Company, Inc.
New York   1975

Published in the United States in 1975.

Copyright © 1974 by Nancy Foy

First published in Great Britain in 1974
under the title *The IBM World*.

All rights reserved. No part of this book
may be reproduced or utilized in any form
or by any means, electronic or mechanical,
including photocopying, recording or by
any information storage and retrieval
system, without permission in writing from
the Publisher. Inquiries should be addressed
to William Morrow and Company, Inc.,
105 Madison Ave., New York, N.Y. 10016.
Printed in the United States of America.
Library of Congress Catalog Card Number
74-21638
ISBN 0-688-02891-8

lovingly dedicated to

FRANCES SURR

my favourite editor, friend
and travelling companion

Contents

Acknowledgments

A book like this owes its entire existence to other people. The function of the author is simply to get out of the way and let the people who were there tell the story. When they are several hundred IBM employees and former employees (or 'graduates' as I shall call them), I am willing to accept a certain collected bias in favour of the corporation.

Because of a certain reticence built into the corporate culture, many of the IBM insiders must remain anonymous. However, I can name a few, and others will know how grateful I am for their help by the absence of their names here. Saul Gellerman and Nate Newkirk deserve special thanks, not only for the time and guidance they gave me early in the research process, but for their patience and insight in reviewing almost every chapter.

The IBM graduates, as their numbers have grown in recent years, seem to have created a new 'IBM Family'. When Charley Smith left World Trade to take a senior position at Bankers' Trust in New York he became a father figure to many of the graduates there. (He also took time to see me at a critical stage in my research.) Another helpful member of the family was Bob McGrath, keeper of its genealogy. He began to publish the *IBM alumni directory* as an avuncular avocation, then discovered there was a healthy demand for such a publication. Among other graduates who devoted time and care to my education about World Trade were Tor Blomquist, Ed Somppi, Werner Lier, Ridley Rhind and the late Frank Smith. At least half a dozen others made major contributions and reviewed chapters perceptively.

The silent heroes of this book are the men who are still inside IBM World Trade — men in more than a dozen countries who purposely or unwittingly gave me current information as well as their own feelings about the company. I am particularly grateful to Robert, who gave me encouragement and empathy at a time when IBM was making it particularly difficult to get through the outer barriers.

I can name with a clear conscience the stalwart corps of IBM Communications people whose task it was to limit the communications, to contain the 'exposure risk' my book seemed to threaten, and sometimes to give real help; not one of them ever told me anything more than he (and IBM) intended I should learn. Most of them did their jobs with tact, individuality and a light touch that made the constant interaction cheerfully challenging. Notable among these are Sandy McGillivray in the United States, Dick Wight in Paris, and Erik Aagesen in Copenhagen who loaned me an IBM 'golfball' typewriter while I completed the final draft.

The one-man UK task force assigned to cope with the 'Foy problem' was Alan Tull, a good-natured and patient friend who understood that I understood his problems, and accepted the artificial adversary situation gracefully. He was admirably backed up by Paul Quin and John Wells at various times. All three had to give 'assistance' when Gil Jones said 'assist!' (and withhold it most of the rest of the time). I must also thank Richard Spiegelberg of *The Times*, Nick Valery of *New Scientist*, Bob Heller of *Management Today*, Keith Richardson of the *Sunday Times* and Angie Pantages of *Datamation* for allowing me to dream up article assignments about IBM and follow them through.

Stuart Hauser, Mogens Boman, Ed Williams and Philip Dorn contributed important outside views that helped me keep the book in perspective as the writing progressed.

As a mother must, mine faithfully read every page of final draft; but few mothers could make such perceptive suggestions for a clearer, better-organized story. She earned the dedication. Finally, there were the people who laboured daily with me. Lauren Williams typed most of the text and administered most of the coffee. John Stokdyk and Adam Spinks proofread and corrected my spelling errors. John also did most of the calculations and charts for the appendix. My long-suffering descendants Ann and John endured hours of interviews, days of shoptalk, weeks of inattention and months of inadequate meals while I finished the text. I appreciate their good sense, sensitivity and sense of humour throughout.

Most of all, I thank the reluctant subject of this book. Very few corporations could become more stimulating and interesting after two years of intense study. IBM World Trade was worth the trouble.

London and Dronningmølle
December 1973

Nancy Foy

Preface

This book was written for a very simple reason: to satisfy my own curiosity about IBM World Trade Corporation.

Many outsiders realize that International Business Machines is one of the largest and most profitable multinational corporations in the world. We know that it dominates the computer industry and determines many of its directions. But why? After eight years around the computer industry and four as an international journalist, I realized that in fact I knew very little about the internal mechanisms of this extraordinary company. Neither did anyone else I could find outside. For such a huge organization it was astonishingly opaque.

I wanted to know why IBM was so big and so successful when others who started with similar technology and resources dwindled into insignificance when computers came along. There might be useful lessons for other organizations to be gleaned from close study of this one. A clearer understanding of IBM and IBM World Trade would certainly be useful to every organization that has to compete with or patronize the giant company — and to governments who are worried about how to control this major force that seems to have a very large part to play in handling national information resources.

Virtually all IBM's growth came from inside, not from clever acquisitions or mergers. Success didn't seem to have much to do with financial ratios or creative accounting, or even technical innovation. The reasons for its spectacular achievement must also lie inside, well protected from prying outside eyes. IBM cherishes its privacy.

A chance anecdote on a train journey gave me the first thread — a glimpse into IBM World Trade. The threads one IBM veteran helped me untwine led to other people, other events, other points of view. But the views were almost unanimously pro-IBM among the many graduates.

Two things became clear almost immediately. First, although IBM operates with a single strong culture and a unified set of goals, it is really two separate companies, with completely different characteristics and corporate personalities. The company that operates in the United States — insiders call it 'Domestic' (and so shall I) — is monolithic, tightly knit, superbly administered. The international company — 'World Trade' to members of the IBM Family — is more loosely knit together, sometimes threatening to unravel around the edges a little as different national companies compete fiercely for corporate prizes. Yet somehow IBM had evolved methods for discussion, debate, even passionate argument between and within its two elements — methods that leave everybody more or less intact and ready to charge ahead in a single direction with IBM's characteristic energy once a decision has been taken. Furthermore, the corporation's natural division into two sibling halves gave each half a real competitor — the other half — in a market so dominated by IBM that one would expect complacency instead of competition. Given two IBMs, I immediately chose the younger, less-organized half for my attentions. Domestic and World Trade can never be separated entirely; like the two men who pushed them to their present stature, they were given life and form by a single progenitor: Thomas J. Watson Senior, an extraordinary, autocratic man with vision far beyond his time.

The second revelation was equally intriguing. The more I talked to people about the inside operations of IBM, the more I began to see that the so-called 'secrets' of success lay in the beliefs and the behaviour patterns of the many individuals who made up the corporation. In other words, the success was based in the culture. Thus I had to enlarge my own viewpoint. People are much more interesting than machines. Certain mechanisms of this fluid company moved them about and changed the shapes of their groups, but the internal culture provided a skeleton that gave form and continuity to the changing patterns. I wanted to know how much of this was conscious — 'management skill' — and how much was unconscious — call it 'corporate intuition'.

The real insights came not from books or articles but from the people who had experienced the IBM culture themselves. Most of them, even after years away from 'Mother IBM', still had Think signs in their offices and a curious nostalgia for the alma mater. Their reactions were similar to those of university graduates, discussing the good old days.

A 1972 *Fortune* article[1] takes companies like IBM to task for a closed attitude towards the outside world:

> The public needs to know more than it does about business — about its products, its processes, its performance, its profits, its inventions, its internal relationships, and the ways all these are changing . . . business should do a better job of explaining itself. Until it does, it will not be able to defend itself, much less to counter-attack its critics.

IBM has grown particularly opaque. An entirely unnecessary mystery shrouds the internal workings of a company whose actions are clearly a matter of public interest far beyond the confines of the computer industry. Some of this heavy silence is due to IBM's neurotic fear of the 'risk of exposure' — an understandable and fairly healthy neurosis when you suffer major anti-trust suits every fifteen or twenty years. Some dates back to two revealing *Fortune* articles in 1966. Some is over-reaction to the progenitor's over-publicized pronouncements. IBM has been able to afford its share of mistakes, and some of them are discussed herein. I find them to be relatively innocuous, sometimes poignant little mistakes or failures. Talking about them openly may be instructive to IBM as well as other organizations. It can certainly do IBM no harm. A study of the success patterns may be less dramatic, but more useful.

Many people, especially people inside IBM, will take this book to be critical of the corporation's beliefs and the way its people live each business day. My intent is not criticism but clarity. Non-IBM readers will probably notice more quickly that the overall picture that builds up is one of a competent organization.

I have tried to minimize my own opinions and simply present a clear report of the behaviour and opinions of IBM people. Like most journalists, I began with a built-in bias against anything big — and IBM looks large indeed from outside. However, I was less interested in the moral question of whether IBM should be so big and profitable, and wondered instead about the pragmatic question of how it got that way. To find this out I had to concentrate on the graduates, rather than the competitors and outsiders (whose opinions are much more available in the press anyway). IBM is contagious. One result of this approach was that I caught the enthusiasm of the graduates to some extent, becoming more pro-IBM than I expected at the outset. Hopefully their useful insights and assorted techniques for managing or getting action from IBM will balance against the collected bias in favour of the corporation.

In addition to whether IBM should be big, I have virtually ignored other 'moral' questions: whether IBM training is good or bad for an individual, for example; or what governments should do about IBM (I chose instead to present them with some practical ways of influencing the company); or whether the final say on decisions that affect the import/export balances of nations belong in the hands of corporations. I would rather give information about the little-understood company so each reader can make up his or her own mind about these broader questions. Editorials on the subject these days are relatively common, while information about what really makes IBM tick is rare. For the same reason I have tried to compress into a single appendix all the awesome statistics about IBM's bigness, adding some comparisons of my own between Domestic and World Trade growth patterns.

The book is really about the IBM culture. My own conclusion is that external forces such as anti-trust suits in the United States or economic nationalism abroad weigh less in IBM's ultimate success than the attention it pays to internal forces, built into this culture. It is important to capture its essential points in examples rather than theories or lectures. All the apocryphal stories herein are true — in that they are part of the IBM folklore. Sometimes the culturally embellished story tells more about the company than the original version.

Throughout I have tried to refer to people by the names their colleagues use, rather than the formal names imprinted on their business cards. The former US ambassador to France, Arthur K. Watson, is known throughout IBM as 'Dick'.* His brother Thomas J. Watson Junior is 'Tom' (or 'Tom Junior' to older IBMers), and their father Thomas J. Watson Senior is recalled with awe or bemusement as 'the Old Man'.

* Sadly, Arthur K. Watson died on July 26, 1974, as the result of an accident in his home in New Canaan, Connecticut.

The history of the Old Man and the early days of the company he built are told in two books: *Think*[2] (written with 'the active non-cooperation of the company') and *The Lengthening Shadow*[3] (a politer tome which insiders call 'the approved version'). These describe his early days as a successful travelling salesman, his rise through the ranks of NCR, and many factors there that helped create the patterns for IBM's own well-managed culture.

From a 1970s viewpoint, the Old Man's world was perhaps *too* well managed. One day I sat in the New York Public Library and looked through *World Trade News* from World Trade's inception in 1949 to 1957 when the corporation stopped sending so many internal journals outside. Seven years of *World Trade News* at once was an overwhelming experience. As open-minded World Traders sometimes found out for themselves, an overindulgence in IBM culture in its original Watsonian form could cause indigestion. Certain phrases kept recurring: '100 percent success', 'deserved promotion', 'outstanding effort'. Each issue overflowed with sales-school photos, visits with royalty, Christmas parties for 1,200 or 2,400 IBMers, World Traders honoured by civic organizations, presentations of awards for the suggestion or safety programmes, Watson's own honours, advice or speeches (including such simplistic expositions on world affairs as: 'French North Africa progresses as a result of industrial growth'). Each page blazoned out the motto: World Peace Through World Trade.

All these pictures of all these good, earnest World Traders in their good, ever-onward jobs and teams, continuing to expand in this best of all possible worlds — it was too simple. It had no humour. It revealed no problems. Both the journals and the company had come a long way from 1957 to 1973. But IBM's policy of turning a closed face to the outside world remains relatively unchanged, so the public image remains fixed in grey-flannel yes-men, unbelievably Good Deeds, and superannuated mottoes.

The people in IBM World Trade deserve better, whether the corporation likes it or not.

Nancy Foy

The Sun
Never
Sets
on
IBM

1
The
IBM culture

'Hello. I'm from IBM.' The young man stood at the
door, less than two hours after the company had received an inquiry
for a single typewriter. He wore a dark suit, white shirt and a club tie.
He was about 24 years old, a little over six feet tall, with well-styled
hair and a healthy, handsome face. A perfect specimen of young British
manhood, IBM style. When the sale was consummated within 20
minutes he went back to his dark green MGB and from among the
golf clubs in the boot he extracted a spare typewriter, a 'loaner'
until the purchased one could be delivered. The following day he
would be credited with 'points' back at the office. His own
attitudes seemed happily merged with those of the company, to
both their benefits. Business was great, and so was IBM, in his view.

The IBM sales manager in another country is hawk-like and patrician
in his late thirties. He is deservedly arrogant about the Hundred
Percent Clubs and Golden Circle memberships that are his reward
for a fine sales record. He has come up through the ranks. His
attire and attitude are completely his own. He speaks out force-
fully, first for himself, then for his country, only third for IBM.
He also acknowledges that he can only afford such a priority
structure so long as he rests on that fine sales record and a network
of aristocratic contacts in his country's government and industrial
networks. Nonetheless, he credits his own success and that of 'his

people' to the strong ties the company builds into them — the Hundred Percent Club conventions, the Family Dinners, the common language, the uniforms. He may eschew these for himself, but he imposes them firmly on all his salesmen.

The 26-year-old public relations man is on assignment from his country organization to IBM headquarters in Armonk. He still keeps his hair a little longer than most Americans; his collar is striped, but he has given up the mauve shirts and purple ties that used to be his mark of independence. He is short by IBM standards, but makes up for missing inches by alertness, a wary involvement. He has changed his ambitions. He used to want a career in art or motor racing. He now sees his future inside the IBM hierarchy; every time he began to be restless there was another promotion or move to cope with. But he will soon have to decide between his own country or an international career, and between his own speciality or a general management position. His outlook seems crisply optimistic.

The IBM personnel manager is well past 40, and looks slightly crumpled by recent events. His country has not met its quotas, and he has to carry out the personnel policies under conditions of faltering morale and hiring freeze. He is beginning to question his own role, and has rather gloomy views about staying in the company for 15 or 20 more years when he has already reached the top of his speciality. A move to another country is impossible at present; he wouldn't take his children out of their home country so late in their schooling. In several more years he thinks it will be too late to leave IBM to work for himself or another company. His attire is mildly non-uniform — a combination of rebellion, forgetfulness, and the dejected feeling that nobody notices. No one from head-quarters has visited for several years. He will bring out the crisp white shirts when or if that happens.

These are not archetypes; they are people — members of the IBM Family in four countries. They have different jobs, attitudes, problems, national cultures, but they have all been through the same process of selection, training, achievement, promotion and involvement in the single culture of IBM. To understand IBM's multinational operations, one must understand something of the coherent behaviour and beliefs that have built up over 60 years of a Watson management. From the individual's viewpoint, the 'culture' is a set of instinctive behaviour patterns and a set of values — our Basic Beliefs — built in through IBM's extraordinary training system. The company takes most of its people right out of university or after one job, then trains them twice as long as any other computer company, and keeps refreshing, retraining and reinforcing the cultural patterns throughout their working lives. The preferred behaviour patterns are accompanied by sanctions against those who do not observe them. The individual's goal seems to be 'belonging', and the punishment 'not-belonging'. People within any culture are parochial; they tend to think their own ways are the best, indeed the only sensible way of doing things. Any criticism of the culture, from inside or outside, is taken as an affront to the member and the group. A culture has its own language, mannerisms, code of behaviour, commandments (punishment or/and expulsion for breaking them), and sense of community.

Jargon is an important part of any culture — a separate language that can only be understood by other members of the same culture. IBM with its coherent history is particularly rich in jargon, sometimes forcing its own terms to become industry-standard — such as 'byte' for the eight-bit subdivision of a computer word, a phenomenon IBM introduced in 1964 when people were accustomed to six-bit 'characters'.

People with jargon enjoy private jokes which use the jargon. IBMers work their own terms into everyday conversation; thus someone not-too-bright might be described as 'CPU-bound', or a promiscuous lady as 'serially re-usable' or 're-entrant', or someone gazing out the window might have gone into a 'wait state'.

One graduate who collects IBM jokes notes that main sources of humour inside are the ideas that salesmen are always promising the earth, that they don't know one end of a computer from the other, and that their profound interest in the customer, his children, golf, and DP problems vanishes the moment the order is signed. He gives the following example:

The bride had had three previous husbands, so it came as some surprise to the groom on their wedding night to discover she was still a maid. Questioned about this the following morning, the bride blushed and said, 'yes, I was. You see, the first was too young, and the second was too old. The third was an IBM salesman — and he just sat on the end of the bed saying how fantastic it was going to be.'

'Our company is known by the men it keeps'

Throughout the world, and throughout IBM's history, ethics and appearance have been an important part of the corporate culture. In 1914 when the Old Man took over C-T-R, a faltering little conglomerate, salesmen generally had disreputable reputations. As Tom Junior noted sixty years later: 'The average salesman in those days wore a green silk shirt with pleats in front, a houndstooth jacket, a great watch chain across his front, striped socks and two-toned shoes. Father realized that a man dressed like this couldn't sell a cash register to a conservative banker.' The senior Watson was himself still under criminal indictment for NCR's monopolistic sales tactics, so he felt the need not only to be ethical, but to be seen to be ethical and respectable.

Absolute rectitude was Watson's pattern, in finance, personnel, community relations, everything, and he expected every IBMer to behave with similar righteousness. The Old Man also wanted uniformity, to knit together the tattered remnants of three separate organizations. He knew that people were respectable to bankers (and himself) in white shirts and blue serge suits, with conservative ties. That was his uniform, and it became theirs. He wore paper collars, so they wore paper collars, less by fiat than by example. (IBMers say that the last paper collar company in the United States was kept alive for many extra years by mail orders from IBM people.)

Then one day Tom Junior, then executive vice president, came to work in a button-down collar. (He had been suffering headaches which his doctor naturally attributed to the stiff paper collar.) Paper collars were abandoned instantly. The day he came to work in a pale blue shirt for a TV interview the news shot through the company, by then several hundred thousand employees. Yet in 1971 that same Tom Junior reminded IBM people — at that time demoralized by the recession and the anti-trust suits — that they looked best in white collars and short hair. In IBM mythology it is said that Tom Junior had been visiting a bank customer. As he stepped into the lift with an official of the bank a 'weirdo' (by Tom Junior's standards) emerged. 'Trendy employees you have,' said Tom Junior. 'That was one of yours,' came the reply. The directive, IBMers say, was issued the next day. This drew amused comment from the press, but some IBMers said it made them feel like members of the Old Man's IBM Family again. Today, an IBM man (particularly in Europe) may wear a coloured shirt, or even a small tidy beard. He still wears his membership visibly though; he will be the one who is particularly presentable in any gathering. Most of all, in every country, he can be identified by an open, confident, engaging manner. IBM people everywhere are nice people — the kind of men who like their wives, children, dogs, gardens, and fellow men.

From the vantage point of the employee himself, the culture has certain ever-present, ever-onward elements. He works hard and long; he takes an interest in his community; he reveres education; his views are moderately liberal. He travels often and easily. He approves of art and music, whether or not he has time to learn more about them. At work he is accustomed to working in temporary task • forces and communicating by means of flipcharts. (The presentation maxim is: 'Tell them what you're going to tell them; then tell them; then tell them what you've told them'.)

The world these people live in is consistent. It changes, but the changes occur in an evolutionary and sober way. One graduate said that the reason IBM has been singularly free from unions goes back to the consistent fairness that permeates the culture: 'universal use of christian names; no distinction between dining rooms, loos or other facilities for managers and everyone else; all these things follow naturally from IBM's assumptions about the nature of man.'

From the corporate vantage, the culture has three characteristics that must be called secrets of success. They are also at the root of the most pressing problems IBM faces. The first is the way in which the corporate culture dovetails (or clashes) with the national culture in about 130 countries. The second is the fluidity with which the company moves its people and organizations around. The third is IBM's Midas touch — the ever-increasing inflow of money, which grows more embarrassing as the uses to which it can be put are constantly narrowing.

The ubiquitous flipchart illustrates the problem of national cultures versus the IBM culture. Throughout the world IBM offices or conference rooms have wall-mounted clamps or locking cabinets as well as stand-up easels to hold the flipcharts. Every training programme includes lessons on lettering flipcharts and standing beside them comfortably to deliver presentations on anything from the 15-year plan to next month's quota in the Shetland Islands. But there are inherent national differences in the use of the flip-charts.

One French manager had for years been making expansion proposals for his activity. Invariably his national management would approve his plans, complimenting him on the impeccable logic — Cartesian logic — of his presentations. He would then fly to World Trade headquarters in New York. Invariably, he would be turned down, often before he had finished his colourful presentation, building up in the French manner to a final grand flourish as he reached the last chart that summarized all the points which had been built up with the traditional progression. Dejected, the manager kept trying, in good IBM fashion. One day in New York, more rattled than usual at the inevitable rejection ahead, he dropped all the charts just moments before he was due to go into the briefing room. A secretary swept them back together and mounted them for him. She had picked them up in reverse order, so the summary chart that he always saved for last was the first to be uncovered. Faced with this one more minor disaster, he gave a Gallic shrug and proceeded, giving his spiel backwards in spite of the damage it did to his inexorable logic. Before he got to the fourth chart there were nods of agreement, and his proposal was approved.

Even though the logic of a flipchart presentation differs from one country to another, sometimes with disastrous results for IBMers, the national differences are part of IBM's strength. IBM was one of the first American companies to insist that foreign nationals must run its foreign subsidiaries. Until 1926 the European outposts were managed by Americans; most of them were losing money, and the situation was particularly bad in France. On his trip to Paris that summer the Old Man sent the resident Americans home and turned the operation over to Camille Delcour, a French IBMer. When Watson returned two years later things were humming, and the profitable French company was expanding with Watsonian verve. During the inevitable Family Dinner that accompanies a Watson visit, the Old Man turned over the floor to Delcour, asking his secret of success. In his heavy accent the Frenchman gave the shortest speech in IBM history: 'Work, work, work,' he intoned cheerfully, then sat down.

'My country or my company?'

Each country has its own organization in World Trade, a 'national company' whether it be a ten-man sales and service office or a ten-thousand-man enterprise. Even the smaller IBM country organizations are among the most important industrial elements of their host countries. Each one is staffed almost entirely by people from that country. Of 115,300 World Traders in 1973, 115,000 were not Americans. Yet the travelling IBMer can walk into the IBM office in Bangkok or Beirut and find someone who speaks his language, who can cash his cheque, sort out his travel problems, or get a message through to his home office. The office will look the same and people inside it will talk his language, not only English but IBMese. All World Trade management people are supposed to know

English, but unless children in the country learn English in school, most of a country's IBM employees will speak primarily their native language.

The corporate culture runs along beneath the national culture, seldom visible from outside unless one knows its characteristics. The jargon, the business card formats, the definition of 'presentable', even the job titles change from country to country. Inside IBM the head of each country organization is known as the 'general manager'. But in France he is (to the outside world) le directeur général; in Britain he is the managing director; somewhere else the local outsiders will call him the president. Inside IBM he has two 'reporting lines': a visible line to an eminent local chairman or the founding father of that IBM company who has been gracefully retired to the chairmanship, or conceivably to one of the IBM World Trade executives who as chairman is keeping a closer eye on that country. Except for the latter case, the general manager's real line of control runs through several more layers of World Trade before the national chief has contact with World Trade's president or chairman, much less the IBM chairman.

Seldom do these separate national cultures clash directly and overtly with the IBM culture except for natural differences like Cartesian logic. The main conflict between IBM and the various elements of IBM World Trade is simple and structural; World Trade is a mosaic; Domestic is a monolith. Somehow the Old Man and his sons welded them together in a workable fashion. As Tom Junior said in 1962: 'We are not, as many large companies are, a grouping of unrelated or merely partly related businesses. We are one business and, for the most part, a business with a single mission.'

'Economic nationalism' is IBM's name for the problems related to this mosaic. Externally, there is the concern on the part of host governments that they are dependent on an American company for their computing know-how. They sometimes refer to 'corporate colonialism'. These are the problems to which IBM pays most attention. Internally there are problems of equal gravity, although they don't always command similarly grave attention. These come under the heading of 'loyalty'. Does an IBM man belong to his country first, or his company? This pressure is increasing. The situation is exacerbated by the feeling inside IBM that foreigners do not have equal opportunity to rise to the highest altitudes at Armonk; Jacques Maisonrouge, a fluent and gifted French engineer who had joined the company in 1948 and who is now World Trade president, is still regarded by most World Traders as the exception that proves the rule rather than the first crocus of a European spring, even though the men who run IBM from New York are trying to develop other Europeans who can operate at the top. These problems are not unique to IBM. Every multinational company suffers them. IBM was one of the first to use foreign nationals to run its foreign companies, and Maisonrouge was one of the first foreigners to have an impact in American decision-making. However, this very preponderance of foreigners and the optimistic expectations that are built into IBM people world-wide have made the problems of country versus company particularly critical at IBM — more so than in companies which are clearly run by Americans, where overseas employees expect nothing better than local promotion.

'I belong to IBM's movable family'

One reason such expectations move so rapidly throughout IBM — along with every other aspect of the corporate culture — is the fluidity of IBM employees. This phenomenon explains a great deal about the company and its success; the possibility that it may be curtailed to some extent is one of IBM's most serious problems today.

The reward for doing a good job in IBM is usually a new job, but seldom your boss's job. It is a different job, but not necessarily a 'better' job, because different is, by IBM definition, inherently better. This single aspect of the company does more to explain IBM than any other fact, event or belief. IBM recruits people who value learning, change, and group achievement. It reinforces these values with the double-length training and constant brush-up courses that are considered rewards in themselves. The neophyte IBMer gains confidence as he learns to cope with more functions and situations. His sense of membership in the IBM Family grows. If a new technology comes along, IBM is likely to create experts rather than buying them.

IBM often refers to itself (self-consciously but truthfully) as an 'agent of change'. The term 'technology transfer' crops up in almost every international IBM speech, part of IBM's answer to corporate-colonialism charges. The best way to transfer technology is to transfer people — to move the man who understands a technique to the place that needs to know about it.

With this fluidity IBM is not so much 'institutionalizing' knowledge as communicating it a little better than most corporations.

Every time people transfer within the company, the IBM ethic as well as the technology goes with them, so the organization retains a cohesiveness, an internal unity that is self-grown, relatively undisturbed by outside forces. But it is a dynamic organization, one that never has a chance to set or freeze. IBM is hierarchical, but the hierarchies are temporary. IBM values flexibility in its people, and gets flexible organizations as a result. There is less bureaucracy; managers are seldom in their jobs long enough to become bureaucrats or build empires, so the organization stays relatively lithe.

It is important to make two disclaimers at this point. First, IBM is not completely 'free from bureaucracy' because of the moving. In fact, many IBM people complained to me in the early seventies about growing bureaucracy or overcontrol. But the company has less bureaucracy than most, even today.

The second disclaimer concerns the idea that all IBM people are constantly moving around. They aren't. The majority stay in one location or at least one country for most of their working lives. They are the skeleton of the company, or its muscle cells and nerve cells for specific parts of the organism. But running through this stable portion, feeding it and keeping it healthy, is a strong blood-stream of people who move regularly and rationally, nourishing other cells as they move through.

This ability to move people around but keep them together was based on the concept of the IBM Family which often took precedence over the IBMer's family. The Old Man believed that people who played well together worked well together. Like a military outpost, each country organization hosted an endless succession of family picnics, Christmas parties for a thousand children, basketball, rugby or cricket teams, and the ubiquitous Family Dinners.

Like the Hundred Percent Clubs, the Family Dinners go back to the Old Man's time. They remain an important part of IBM even today, though they are now held less frequently, with smaller groups of employees, and a few countries like France have almost entirely eliminated them. Even so, the dinners were and are part of the cultural 'glue' that still holds the huge corporation together. In the olden days, whenever the Old Man, one of his sons or lieutenants arrived in an IBM outpost, there was sure to be a carefully staged evening out, paid for by IBM and obligatory for every IBMer and his wife. (The Old Man was always inordinately pleased at this 'voluntary' display of love and loyalty for IBM.)

Often more than a thousand people would turn out fervently or dutifully for these staid, speech-ful, booze-less occasions. As one veteran described the dinners of that era: 'After the superb food and mineral water, you sat there glassy-eyed, listening to lots of long laudatory speeches. There were usually a few funny remarks from the wiseacres here or there in the audience, but basically most of you left rededicated to the cause.'

The no-drinking rule about Family Dinners (or IBM facilities in general) became an issue in Europe. No less than three countries (France, Italy and the Netherlands) claim the first wine served at an IBM function. This may be one means of expressing national loyalties on a peripheral but culturally important basis. One American graduate still remembers the awe of his brethren when he came back from a Dutch meeting in 1963 with a wine-glass engraved 'IBM'.

IBM demands great loyalty from members of this family, but it has always given them loyalty in return — a full-employment policy that essentially guarantees they will not be let go so long as they obey the rules of the culture, and the promise of change for the young managers, particularly American managers, whom IBM has trained to value new challenges. Now the company is hoist with its own petard. Like other companies in expanding industries, it always assumed that getting good people was crucial to success. Now, as the computer industry matures and manufacturing technology improves, getting rid of people is a primary problem. The moves are less often for the development of the individual and more often for the convenience of the corporation. IBM is over-populated with good people. The cultural belief that expulsion was the greatest punishment, and its corollary that deciding to leave was the greatest disloyalty, are being re-examined. Because fluidity was such an inherent part of the IBM structure, these changes have had major effects on morale.

'IBM has the Midas touch'

Most companies would like to have IBM's third major problem: an embarrassment of riches. From the outside it seems that everything IBM touches turns to gold, as if the corporation had passed the point where it could ever again make a mistake. Competitors complain that whatever IBM decides to design into its equipment, that feature immediately becomes an industry standard, simply because more than two-thirds of the world's computers come from IBM. Competitors also complain, with some merit, that every advance in the industry has been available from some other company, better, sooner and cheaper than from IBM. Yet customers remain devoted to the IBM equipment. It is always safest to choose IBM, and the sixty-year reputation for good service is unique in the computer industry and most other industries.

Although this is not a book about the computer industry, one aspect of it must be understood if one is to understand IBM. Most machines are rented rather than sold. This is one more instance of IBM policy becoming an industry standard. Until Tom Junior signed the 1956 consent decree with the US government's anti-trust forces, all IBM computers were rented. Then IBM was forced to find a reasonable formula by which to sell them to those customers who preferred to own their own machines. The formula selected then was 48 times the monthly rental for most equipment. (Some go at multiples of 56 or 64 now.) The majority of customers continued to lease their machines from IBM.

It takes tremendous amounts of money to get into a business when you don't sell your product. Although the manufacturer can entice the customer by charging only about 2 percent of the total value per month, money must be found somewhere to pay for the people and facilities it takes to build the machines and carry them through the 48th month of use, when the costs and profits have been amortized. Thus for most of its early years, IBM was constantly cash-hungry, in direct proportion to its rate of expansion. It was trying to fill an ever-increasing diameter pipeline with money, while the trickle flowing out the other end came from a narrower part of the pipe. The Old Man hated borrowing, but he hated diluting his own shares of IBM (never more than 5 percent) even more. So he borrowed, sums that seemed gigantic in his day, though moderate in modern terms. But he limited his borrowing to the amounts he needed to fill the pipeline, and he limited the expansion of the pipeline itself to the amount that current revenues and borrowings could cover. Today, when 'growth' so often means acquisitions, mergers and flotations, this attitude is hard to understand. IBM did all its growing from within.

Once IBM was forced to sell its machines as well as rent them, it became harder to control the dimensions of the pipeline. When a few financial people discovered in the late sixties that IBM computers could be written off over a ten-year period instead of IBM's four-year period, a new industry bloomed: 'third-party leasing'. An entrepreneur with a good line of credit could buy the IBM computer outright, and lease it to the end-user for a monthly rate that was up to 25 percent lower than IBM's rate. By writing off the machine over a less conservative period, he created instant assets and a large cash flow, with very little effort. This sub-industry was particularly threatening to IBM because it could cause wild fluctuations in the revenues and profits that had to be reported — and matched from year to year. IBM is a company which prefers smooth, gentle curves on its performance charts, not wild up-and-down swings to disturb the shareholders and employees. In the 1970 era IBM began introducing new computers which sold at perhaps 56 times the monthly rental, effectively lowering prices. It also had the power to introduce new machines, thereby making obsolete many of the old ones that were not yet ten years old, as well as putting copycat competitors to inconvenience and expense. IBM's diversification into the lawsuit business started with retaliatory moves from the third-party leasing companies and competitors; this issue will continue to be delicate for many years.

When you continue to own your product after a sale you design it, market it, and take care of it more carefully than you would if you never have to see it again once it leaves the factory. The Old Man understood this; he built his company's philosophy on the three Basic Beliefs: customer service, loyal and happy employees, and a boy-scout-like striving for excellence. These combined to create the customer loyalty that made IBM invulnerable to competitors, even when their products were better, cheaper or more innovative.

Even with the depradations of the leasing companies, the pipeline inexorably filled, to the point of overflowing as the Domestic growth rate slowed down at the end of the sixties. Manufacturing advances meant that it cost less to produce the computers. Expansion rates were more gentle. The emphasis on customer service meant that IBM designers were finding cheaper, more reliable and more efficient ways to keep the machines running. IBM was able to go on expanding, turning more of its energies to the less mature international markets, while the money kept pouring out of the pipeline into IBM's pockets at an increasing rate, and the need for major investment and an increasing workforce dwindled. Cash and negotiable securities crept from $1 billion to about $3.3 billion by the end of 1972.

An enviable situation, and one the competitors envied. But what is IBM to do with all that money? The bigness that has resulted from 60 years of coherent management in itself restricts IBM's freedom to act. It would make sense, for example, to reduce prices on many models; IBM's 30 percent profit margin keeps creeping up, attracting anti-trust attention and fuelling the feelings that anything as big as IBM must be inherently bad. But any move to reduce prices draws instant complaints from competitors that IBM is trying to force them out of business. Similarly, IBM cannot buy other companies or diversify into other businesses without drawing dreaded anti-trust attention. Even special cash dividends to shareholders are restricted by government regulations. In this sense IBM is a creation of two men: Thomas J. Watson Senior and Senator John Sherman, the author of the 1890 anti-trust law in the US. As one IBMer commented: 'IBM should build a statue to Sherman's memory.' The intent of the law was to prevent monopoly, but because of its form IBM has been impelled to grow from within, and to build that growth on an ethical and educational base. This it has done so successfully that the latest anti-trust threats are more concerned with bigness alone than particular monopolistic practices. Every employee has to sign an annual statement that he has read, understood, and will comply with an IBM 'business conduct practices' manual that includes the text of the 1956 consent decree. The Watsons have always been hypersensitive to the threat of break-up by the US government, with good reason. The Old Man came into IBM with an anti-trust conviction from NCR hanging over his head. He fought two more anti-trust battles, from 1932 to 1934, and from 1952 to 1956. When Tom Junior insisted on signing the 1956 consent decree, his father finally handed over control of IBM.

So prices can only be lowered a fraction. Most avenues for diversification are automatically blocked, because potential new competitors would howl that IBM was looking for new fields to monopolize.

How did IBM get this big? How does it manage itself so efficiently when it has grown to more than a quarter of a million people? Which of its problems are common to all multinational companies and which are unique to IBM? What can other organizations learn from IBM's story? How can governments and competitors achieve peaceful coexistence with this giant phenomenon? Can IBM be controlled? What would happen if it were broken up? And where does its future lie? These are the questions we must ask. The answers to some of them lie in the history of the Watsons and their beliefs.

2
The Watsons, the war, & the wall

Thomas John Watson Senior was an extraordinary man. Extraordinary not so much for his successful concepts, which were mostly borrowed, but for his singleminded belief in them, and his missionary zeal to make sure each member of the IBM Family pursued them with equal fervour. By 1974, one hundred years after his birth, the company he created had become the world's most successful multinational corporation.

'Watson copied people — selectively'

Born to a family of Scots descent in a farmhouse in upstate New York, Thomas Watson was an asthmatic child with a fierce temper, unsure of himself with his contemporaries. He showed no early signs of greatness. At the age of 18 the young man gave up a $6-a-week bookkeeping job to join a friend named George Cornwell selling pianos, organs, sewing machines and caskets around the countryside for a $10-a-week salary. He observed Cornwell's easy manner and developed a skill at bartering sewing machines for bolts of calico or pianos for pigs.

Then Watson met the second salesman who would influence his style, a lively individual called C.B. Barron, who wanted to set up a business selling stock shares door-to-door. Barron believed that first impressions (preferably prosperous first impressions) were vital. 'Sell yourself and you sell your product,' he advised his young associate. Splendidly attired, Barron would have himself paged in his hotel to impress the local people whenever he arrived in a new town. (Eighty years later a young IBM graduate remarked wistfully: 'The thing I miss most is not being paged when I get to a foreign airport.') Watson began to pay more attention to clothing and to copy Barron's overlay of assurance. However, Barron's ethical style was somewhat less splendid than his wardrobe or sales style; he soon absconded with most of the funds of the new venture, leaving the 21-year-old Watson to find a new employer.

That's when the young man encountered the third salesman to influence his life, and through him the company that was to provide the blueprint for much of IBM's culture. Working under a National Cash Register manager named John Range, Watson first encountered the carrot-and-stick style of motivation, with lavish pay for success and even more lavish tongue-lashing for failure. But after each scolding the senior man would patch together the tattered ego of his disciple and gently show him how to do better next time (a technique that IBM salesmen still know very well). Range was well-versed in the style NCR's powerful John Patterson demanded. Training was vital, and the tongue-lashings were simply a 'character-building' aspect of the training. The senior man accompanied his new salesman on sales calls, demonstrating successful techniques in impossible situations. Range sold the machine as a useful tool that would make the customer more efficient and successful. Customers were handled gently, given confidence, convinced that they were in charge of the situation, but mesmerized by the constantly recurring punctuation of the bell ringing up a sale. (Modern IBM customers are wooed with gaudy flashing lights on a 370 computer console, or the soothing clatter of a busy line printer.)

Watson learned quickly. On 15 percent commissions he made $1,200 in one record week in Buffalo. By 1899 Patterson himself invited the successful young salesman to take over as sales agent in a branch office in Rochester, New York, on 25 percent commission. There Watson joined the local Chamber of Commerce and moved his parents and sisters into a pleasant home. In Rochester, working on his own (with the occasional help of his sister), Watson sometimes used fierce methods to beat the competition. In four years Watson brought the Rochester office from the bottom of the NCR list to one of the top in the country. In the process he eliminated a number of local competitors, thus bringing joy to the heart of Patterson, who believed the market was his God-given right, but seemed to operate on the premise that God helped those who helped themselves.

In 1903 Watson was tapped to be Patterson's instrument in a national campaign to this effect. Armed with a million dollars of NCR money, Watson went out to various cities, setting up cut-rate cash register outlets, ostensibly independent, to buy up or drive out the competitors.

Watson's success brought him back to headquarters and proximity to Patterson — never a comfortable phenomenon (no more so than proximity to Watson himself in later years) but an educational one. Sponge-like, he absorbed everything he could.

Patterson's approach to sales was ferocious, but his under-standing of salesmen was superb. In addition to the carrot/stick style of sales management and an over-detailed sales manual that had to be learned by heart, he used such techniques as high commissions, Hundred Point Clubs (the direct model for IBM's Hundred Percent Clubs), sales conventions with almost revival-meeting overtones, a quota system, guaranteed sales territories, and a company school built on his own farm. Even the famous 'Think' signs for which IBM is so uncomfortably famous gained impetus from Patterson. Watson used the word one day as he improvised during an inspirational NCR sales meeting. Patterson was so taken with the simple message that he had 'Think' signs made and put up in every department at NCR.

While Patterson was personally offended by competition from other companies, he approved of it among his own salesmen; he set them working against each other to achieve the highest sales records with a constant stream of contests, each endowed with valuable prizes. (IBM in later years had accounts with Tiffany's and similar shops for contest prizes and special awards.) Patterson's men were taught how to handle every nuance of their memorized sales spiels. They were trained to give their talks using red chalk in front of an easel. (In modern IBM the chalk has evolved into coloured felt-tip pens.)

Watson copied Patterson with discretion, though. In later years it was understood in IBM that the Old Man had never approved of NCR's knockout machines or the memorized sales manuals.

Patterson's influence on Watson's management beliefs extended far beyond sales. He believed that his employees and managers must be healthy; at one point he banned not only cigarettes and tea but also butter, eggs and condiments from all NCR tables, including customer tables. (It is no wonder Watson had no compunctions later about merely depriving IBM's customers of their alcoholic refreshments.)

Patterson demanded loyalty, and young Watson approved. (An IBM internal newspaper in later years stated unequivocally: 'If you are loyal you are successful.') Patterson's (and later Watson's) subordinates may not have been exactly 'yes-men', but they quickly learned to keep their disagreements to themselves and present a unified and cooperative front to the boss. Differences were sorted out before they entered the Presence.

NCR's own Old Man blew hot and cold on people, sometimes banishing a man from the corridors of power simply because he had been there too long. Like IBM people in later years, the deposed ones would be put in visible purdah. (But the IBM people always knew why.) Watson himself suffered the agonizing experience of weeks without phone calls or mail when Patterson was trying to force him to resign in 1913.

Patterson believed in the importance of industry (notably NCR) to the community (notably Dayton, Ohio). His employees worked in relative prosperity and uncommon comfort in a big glass-walled factory he built on his hilltop farm there. (Watson later showed a similar affinity for Endicott, New York, where he created comfortable amenities including an employee golf club.) Watson rose quickly through this organization, obedient to those above him (eventually only Patterson himself) and usually fair but demanding to those beneath him. For one pleasant two-year period, Patterson left him completely in charge in Dayton while the tycoon toured Europe attending social functions 'high up amongst the first aristocracy.'[1]

Two events at the end of his NCR career were to have a major effect on Watson's beliefs. The first was the anti-trust lawsuit filed in Ohio in 1912, when Watson discovered that he might be personally and criminally liable for NCR's violations of the Sherman Anti-Trust Act of 1890. Although Watson's career at NCR was already drawing to an end, he was convicted in February 1913 along with other NCR officers, fined $5,000, and given a one-year jail sentence which was held in abeyance while appeals progressed.

The appeals were still under discussion six weeks later when great floods swept Dayton — and swept Watson and Patterson into prominence as national heroes. While Watson remained in New York,

Patterson returned to Dayton on the last train to get through before the floods closed the railway; immediately the two men swung into unified action. NCR on its hilltop had the only remaining telegraph line open from Dayton to the outside world. Patterson opened NCR's canteen, its often-ridiculed employee recreation centre, and its medical facilities to the local people. Watson launched national appeals for help, coordinated supplies and served as the nation's only source of news about Dayton. After the two men 'saved the city' (as it was written at the time), they poured further energy into raising money to reconstruct Dayton and build a proper flood control system. (In the 1960s IBM's Corbeil-Essonnes employees helped out in a local flood.)

Immediately after the flood crisis Watson married 29-year-old Jeannette Kittredge. Then in mid-1913 Patterson finally fired him. It was a dark time. Watson — no longer 'young Watson' as his fortieth birthday loomed — was still under threat of the one-year jail sentence, and his wife was already expecting their first child (Thomas J. Watson Junior). On the credit side he had the benefit of 15 years' experience under the capricious Patterson — none of it wasted as events were to prove.

Next to Patterson the most important influence on the Old Man's life and style at IBM was Jeannette Kittredge, who stuck through the anti-trust and Dayton troubles to become his wife. Her gentle exterior manner masked internal convictions that were much deeper than his own pragmatic observations and formed a skeleton system of rectitude for the motivational muscle he had acquired in his working life.

Watson's sponge-like ability to absorb other people's ideas or 'models' of behaviour — or values — helps explain one of the most intriguing paradoxes in this paradoxical organization. To resolve the images of fierce and sometimes ruthless competition on the one hand and absolutely ethical behaviour on the other, an observer need only look at Watson's two greatest influences: John Patterson and Jeannette Watson. In a sense she 'focussed' his own combination of Scots morality and Victorian morality. However resolving the images inside the organization is not as easy as seeing their causes from outside.

Jeannette came from a socially prominent Dayton family with strong Presbyterian persuasions and an equally strong sense of morality. She believed firmly in the Golden Rule. Watson transformed this into part of the IBM creed and even lectured in a 1939 broadcast to Hitler about doing unto others as he would have them do unto him. Through Jeannette, Watson glimpsed the benefits of art, culture, and social acceptance.

Watson was never particularly religious, but he believed that churchgoing was good for his people. His parents were Methodist. In his Endicott days he was Episcopalian; as his horizons expanded with Jeannette and IBM he joined the élite Presbyterian church in Manhattan, where his funeral service was held in 1956. IBM people were also expected to go to church.

Similarly, his view of drinking seemed to be more operational than the ideological conviction of the Kittredges. He viewed his no-drinking edict to IBMers as good business and good morals, contributing to the spotless reputation he needed. In his own home he sometimes served cocktails to eminent visitors in later years, even though no customer could ever have a drink on IBM premises, and early employees knew they could be dismissed for being seen in saloons during working hours or displaying obvious drunkenness.

The employees (later including his own sons) tended to take the Watson edict against drinking in a practical vein themselves. In the thirties an informal 'information service' existed between the IBM secretaries on Watson's 17th floor of the New York headquarters and girls on other floors. The men all kept clean paper collars handy in case he called them in, and if he started to wander inside the building the girls telephoned advance warning. As soon as he left in the evening the grapevine carried the news, and as one European described it: 'We would immediately run two blocks to the St Regis Hotel and throw three whiskeys down the hatch.'

Europe generally disregarded the no-drinking policy. When the French plant was built in 1924 wine was naturally served in the employee canteen. Later the Italian government decreed that each company must buy a certain quantity of wine. IBM at first resisted nobly, but eventually acceded to the government's wishes (and those of its Italian employees). In 1969 the corporate Management Committee finally decided to relax the rules to the extent of allowing drinks to be served at social events sponsored by the Domestic company.

Watson became a minor patron of the arts, with strong tastes of his own. He liked the work of Grandma Moses, for example, long before she became famous. He had a pleasant though bland collection of art that gave him social confidence as well as aesthetic pleasure. As usual, this interest was immediately extended to IBM. He stated firmly that art and business benefited each other. A company art collection was begun and eventually seen by millions of people as it toured galleries and museums at IBM's expense. In 1940 President Roosevelt appointed Watson to head a National Week of Art

Music was also a good thing in the Old Man's eyes. He once commissioned Vittorio Giannini to create an IBM symphony. The resulting opus was redolent with themes from IBM company songs.

Besides the salesmen, Patterson and Jeannette, the other major influences in Watson's life were well-known tycoons, politicians and professors. The man who took him out of his despondent period after the NCR events was Charles Flint, known as the 'father of trusts' but also the father of conglomerates as we know them today. Flint believed in survival of the fittest and the ultimate morality of monopolies, a point which Watson did not quite accept after his NCR experience. Nonetheless, Flint was concerned about the financial wobbles of a little conglomerate called C-T-R (Computing Tabulating Recording company), which he had put together in 1911 from the remains of 13 preceding companies. Watson was hired to put it on its feet, with a salary of $25,000 and 5 percent of any profits he could wring out of it (an arrangement that was later to make him the highest paid executive in America). Watson became general manager, not president, of 'the C-T-R' in May 1914, four months after the birth of his first son. On 13 March 1915, the anti-trust judgment against the NCR men was set aside on appeal, and a new trial was called for. Two days later on 15 March Watson became president of the C-T-R. After the Dayton heroism the new trial was never pursued.

The other C-T-R man who influenced Watson was George Fairchild, its chairman and largest shareholder. Watson was characteristically submissive to the overwhelming chairman, though he carried on a running battle with Herman Hollerith, a technical genius whose C-T-R company made the tabulating machines ('Hollerith Statistical Pianos') which were precursors to computers as we know them today. In Watson's view Hollerith's technical brilliance was not matched by his business brilliance. The constant internal warfare between them may have influenced Watson; for the rest of his life he would line up with his sales people in any dispute with the technical boffins (an approach Tom Junior also seemed to favour), even though he was impressed by technical achievement.

'IBM girdles the globe'

By 1924 the company had tripled under Watson, but he still kept a low profile and stayed out of the way of the fierce Fairchild. Within a two-year period, though, the two parental figures died, Flint in 1922 and Fairchild in 1924. The 50-year-old Watson was finally on his own. A few months before Fairchild's death Watson changed C-T-R's name to International Business Machines.

John Patterson had had the motto 'The World Is Our Field', but a Canadian named Larry Hubbard deserves some credit for the name change; he suggested using the word 'international' in the company's name after Watson gave him the C-T-R agency in Canada.

C-T-R had already been active internationally before Watson arrived in 1914. He pursued this direction energetically, more for the involvement and potential than the current income, which was negligible until the thirties. Hollerith's first tabulating machine patent had been filed in 1884, when Watson was only ten years old. As early as 1890 Hollerith filed for a broad German patent and began to introduce his machines abroad.

In 1904 an Englishman named C. Everard Greene formed a syndicate to develop the use of Hollerith machines. In 1907 Greene's group became the British Tabulating Machine Company (BTM). Hollerith awarded them licenses to build and distribute his machines throughout the British Empire except for Canada. The British company made its own patentable amendments to the machines, not only to handle sterling calculations but also to speed the operation. A wary relationship continued between BTM and C-T-R, with frequent discomfort and distrust, until they parted when IBM World Trade was formed in 1949. BTM then became the progenitor of Britain's computer company, ICL.

In 1910 Hollerith set up similar arrangements with Willy Heidinger's German-financed company in Berlin, Deutsche Hollerith Maschinen Gesellschaft mbH (known as 'Dehomag'). The Germans were as adept as the English at altering the machines and patenting the improvements.

During World War I Dehomag was unable to pay C-T-R the licence fees and royalties it owed. Watson grew progressively less interested in leaving the majority of his European business in German hands as the sum grew. By 1922 — the year the German money went wild — the Dehomag debt had grown to about $100,000, not a large sum in dollars but an impossible 100,000,000 million marks for Dehomag. In a settlement that was fairer than most in inflation-torn Germany that year, IBM took over the company, but gave its founder Heidinger a 10 percent interest, simultaneously drawing Dehomag's boundaries back to the physical boundaries of Germany and handing out the rest of Europe to agents of Watson's own choosing.

Manufacturing or assembling abroad not only eased cash problems in moving equipment from one country to another but also avoided the import barriers that were already beginning in Europe. Competition had also begun. James Powers, a colleague of Hollerith's from the US Census Bureau (which had commissioned the first tabulators) began to make a mechanical model that was fairly similar to Hollerith's electric machine but had new (and patented) twists to it. Powers and Hollerith began racing around Europe setting up marketing outlets. C-T-R usually depended on local money while Powers (later absorbed into Remington Rand) normally used American money.

Watson saw the potential for international business very early. Monopoly might be considered poor form at home, but he felt it was his patriotic duty to make sure his people overseas gained as much of the market as possible for the American free enterprise system. By 1924, the company had installations all over Europe. Watson's first 'World Trader' was Otto Braitmayer, who had once been Hollerith's office boy. Eventually rising to vice president, Braitmayer was sent to Germany in 1924 to open a new plant at Sindelfingen and begin work towards a Paris plant, which opened in 1925. In 1926 Braitmayer went to China and the Philippines, then Australia and New Zealand. The Old Man proclaimed proudly: 'Everywhere he stops there will be IBM machines in use. The sun never sets on IBM!' In official company transcriptions of Watson's speeches this motif sometimes appeared as 'International Business Machines girdles the globe.'[3]

By the thirties the primary competitors in the tabulating field in Europe were the American companies of Powers and Remington Rand and the Bull company, named for a Norwegian inventor but set up in France when his patents were purchased from Bull's estate by an entrepreneur named Emile Genon. In 1933 the various Bull elements were rationalized with a contract under which the French company would make the machines and the Swiss company would be the sole distributor outside France. After two years of secret negotiations, IBM in late 1935 bought 86 percent of the outstanding shares of Swiss Bull and Genon became head of IBM Swiss Bull for a while. As soon as the American competitor bought its Swiss marketing company, and thus a stranglehold on Bull's exports, the French company broke off the exclusive sales contract, initiating a chain of lawsuits that lasted for decades over the ownership, contracts and patents.

Although Jeannette had by this time produced three more children, two daughters and then in 1919 Arthur Kittredge Watson (known as 'Dick'), she usually accompanied her husband on his business trips to Europe; as the children grew older they went along too. Both sons were as overwhelmed by their father as his employees were. Only Jeannette seemed able to penetrate his growing power and certainty. Whenever she went along the trips took on culturally enriching overtones. One day in Geneva during the late thirties they had been to see an exhibition of Spanish masterpieces. That evening their European hostess, an IBM wife, politely asked Dick what he thought of the paintings. The teenager, afraid to say the wrong thing, turned to his older sister: 'What did we think of the exhibition, Helen?'

By this time Watson was demanding and getting a much faster rate of growth from the company. The cash famine in his early C-T-R years had left its mark, and he had a firm policy of ploughing back profits to support growth. Even so, as the great depression advanced his patriotism and optimism kept him building machines at an ever-increasing rate, well beyond what could have been considered prudent at the time. The gamble paid off, though. (He probably never viewed it as a gamble.) A large contract from the new US Social Security department was won in 1935 because IBM could begin delivering machines immediately from its overflowing warehouses.

Watson approved of taxes — just as he approved of authority — as much as he disliked debt. By 1935 he had paid off the $187,500 mortgage on IBM's old headquarters at 310 Fifth Avenue in New York. In 1935 Watson also began to build up reserves to protect IBM's profits in blocked-currency countries. (One of the ways IBM later coped with blocked currencies in Spain was to hold Hundred Percent Club meetings there every three years.)

Tom Junior was later to look back on the cash famine with bemused objectivity: 'We constantly acted as though we were much bigger, much more sophisticated, much more successful than any current balance sheet might bear out.' During a series of lectures in 1962 he also noted:[4]

In the early days C-T-R was working so close to the line that there was no money available to duplicate Patterson's handsome factory buildings and his generous benefits programmes. Father used showmanship instead. He staged band concerts and picnics and made scores of speeches. Almost every kind of fanfare was tried to create enthusiasm. The more substantial things — above-average wages and benefits — came later.

This sleight of hand extended to the calendar too. In 1924 Watson formed a Quarter Century Club for employees of the 13-year-old company, by extending memberships and honours to the people who had come from predecessor firms. He moved date lines the other way in 1939 by celebrating his own quarter-century with the company as if it were IBM's 25th anniversary. By these counting methods 1974, his own centenary, is the 75th, 60th and 50th anniversary of IBM, as well as the 25th anniversary of World Trade.

As the company expanded, so did Watson's horizons. In 1933 he became president of the American section of the International Chamber of Commerce. In 1937 he became international president. During the 1920s he had invented the slogan that is still used by IBM and the international chamber: World Peace Through World Trade.

Watson always exhibited a near-reverence for authority. He was submissive to his own bosses in the days when he had them and to those he considered his betters in the social, political or academic communities. In turn, he expected submission from his subordinates and his sons. This reverence for authority may help explain the shifts in his political support — a practical kind of respect for the party in power. Although he was a nominal Democrat he revered Republican president Coolidge, not to mention his close friend, the (equally nominal) Republican Dwight Eisenhower. His sons followed his footsteps closely in many respects. They supported different political parties (a phenomenon in the Nixon era which helped win Dick an ambassadorship and Tom Junior a place on the notorious White House 'enemies list' for giving money to Muskie), yet they exhibited almost no visible ideological conflicts. Their father gave not only reverent respect but also helpful advice to American presidents. Once or twice a week Franklin Roosevelt received Watson letters full of homilies and ideas. Now and then in return the president telegraphed his blessings to an IBM gathering.

Watson's reverence for political leaders helped him earn 32 decorations from American and foreign governments, though he was ambivalent about accepting an ambassadorship from Roosevelt which would have meant leaving his own IBM. The fondness for international gestures and decorations sometimes got the Old Man into trouble. In 1933 he embarrassed many fellow businessmen with a speech telling Americans in essence to stop criticizing the duly appointed government of Russia, communist or no, and let it get on with its own business. That year he also gave glowing tributes to Benito Mussolini, whom he felt was bringing an admirable order out of the chaos in Italy. (These remarks have since been expunged from corporate histories.) Hitler bestowed upon him the Order of Merit of the German Eagle with Star in 1937 and gracious words flowed between them, though there was a noticeable lack of rapport.

In Dwight Eisenhower, Watson's delight in politicians, military leaders and academic people combined. The two men with their simple beliefs, great optimisms, and great drive were close friends. Watson by the mid-forties was a trustee for Columbia University. When Eisenhower was about to return from Europe Watson overcame the opposition of a number of other trustees and Eisenhower became Columbia's new chief, a position admirably suited to keeping him visible until the next presidential election.

Watson was impressed by foreign dignitaries, particularly those with royal titles. From 1927 through 1943 IBM officially documented the state visits of dozens of them (keeping a network of embassy informants busy finding out which dignitaries were scheduled to make official visits). The visitors ranged from minor Latin American dictators to Madame Chiang Kai-Shek at the height of her US popularity. Each visit was recorded in an elegant slim book, full of photographic mementoes of Watson with the great people (heralded as 'Citizen, Patriot, Soldier,' or 'El Gran Presidente'). Thus it was no surprise that as the company grew in Europe it collected among its employees a certain number of noble or near-noble gentlemen, as well as some heroes and near-heroes. Sales to big clients (often governments) in those days usually depended on having salesmen who were on a social par with the upper-crust customers.

Baron Christian de Waldner, who was hired in 1934, and was eventually promoted to head of IBM France, became 'Mr IBM France' until his retirement in 1973. He was both nobility *and* hero. He was also firmly entrenched in the appropriate French corridors, where his ability to 'talk to de Gaulle' allowed him to keep interference from American IBM experts to a healthy minimum. His willingness to resign whenever matters from headquarters didn't suit his fancy caused discomfort to the men who came over to 'tidy up Europe' in the sixties.

George Daubek, who brought the British Empire into the IBM empire after 1950 and headed IBM Austria for many years thereafter, came from an aristocratic Czech family. Henrik Lykke-Hansen in Denmark was able to take a visiting IBM American to lunch with the king.

Many of the Old Boys were the entrepreneurial types who could make the grand gestures the Old Man loved so well. In 1927 an IBMer in New York placed one of the world's first transatlantic telephone calls, relaying a message from IBM Chicago to IBM London. When the Old Man made much of this, Valentin Boucas who was IBM's agent in Brazil took note, and when the Latin American telephone link was opened Boucas used it immediately to book his seat on the first flight of the Graf Zeppelin from Pernambuco to New York. The Old Man was delighted. In his eyes this was not an expensive boondoggle; it was a Great Step Forward in Transportation and Communication.

Whether their credentials were aristocratic, heroic, political or entrepreneurial, these Old Boys became IBM's Old Gentlemen. They remained sacred in the youthful IBM culture long after the Old Man who hired them was gone. George Daubek, for example, although he was semi-retired at the age of 82, still had a large executive office and a secretary at IBM Austria in 1972 — the year IBM decreed that top executives must retire at 60.

'Some of IBM's German profits went to the Resistance'

The Old Man was a patriot as well as an optimist. In 1937 Adolf Hitler had assured him: 'There is to be no war.' Watson went home, not necessarily satisfied with the assurances, but believing that his counterparts in the German business community would be able to keep reins on Hitler. He held on to his optimism quite late. In September 1939 he bought the Place Vendôme building in beleagured Paris. 'Peace' signs began to sprout next to 'Think' signs on IBM desks. Then in 1940 when events proved him wrong, Watson took to the airwaves to lecture his former host, then severed diplomatic relations by sending back his 1937 medal. Hitler retaliated by forbidding Watson ever to set foot on German soil. (In Basle after the war, Watson had the last word, gleefully walking across the bridge to Germany and back.)

Like the 1914-18 war, World War II sent IBM's domestic business soaring as America again became the world's armoury. As the war began in Europe, IBM in the United States established a 94 percent interest in Munitions Manufacturing Corporation, which began to make bombsights, machine guns, then airplane engine parts, timing devices — eventually $200 million worth. The 40-hour week became a fond memory, and women infiltrated IBM for the first time. The Old Man decreed that each American IBM soldier should have one week's pay each month he was away. (Americans who go from IBM to the armed forces still get extra pay for up to two years.)

The war gave impetus to grand designs for huge calculating machines. IBM turned down a project offered by two young men named Eckert and Mauchley for something they called 'ENIAC'. This 'first computer' was eventually sponsored by the US Army and Remington Rand, and became a precursor of the Univac computers. Meanwhile Watson and the US Navy were sponsoring Dr Howard Aiken at Harvard University, who was trying to produce a calculating monster called Mark 1.

Although the war gave impetus to IBM's growth, Watson refused to profiteer. First he limited his own remuneration (by then well known to be the highest in the United States) to its 1939 level. Then he imposed a limit of 1½ percent on IBM's net profits on the war work, and even that profit was set aside in the widows and orphans fund. Domestic revenues more than doubled from $60 million to $138 million from 1941 to 1945, but profits rose only slightly from $9.8 million to $10.9 million. It is often said that IBM's business from abroad dropped during the war. Yet even with Watson's huge reserves for blocked foreign profits and most of the major European countries out of touch, the amount of money returned to the parent corporation from foreign operations went up from $239,000 in 1940 to almost $2 million in 1945. In 1946 it jumped to $3.3 million.

One of the most intriguing phenomena during the war in Europe was the way IBM employees demonstrated a Watson-like loyalty to the company, keeping IBM's machines running even when it sometimes clashed with national loyalty. One apocryphal story among the IBM international men tells of the IBMer who joined the Royal Canadian Air Force as a bombardier at the beginning of the war. At the height of the German bombings he was given the assignment to bomb the IBM factory (still known as Dehomag) at Sindelfingen. According to the story (told me by half a dozen IBMers), the man suffered an agony of torn loyalties as his plane droned across the Channel, and when the moment of Truth finally arrived, he contrived to drop the bombs on the Mercedes plant, across the railroad tracks from IBM's plant. (Only one of the informants wondered what the Mercedes bombardier was doing that night.)

The truth was in fact intriguing. The man who dropped the bombs on Sindelfingen was Frank McCarthy, personnel manager for IBM's Office Products group in Canada. His story is quite different. 'I had been working for IBM for about a year when I went into the Air Force. The fact that I might have bombed IBM didn't ring any bell with me really until I was looking through my log book after the war and realized that we had dropped bombs on both Berlin and Sindelfingen. I mentioned that to Harold Christensen, who said: "What a thing, dropping bombs on us!" I explained that the target was the town, not the company and when you got over a target in the dark with the searchlights and flak you might have been hitting any place. At the time I didn't even know we had a plant in Sindelfingen. I just hoped afterwards that I hadn't hit any IBM people. Chris reassured me, describing the bomb shelters in both plants.'

The inflation of McCarthy's experience explains something about the IBM culture — and the lengths to which loyalty can be expected to go within it. The belief that the man would change his target tells more than his natural concern for the welfare of his corporate brethren, discovered after the fact.

In Europe the war created three major kinds of problems. What were the IBM companies to do about their money, machines, and men? Many, particularly in Eastern Europe, had Jewish employees in the path of the Nazi machine. In Poland, for example, IBM's man Janusz Zaporsky did as much as he could to assure service to his customers; then as the Germans and Russians approached he escaped at the last moment to Brazil, where he eventually headed the IBM company. Much of the equipment he left behind was eventually damaged or destroyed.

Despite Dehomag's experience during and after World War I, its founder Heidinger believed, like most Germans of his time, that Germany would eventually be bringing order to most of Europe. Like any enterprising young IBM manager, the veteran Heidinger made stirring pleas to the company for more

resources to meet the expected need. At the same time he began
a battle to get IBM to draw the Dehomag boundaries beyond
Germany's physical boundaries on the IBM map of Europe. IBM's
Harrison Chauncey spent a night in a German jail during these
1940 negotiations.

National and company loyalty conflicts had finally bubbled to
the surface. As Heidinger battled for control of the company he
had founded, IBM took two steps to sidestep confrontation.
First, full power over IBM's 90 percent interest in Dehomag and
other European holdings was given to a Swiss, Werner Lier, who
became manager of the European headquarters in Geneva when
the Americans went home in 1940. Quite a few American companies
with German holdings adopted this approach as war loomed.

Then Lier went to Germany, just before Pearl Harbour in
October 1941, to offer 5 percent of the German holdings to
Dr Otto C. Kiep, one of the Dehomag directors, if he would look
after IBM's interests — something Heidinger was clearly not going
to do if they conflicted with his own or his country's interests.
Kiep, who had met Watson while he was Germany's Consul General
in New York, declined the offer, writing to Watson (via Lier)
that there was considerable animosity in public opinion in
Germany against American-owned companies. He remained on
the Dehomag board, though, and reported regularly to Lier, who
was also receiving production and shipping reports from the
German company.

Kiep died a tragic death, though he had no actual involvement
in the war. During the investigations after the plot to kill Hitler
failed in 1944, Kiep's name was found on some list of 'men of
reason' who might be asked to help run the country after the
assassination. Kiep was tortured, then condemned on 16 August
1944 and hanged ten days later. When the situation became
known to Watson after the war, Kiep's widow was made a director
of IBM Deutschland; in 1950 she made a speech at the company's
Berlin convention banquet.

As in America, the IBM companies in Europe were considered
essential to the war effort, not so much for their ability to make
ordnance or special devices (manufacturing was still rudimentary
in most of them), but because the punch card machines they
normally rented and serviced were often essential to their
customers who then (as now) were the giants of industry and the
major government departments. Information about IBM installations and shipments had intelligence value. A key man in this

aspect of IBM's wartime business was Lier, an army captain. Swiss laws were very strict about 'anti-neutral' activities, particularly for officers in the Swiss Army. Thus he took many risks during the war years. Information came in to Lier from Kiep in Germany and Roger Virgile in Paris among others, then found its way to the US State Department, as well as Watson.

Money continued to flow from Dehomag into Geneva because the German operations, like those in wartime America, were strongly profitable. Lier and Watson had a number of bright ideas about how to spend these blocked profits. After Paris fell, for example, the Americans maintained an embassy in Vichy, although it was cut off from normal communications with the United States. Lier used to make dramatic night trips through occupied territory to visit the embassy, carrying Dehomag funds which were used to pay the salaries of the Americans.

Watson also instructed Lier to use $10,000 of the German profits to create in Geneva an office for USAFI (US Armed Forces Institute) to help POWs in Germany. USAFI's main work was to expedite scholastic literature to the US prisoners in Germany. Later, with the help of General Barney Legge, who was US military attaché in Berne, and Sam E. Woods, then the US Consul-General in Zurich, some of the money was diverted to help in repatriating pilots back to the UK through 'unknown channels.'

While some of the IBM money was being used to help POWs disappear, other funds were used to keep track of them. Watson instructed Lier to get every machine that was not being used by customers and organize a punch-card system for the Red Cross in Geneva, to trace POWs. (This was naturally called 'the Watson service' and received a great deal of publicity at the time.)

The original $62,000 investment in Dehomag had already earned IBM $4.5 million income before the war. Equipment which had come from America before the war had to be built locally, so Dehomag emerged from the war with a new plant. Some parts were shipped out to other IBM companies via neutral Switzerland and Sweden — an act of company loyalty which could have been a death warrant for the Dehomag people if the ultimate destinations were known. The normal approach to such commerce (even today) is what insiders call 'equipment that fell off the back of a truck somewhere' — trans-shipment to an independent company in a neutral country, which subsequently (and quietly) resells or 'loses' the machines.

Some of the IBM companies closed down completely during

the war; others ticked over under occupation; and a few expanded under the Germans. In Yokohama IBM Japan (then known as 'Watson Business Machines Company) was seized by the government as enemy property on 8 December 1941, the day after the Pearl Harbour attack. The assets were sold in 1943 to the newly formed Japan Tabulating Company which maintained the installed equipment. (They were restored to IBM in 1949.)

To keep an IBM company alive during the war, the IBMers had to keep the IBM machines running. For the American-based company, maintenance was a major problem in Europe during the war. When spare parts were unavailable it took the form of cannibalism — breaking down one machine into spare parts for the others. Old parts were reclaimed and refurbished with whatever materials were at hand. Most of the country organizations learned to make their own cards, and those with card presses or spare parts in abundance tried to help their less fortunate IBM neighbours.

James Connolly[5] described the Belgian experience, which was characteristic of IBM companies in several other countries. Genon, who had master-minded the IBM Swiss Bull deal, had eventually been rewarded for his efforts with leadership of the Belgian IBM company when it was taken over from the former agency in 1936. As the Germans approached, Genon fled into France and then back to Switzerland, leaving IBM Belgium in the hands of Louis Bosman and Walter Galland. Galland immediately courted Herr Garbrecht, the German who was given custody of IBM Belgium and IBM Netherlands in 1942. Garbrecht was encouraged to see himself in a chairman-like role, delegating to subordinates (like Galland) the day-to-day running of the enterprise but maintaining a chairmanly liaison with the military government whenever 'his' companies needed supplies, favours or information.

Some of the spare parts manufacturing in Belgium was done in secret with materials stolen or coaxed from the Germans. Old machines were taken off the scrap list and refurbished. Until the last few months of the war they were able to keep IBM machines from being sent out of the country by having access not only to information about which machines were to be requisitioned, but also a large network of high-level acquaintances. Thus customers could be warned in advance and the official machinery set in motion early.

Thus by the end of the war IBM Belgium revenues were 20 percent higher than they had been when Garbrecht took over the company in 1942. Finally, just before Brussels was liberated, the Germans decided to ship some machines back to Germany. An IBM employee named Adolphe Mulkens supervised the loading, carefully removing one essential part from each machine. The Germans never discovered the perfidy; a few months later the machines were found abandoned in a railroad yard a few miles from the German frontier.

Saving IBM men was a vital concern throughout Europe. In Belgium Galland and Garbrecht had been able to keep their 'essential' customer engineers through most of the war. When they were no longer able to evade the requisitions for compulsory labour in Germany, they informed the men and some of the younger ones joined the Maquis, where IBM Belgium supplied them with money and food (politely, without Garbrecht's knowledge).

The Dutch IBM company, also working under Garbrecht, had similar experiences holding on to machines and men. The Dutch manager Pieter Van Ommeren managed to cannibalize and retrieve from the scrap heap enough equipment to increase the Dutch installed base by more than 10 percent during the war. However, pleas from Garbrecht and customers were less successful with the Nazis in Holland; thus about half the equipment had been taken over and shipped away by the end of the war. But IBM could sometimes turn the tables. In 1943 Van Ommeren discovered that 34 ancient machines that had once been used by the Russians were sitting in the Hamburg port, where they had been rusting gently for several years. Garbrecht pulled the necessary strings.

IBM Hungary managed to keep custody of its own machines and people through the war, working with Dehomag and IBM Switzerland for supplies. In Greece, Austria and most of Eastern Europe, the Germans took over the machines and ran them during the war. In the massive sorting-out after 1945, IBM agencies were again set up in most of these countries to take over service to whatever installations remained.

In Italy the IBM company was under the care of Giulio Vuccino, who managed to keep a low profile and slowly build up his manufacturing capability. At one point soldiers removed machines from some customer installations at gunpoint. Later in the war German SS officers arrested Dr Samarughi, who headed IBM's Rome office, and kept him in jail for three days while they seized equipment from IBM's Rome customers. Very little of the equipment

34

thus requisitioned did much good for the war effort. Although it was fed into the coagulating transport system, like other IBM machines in Europe much of it was discovered in railroad yards after the war, rusted badly, with key parts missing.

Vuccino also had a problem protecting men who were about to be taken for interrogation or forced labour. He set up an information network to find out who was going to be taken, and if official intervention ('essential to the cause' testaments) didn't work, he would send them underground. IBM Italy supported its fair share of resistance people too!

France was one of the key countries in the IBM empire, with major manufacturing plants and a large organization. A new plant was opened at Corbeil-Essonnes, 20 miles outside Paris, in 1941. Roger Virgile remained in Paris and the Germans put an SS officer in charge of IBM France. He was Captain Westerholt — a graduate of Dehomag. Westerholt carefully looked the other way whenever Virgile passed on his detailed reports to Lier in Switzerland. The other custodian in France was another Dehomag man by the name of Oskar Hoerrmann, who managed to keep IBM France out of the Wanderer Werke conglomerate the German officials were planning, which was to include Remington, Powers and Bull, too. He delayed negotiations, filed lawsuits for unfair competition against Bull and generally traded on the difference between French and German machines and applications. Hoerrmann also gave his loyalty to his IBM brothers instead of his German bosses when he protected inventor Jean Ghertman from concentration camp — once under threat of having to take Ghertman's place if he didn't produce the technical man within 24 hours. As usual, high-level contacts were more reliable than heroics; the man who issued the order was transferred the same day, and the arrest documents discreetly disappeared. Hoerrmann also kept exquisite records, complete in every detail — to the extent that all machines commandeered by the Germans from IBM France and its customers were restored with astonishing ease after the war.

IBM specialized in escapes, dramatic or otherwise. In addition to the men who went underground with IBM support in occupied countries, there were young IBM men like Pierre Louis who escaped twice from prison camps in Germany. Others like Michel Brindejoint in France elected to spend five years as a prisoner rather than direct operation of a group of IBM machines for the Germans. Ed Corwin, an IBM salesman in Poland, spent most of the war in a concentration camp. When he was released IBM paid him all his back salary for the war years and whisked him off to Endicott, where he became an engineer. Lier himself had to make a dramatic escape from Switzerland in early 1945. General Legge called him in one evening to organize his getaway as he was about to be arrested by his own countrymen for unauthorized (un-neutral) activities. The Americans who had been funnelling his information through to the US State Department for five years whisked him to London, then the United States, where Watson treated him as a hero and the US government gave him its highest civilian award, the Medal of Freedom.

Finally the IBM men began marching home from war. In New York Watson welcomed them with parades and banquests. In Europe there was less time for festivities, but memorial plaques went up in IBM offices in every city. In 1945 the US military authorities appointed custodians of Dehomag, which moved its headquarters to Sindelfingen and finally became IBM Deutschland in 1949. Heidinger and the fight for control had died a natural death in 1944.

More than 25 years later, a veteran executive who had served in IBM World Trade remarked: 'There were a lot of loyal IBMers in the German command. They protected a great deal of our property'.

'No matter who his father was, Tom Junior would have become chairman'
One of the beliefs the Old Man held most dear was the concept of family. Watson was a loving, albeit autocratic father. Whether or not he had a sense of humour, the household he dominated carried a sense of fun, and he enjoyed playing practical jokes on his children. He once said:[6] 'Our wives are all part of the business. We started with just a few hundred people in 1914 and decided that no matter how large we grew we would carry it on in the same spirit. We always refer to our people as the IBM Family, and we mean the wives and children as well as the men.' In a 1929 speech[7] he said with equal fervour: 'Our sons and grandsons can follow us in this business because it is an institution that will live forever.' Jeannette was a vital part of the IBM Family as well as the Watson family. She not only accompanied him on trips but also sat on the World Trade board of directors. At his death she resigned that position to accept a seat on the main board.

Given their overpowering father and the involvement and certainty of their mother, the two sons achieved astonishing success

in their own rights. Like their father, the boys showed no early
signs of greatness. Both were handsome and eventually elegant men;
both were tall and slender, later endowed with prematurely white
hair. But both combined their father's temper with a visible lack of
confidence. Neither was an outstanding scholar — yet both have
followed their father's pattern of respect and support for educational
institutions. Both went through rebellious phases, drank enthusiastically as youthful IBMers. It was much easier to be Watson than to
be a son of Watson: though the father thrived into his eighties, both
sons were slowed down by heart attacks in their fifties.

The boys seemed to be understandably ill-at-ease around their
father, but carried on his reverence for families, both their own and
the IBM Family. Both eventually produced six offspring, but there
is no sign that another generation of Watsons will be deeply involved
in IBM's management. Tom Junior's only son served as a systems
analyst for IBM UK for a year, then left to practise law in Boston.

Watson never directly demanded that his sons follow in his
footsteps, but they understood his wishes. Tom Junior sometimes
recalls the day when he was about 11 and went to his mother in
tears. 'Mother, I don't want to join that IBM company.' he wailed.
'Nobody is asking you to join the IBM company,' she replied
soothingly. But as the years passed the Watson family and the IBM
Family grew even more inextricable. Tom Junior gave his first
speech on a sales convention podium at the age of 12, and several
World Traders remember the time Dick, an expert yodeller, was
obliged to perform publically at his father's request.

Tom Junior graduated from Brown University in 1937 and
immediately joined the company — as his father wished. Then at
the outset of the war he went into the US Army Air Corps for
five years, spending most of them overseas piloting senior officers.
His official biography still notes his wartime achievements: senior
pilot rating and Lieutenant Colonel rank, with an Air Medal and an
Army Commendation Ribbon. After the war he came back to IBM
and suffered the embarrassment of a meteoric career, demonstrating
what his father had always claimed — that any man who worked
hard could achieve the same pinnacle of success and power that
Watson himself enjoyed. This could not have been easy for the
sensitive young man as he kept getting choice assignments or
territories, but he took on each task earnestly and earned the
respect of his colleagues on his own merits. In January 1952 he
was elected president of IBM, but his father still held complete
control as chairman and chief executive (a position that has always
overshadowed the presidency at IBM).

Then in late 1955 Tom Junior took the independent step that
was to make him chief executive in fact as well as in title. IBM had
already suffered one anti-trust lawsuit in 1932-4, settled by
'consent decree' in which the company agreed to change its
practices without admitting guilt for monopolistic behaviour. In
1952 the government had again sued IBM for its domination of the
tabulating machinery market. Almost all of IBM's growth had come
from within, rather than through acquisitions; the Old Man reacted
strongly as the government kept pestering his company with more
and more demands for information. Tom Junior realized that his
father was getting older — he was almost 82 at the time — and was
unable to see the necessity for settlement. So the 42-year-old Tom,
in January 1956 after a blazing battle with his father, marched off
to the government and signed the famous 1956 consent decree. At
that point the Old Man began to hand over real control, and in May
1956 Tom Junior became chief executive officer. Less than six
weeks later, Thomas John Watson Senior died of a heart attack.
From that point on Tom Junior was on his own.

The interests of the two sons, or the Old Man's interpretation of
their interests, created the organizational structure of IBM. Watson
sliced his corporation so the older son, a capable administrator,
should be in charge and run the Domestic portion, while the younger
son who loved languages and travel could oversee the international
portion. Both sons accepted this division of the world, as if they
were saying: 'If that's how father wanted it, that's how it will be.'
One wonders what the organization would have been like if the Old
Man had had one son — or three?

While Dick watched over World Trade, gaining importance
slowly as his part of the corporation grew, Tom Junior's great
moments began almost as soon as his father died. In December of
1956 he held the famous 'Williamsburg meeting', a single three-day
meeting of 110 key IBM men, in which they thrashed out the
details of a grand plan to decentralize the organization — a concept
the Old Man had often talked about but seldom practised, except
by accidental oversight. Tom Junior described his father's
organization in his 1962 lectures:[8]

> Prior to the mid-fifties the company was run essentially by one
> man, Thomas J. Watson senior. He had a terrific team around
> him, but it was he who made the decisions. Had IBM had an
> organization chart at the time, there would have been a
> fascinating number of lines — perhaps thirty in all — running into
> his office.

This was only the first of a series of reorganizations, but it began to set the sweeping pattern — overnight change. 'The real achievement at Williamsburg was not that reorganization but the fact that it made IBM readily reorganizable,' Tom Junior commented in 1973. That first reorganization confirmed in the employees the awareness that no matter how much or how often they were shifted around, IBM would take care of them. This awareness became one of IBM's secrets of success as the company changed from a brittle one-man structure to a more flexible mechanism.

Another step in this direction was Tom Junior's elimination in 1959 of the last real difference between white collars and blue collars. As early as 1934 his father had eliminated piecework. Long before behavioural sciences were fashionable in management, Tom Junior understood that the dignity of the individual was not necessarily consistent with hourly wages. Therefore, he put every IBM employee on salary from the first day of 1959.

Another major achievement in Tom Junior's early days was the decision to borrow a huge sum of money from the Prudential Insurance Company to finance research and development of the 650 computer.

The next great risk was Tom Junior's go-ahead for the 360 computer programme in the early sixties. The achievement was not so much the 360 product itself as creating the one-world product line and an organization that could absorb nearly 100,000 new people in one four-year period. IBM was solid and big, but not so solid and big that an entire changeover of this order couldn't put the corporation in jeopardy.

Then as the computer business went into high gear, IBM shifted from being just a sales company to making its own components as well as assembling them. Each of these has turned out to be the 'right' decision for IBM — but at some point during the 360 development the company that the Watsons were building grew strong enough (and so dominated the computer industry) that *any* decision it took became the right decision.

Over the years Tom Junior did something else that must be classed as brilliant. Somehow he kept the team spirit, the sense of corporate ethic, the emphasis on education, even the 'small company' feeling that had come with his father from NCR. Somehow all the new people — up to 3,000 a month — were indoctrinated with the IBM beliefs, moved around the IBM map, and motivated to take on IBM jobs that had never been done before.

Shortly after he became chief executive Tom Junior began making his famous 'wild duck' speeches, which are frequently misunderstood by outsiders. Concerned that so few of his people argued with him and so many kowtowed to his power — a problem that may be even more crucial in IBM today — Tom Junior told his men a story by the Danish philosopher Kierkegaard:[9]

> He told of a man on the coast of Zealand who liked to watch the wild ducks fly south in great flocks each fall. Out of charity, he took to putting feed for them in a nearby pond. After a while some of the ducks no longer bothered to fly south; they wintered in Denmark on what he fed them.
> In time they flew less and less. When the wild ducks returned, the others would circle up to greet them but then head back to their feeding grounds on the pond. After three or four years they grew so lazy and fat that they found difficulty in flying at all. Kierkegaard drew his point — you can make wild ducks tame, but you can never make tame ducks wild again. One might also add that the duck who is tamed will never go anywhere any more.

'I wanted the guys to maintain their integrity and independence, to be willing to lay their jobs on the line if necessary,' he recalled in 1973 just before his retirement.

The two brothers were very different, but seemed to understand each other well. Both had strong tempers, but the elder brother kept his in check, while the younger one often gave vent to his anger. Dick could be vindictive when he felt he had been slighted; he would sometimes gather information (just like any other IBM manager) to justify firing one of the otherwise sacred employees who had offended him. Both men evoked strong loyalties and occasional allergies in the men who worked close to them. Tom Junior was the more controlled of the two, but one graduate who knew them both said 'I personally found Dick the more charming and comfortable of the two. Tom Junior often gave one a sense of having a florid face and tense muscles, fighting his emotions. Dick exploded often; Tom Junior rarely.'

Relaxing isn't always easy, especially when you live with a ghost like Thomas J. Watson Senior. Early in his life Tom Junior learned to unwind with the elements rather than against them. *Fortune* has in different years carried photos of Tom Junior skiing, sailing, or gliding. All these are sports which are basically using the snow or the wind rather than fighting them.

Both Tom Junior and Dick absorbed their father's belief in the importance of Doing Good (though both downplayed their father's insistence on being *seen* to be Doing Good). They had liberal political ideas, flavoured more with a social ethic than a protestant one. Tom Junior was selected 'Businessman of the Year' by *Saturday Review* in 1967. At that time he was serving on President Johnson's advisory committee on labour-management policy, as well as the boards of Brown University, the California Institute of Technology, Sarah Lawrence (a women's college whose president, Charles DiCarlo, is an IBM graduate) and various other boards and foundations. He was serving his third year as national president of the Boy Scouts of America. He kept his activities as much as possible within the confines of the United States.

Dick on the other hand, carried his outside activities further afield. In 1973 he was a trustee of the Hotchkiss School, the Metropolitan Museum of Art, the American Hospital of Paris, and a fellow of Yale University; he was president (like his father) of the International Chamber of Commerce, and a trustee of the Carnegie Endowment for International Peace. In April 1966 he was awarded the rank of Officer in the National Order of the French Legion of Honour.

Within the carefully divided organization their father had created, each of the brothers demonstrated a quirk. With Dick it was grand human gestures, on a scale with his father's. He was a flyer too; he would sweep into an airport in the company plane, the first pilot to arrive after a ferocious three-day storm, or pour similar energies into American cultural activities in France. With Tom the quirk was architecture. He insisted on first-class, low-profile buildings.

Tom Junior's most important organizational achievements kept a low profile, though they sometimes happened literally overnight. Where his father's IBM empire was almost feudal in character, Tom Junior's tidy organization grew purposefully more decentralized, shifting often and fluidly as it grew, breaking into smaller and smaller units, until even a class of six students is broken down into two discussion groups of three each. The important decisions remained in New York for the years of Tom Junior's reign, but the day-to-day autonomy shifted under his guidance, out to the smallest unit that could handle a job and keep the lines back to headquarters clear and open.

'Dick wanted his company to be separate but equal'

Dick's career was similar to his elder brother's in many respects. He attended Yale but left before graduation to join the Army, where he ended up as a major in ordnance in the Philippine Islands. After the war he wanted to stay there and work in the IBM office, but his father (always a devout adherent to education) turned him down; so Dick dutifully returned to Yale, specializing in languages. He joined IBM when he finished in February 1947 and soon afterwards married Ann Hemingway. The senior Watsons joined them on their honeymoon cruise, which was also a business trip to Europe.

Dick's interests always lay abroad, and the Old Man was quick to grasp this difference and use it in the design of the organization. In 1949 the Old Man folded the last foreign agencies into the corporation and created IBM World Trade Corporation. Perhaps in deference to Dick, Canada was shifted from Domestic to World Trade at this point. Dick immediately became vice president and director, and essentially ran World Trade as what *Fortune* called his 'personal fiefdom' for many years thereafter. In 1954 he became president of World Trade and in 1963, two years after Tom Junior became chairman of the IBM board, Dick was appointed chairman of the World Trade board. It says something about the IBM power structure that never during his years of running World Trade was he based in Europe, though he was an indefatigable international commuter.

Dick had separate but almost equal status with his brother in the corporation itself. He became a vice president and director of IBM in 1959, then head of the corporate staff in 1963. He became senior vice president of IBM in 1964, and the post of vice chairman of the IBM board was created for him in 1966.

IBM today is a corporation whose success has been built on sibling rivalry. This rivalry is not so much between the two brothers as between their corporate entities — Domestic and World Trade. These two separate phenomena began to exhibit a creative tension in the fifties, as the younger son built a wall around his portion of the company and the elder son respected it. Once the wall was built most communication between the two halves had to go up and over the top, through Dick. Tom Junior later acknowledged: 'That wall was plenty high and plenty thick.' Although he had been against the formation of World Trade to begin with (because there were already too few top level managers available and control would be more difficult), once his father had made the decision, Tom Junior kept his hands off. Their father had put Dick into that job, and that settled it.

At first, in the nature of all new subsidiaries, World Trade was treated by Domestic as a 'dumping ground' — a place to send people who didn't quite fit. Then it became an informal resource— good World Traders were wooed to Domestic for choice positions. The highly competitive World Trade people began to turn the tables, though, and use Domestic as their own pool of talent. Whenever an IBM man from Japan, say, would arrive in New York, his first act would be to get in touch with other former Japan hands and ask around to fill his shopping list — 'a good personnel man for Tokyo headquarters', or 'someone who can cope with the Philippine situation'. One graduate credited Dick with an intuitive brilliance about the people he selected. 'Between 1950 and the early sixties, he managed to keep out the professional tourists and international dilettantes who might have come in and screwed it up.'

Tom Junior's 'control' over World Trade — the factor that had influenced his original opposition — was structural rather than operational. Revenues were not allowed to increase faster than profits. Al Williams who was IBM president for many years is generally credited as the architect of this financial structure that gave Dick and World Trade independence at the same time it permitted IBM to keep track of its overseas business.

During the first decade of its existence World Trade grew from $51 million revenues to almost $300 million. By 1963 when Dick shifted more of his attention to corporate matters, World Trade's revenue was up fifteen times from 1950, to $788 million. Profits had risen similarly from about $7 million to almost $105 million.

World Trade's pioneers with Dick during the fifties tended to be Americanized foreigners. Jack Brent from Canada was executive vice president. *Fortune* in 1960[10] said: 'Brent was one of the first men picked to help World Trade get started in 1950. Now his main concern is to strengthen the self sufficiency of managements abroad and cut their need for day-to-day help from New York.' Other key executives were Luigi ('Louis') Castaldi, the Italian-born manager of IBM Europe who spoke five languages, and Klaus Hendrick (part-Jewish nephew of Dehomag founder Heidinger) who had fled to the United States on an IBM training programme in 1936 and stayed through the war.

From the first days of World Trade Dick's erratic and peripatetic brilliance had been anchored to the steady stolidity of a New York accountant, Edwin Goldfuss, known throughout World Trade as 'Eddie'. He was the visible and imperturbable manifestation to World Traders of Al Williams's financial strategies. 'Eddie was an accountant, with provincial views and a simple approach to the world,' said one graduate. 'He made a strange teammate for the urbane Francophile, but it worked.' The strategy was that this year's profits must grow in proportion equal to or more than the growth in this year's revenue. Only this way could the company go

on financing all the new machines customers leased. 'They couldn't
have done it with soapsuds or cars, but they could with computers,'
said the graduate.'On the one hand you had a guy who could
implement this down-to-earth financial control system. On the
other you had Dick, dispensing holy water on the foreign nationals
who could run the country organizations. Domestic fed in the
product and had the sense to leave them alone.'

This separation, which seemed to carry the mark of approval of
the Old Man himself, may have been the right policy for the
wrong reason. The organization that was set up to give the younger
son room for separate growth became a fractured collection of
relatively independent companies, but somehow it worked. 'If
they had used the highly structured, monolithic sales approach of
the Domestic organization they wouldn't be as far ahead,' said a
graduate who later competed with World Trade.

In the early years of World Trade, Dick had worked with a
small entrepreneurial group — Brent from Canada, Castaldi from Italy,
Tommy Cummins from Texas, Jean Ghertman and Raymond
Pailloux from France. As Castaldi and Brent later agreed: 'Titles
didn't mean anything. We didn't have an organization chart.' These
pioneers laid down the patterns for World Trade's later growth.
They took the Old Man's concept of a 'product by plant' manufacturing pattern and Europeanized it. In 1951 Fran Ritz, a
manufacturing man, broke a typewriter into components and laid
them out on a table. He then invited the various Europeans to go
back to their countries and get bids on each part in large quantities.
Thus they created an internal 'Common Market' and began to be
less dependent on Domestic for parts, and more welcome to their
national hosts. They began to set up industry specializations, a
forerunner of the 'centres of competence' of the sixties. They set
out sales territories, labs for European R&D, education programmes,
and accounting procedures that endure today.

'Dick and Brent wanted innovations all the time,' recalled a
colleague who credited the two with the entire atmosphere of
'order from disorder' that helped World Trade grow. Dick's drive
and intelligence, often underestimated outside, attracted and held
these entrepreneurs who imported the Old Man's IBM culture to
Europe and added their own pragmatic flavour to it, encouraging
each country organization to solve as many of its own problems as
possible.

In this sense, the 'internationality' of the equipment came from
the Old Man's vision of pushing his empire's marketing and manufacturing overseas; but the true multinationality of IBM just

'happened' as the enterprising young men in the fifties had to cope with currency limitations and different country situations by helping each other out informally. It was Dick who blasted out of his father's American corporation the less rigid framework that allowed the pioneers to solve their problems on the spot.

Organization men don't lay down cultural patterns, although they can enhance existing ones. They do, on the other hand, know how to bring order out of disorder. Thus, after a dozen years of pioneering, World Trade needed a different kind of international manager. In 1962 Dick's job was enhanced with more New York involvement; Castaldi went to IBM Italy, and Brent back to Canada. Gil Jones came over from Domestic with a cadre of young professionals, bringing with them the more formal budgets, operating plans, organizations and policies from Domestic. Dick seemed less comfortable with these people — and they with him. The men of the fifties invariably spoke of Dick with affection and reverence, even 20 years later. The World Traders of the sixties sometimes had more mixed reactions. From that point on, more of Dick's attention was focussed outside.

Dick was an outside man, at his best when he was calling on ambassadors or accepting international awards or negotiating to free his men in Eastern Europe. In 1963 he arranged to have a Hundred Percent Club meeting in Rome, including an audience with the Pope for the entire Club. (IBM had just given the church a model 650 computer to help translate the Dead Sea scrolls.)

By 1960 Dick was travelling about 50 percent of the time. When he wasn't visiting World Trade organizations he would be in the New York headquarters by 8 a.m. for two hours with a Berlitz language teacher. After French he mastered Spanish, then Portuguese, then German. By the sixties, while he was serving as World Trade's outside man and informal ambassador, the day-to-day operations were in the hands of two men named Smith and Jones — Charley Smith and Gil Jones.

'Gil Jones is probably the best all-around executive I've ever seen,' said one graduate. (The opinion was not quite unanimous; another regarded Jones as 'horribly difficult', while a third called him 'a delightful tough guy.') What Jones added to World Trade in the early sixties, besides management 'flair', was a cadre of 30 or 40 experts from Domestic, who brought with them more of Domestic's procedures and a sense of tightly knit organization that World Trade needed badly after a pioneering decade of rapid growth.

Jones's alter ego was Charles C. Smith (still 'Charley' to the graduates), who had come over as head of marketing, then became World Trade vice president. 'We ran it as a team,' said Charley Gil handled the staff at home, as president. Then in 1963 we Jones handled the staff at home, as president. Then in 1963 we reversed roles, and I served as chief of staff while he looked after the subsidiaries.

Jones believed in changing the assignments for his men all the time, augmenting the fluidity that is still one of the World Trade's greatest assets. Charley Smith, for example, at one time or another had charge of all the different staff groups — personnel, education, marketing, engineering, OP. This kind of management movement on a broad scale quickly developed a central core of men who could cope with anything anywhere. 'People would do things for Charley Smith that they wouldn't for anybody else,' said one graduate. 'If you went to Jones with a problem it would be "your problem". With Charley Smith it was "our problem".'

A fourth key man as Dick's organization grew in the sixties was Maisonrouge. Dick brought him into World Trade headquarters in 1956 as manager of market planning and research. In 1958 (at the worst point in Franco-American political relations), Dick gave Maisonrouge responsibility for a ten-country region in Europe. Then in 1959, extending his father's concept of having nationals run the country organizations, Dick brought Maisonrouge up to be assistant general manager for Europe. Dick's pioneers in the fifties had been 'Americanized' foreigners; but Maisonrouge was (and remained) determinedly French. The need for foreigners at headquarters was already growing obvious to Dick, a decade before most multi-nationals paid much attention to the idea. Maisonrouge went back to World Trade headquarters again in 1962 as a vice president. The token foreigner adapted himself so capably that he was elected president of IBM World Trade Europe (a post created for the occasion) in 1964, and elected a director of World Trade in April 1967. Six months later his meteoric career was crowned with the presidency of IBM World Trade and a coveted IBM vice president position. As in Domestic the chairman — Jones — was chief executive of World Trade. This situation finally changed in late 1972, when Maisonrouge took over as chief executive and Jones, though retaining the World Trade chairmanship, shifted to the Corporate Office at Armonk. (Finally in 1974, Maisonrouge returned to Paris as chairman of a new and seemingly more autonomous IBM Europe, as World Trade split into two parts and began to exercise less visible control.)

Wall construction went into high gear in the early sixties. Separate (and sometimes equal) educational institutions were set up — a management school at Blaricum in the Netherlands or a Systems Research Institute in Geneva, for example. Whether or not these were identical to their counterparts in Endicott and New York City, the need to have them was as much emotional as logical.

So was Dick's management style. 'I'd fire any manager who behaved like Dick,' said one former lieutenant. Another mentioned undignified behaviour. Several attributed the wall to a lack of confidence on Dick's part, a fear of failure that was compounded by the visible success of his elder brother. 'A Dick Watson meeting told a lot about Dick,' said one graduate. 'If you were saying good things about World Trade he would want everybody in the company to come in and hear. If your message was negative, it was just the two of you behind closed doors.' Perhaps because of this aspect of his personality, Dick always prepared himself beautifully for meetings. 'If we were coming in at 10 with a report, Maisonrouge would be there at 9 briefing Dick with all the necessary background. Dick couldn't accept criticism; Tom Junior had room to change his mind, and could read you the riot act one day for "letting him decide wrong" the day before. Not Dick.'

Dick had another problem. He couldn't drink gracefully. Both brothers had gone through periods of ostentatious (and no doubt rebellious) drinking when they were new boys in their father's company, but Tom Junior had learned to have the occasional cocktail with comfort (to the extent that he was once pictured on the cover of *Sports Illustrated* in his ski lodge with drinks clearly in view). Dick's problem was not any compulsion to drink, but a tendency to let his temper go if he did. In his years as IBM's ambassador to the world he attended many formal occasions where a cocktail glass in hand was obligatory. His usual response was to exchange his full glass quietly with a subordinate's near-empty one, avoiding any possibility of behaviour that would reflect badly on IBM. Thus a man who attended such functions with him for 25 years could say truthfully: 'I never saw Dick take a drink,' yet others observed with equal truth: 'He was a terror when he drank.'

One impressive thing about IBM is that whenever something has to be done, no matter how distasteful, IBM does it right. Thus 'when Watsons are wrong, they apologize' (Tom Junior's unequivocal words). In the early sixties, for example, Dick flew to Britain to review the activities of the little UK company, which was not doing as well as its continental counterparts. He went along on a sales visit to an ITT company and was dissatisfied with the way the account was handled. He then called the entire sales force together and tore them to pieces for their inept, un-IBM-like behaviour and results. This was an unfair tongue-lashing at best, and particularly demoralizing to a sales team which was trying to compete with a firmly entrenched UK computer industry, including IBM's former agents who had been given more than 30 years head-start by the Old Man. One of the indignant salesmen wrote a letter complaining about Dick's own un-IBM-like behaviour. Tom Hudson, who headed IBM UK at the time, risked Dick's enmity by letting the letter go through. Within ten days Dick was back, apologizing to the assembled salesmen and characteristically turning the meeting into an educational session.

By 1963 the wall was sufficiently visible that an IBM internal journal codified it under the headline: 'No Walls in IBM' — a kind of affirmation-by-denial that was reminiscent of the Old Man.

3
Organization
&
planning

The credit for IBM's centralized control belongs to Tom Junior (who passes on a good deal of it to Al Williams). The credit for World Trade's decentralized management belongs to Dick. How the two dovetail so effectively is an intriguing question.

'Organization charts are obsolete before they're printed'

Throughout the Old Man's era IBM enjoyed rapid growth, but the lines of control all led directly to his office. Tom Junior's 'Williamsburg meeting' for three days in 1957 marked the first time that overnight reorganization hit IBM managers. Because most of them had grown up within the company, because jobs were assured for all, and because Tom Junior made it clear that this was the beginning of a new era of flexibility in which reorganizations would be the rule rather than the exception, most of them adapted quickly. The former monolith was broken down into three more manageable elements — data processing (DP), office products (OP), and military systems. Those three have continued relatively unchanged, with a further breakdown of the (by then monolithic) DP division in 1972.

In spite of the constantly changing internal organization, there is an ongoing structure, and surprisingly little turnover of people at the top compared to most corporations of IBM's size. All the top men have grown up within IBM. Many of them (like the Watson brothers themselves) have never worked anywhere else.

The top decision-making body at IBM is the Management Review Committee (the MRC), which is a three-man body headed by the chairman.* Normally it meets two or three times a month, hearing presentations from senior staff people or task force leaders about matters of policy. Throughout Tom Junior's era this was a rather democratic group, willing to spend time worrying about the welfare of 26 people in Bulgaria who were going to become government employees with the same earnestness with which it considered the next product line.

Separate three-man committees operate in a similar manner but meet oftener for Domestic (the Management Committee or MC) and World Trade (the Management Operations Committee or MOC). Since the MC, MOC and MRC memberships overlap coordination is rapid and effective. Minutes of the MC and MRC (which became a matter of public record during the Telex anti-trust trial of 1973) show a classic layering of detail.

Agreement is 'engineered' tidily at these levels. All the specialists, staff people and top line managers who are concerned with an issue have a chance to review recommendations and 'concur' or 'non-concur' (both are verbs in IBM language). The same mechanism has already operated from the bottom up, so by the time a final decision is reached, all parties have had an input to it. This may help explain the astonishing speed with which IBM can react once a decision is made. One factor may be that a great deal of time is devoted to 'defining the problem'; by the time this has been thoroughly debated by all parties, the solution is likely to be more universally apparent.

The process was never trouble-free; IBM's decision-makers are men with force and conviction. 'You get some very rough meetings,' Charley Smith once observed. 'There were usually unified opinions worked out among individual groups before they arrived. Engineering would have its own internal combat to determine the chosen approach, and then meet head to head with manufacturing or sales. It used to take a good deal of refereeing. But these were major arguments about directions, and men with convictions would stand up for what they thought was right for the company.'

The convictions were not always first-hand. Computer expert Bob Bemer (architect of several IBM systems and father of the

*In 1974 a top level reorganization replaced the MRC and MC with a larger 'Corporate Management Committee' (CMC). The names change but the style and structure endure.

ASCII standard code for terminals) recalled a time when IBM was trying to decide on a particular business machine. B.O. Evans and his team had designed a '660 system' at Endicott, and Rex Rice led the '750' team at Poughkeepsie. (The chosen machine was to succeed the 650 and 705 systems.) Bemer's applied programming group recommended the 750. 'Unfortunately,' says Bemer, 'the programmers of those days were not yet emancipated and were not allowed to sit in the highest councils of decision at IBM. Our decision had to be relayed by Roger Bury, manager of education. Unfortunately, Bury somehow got it backward, and said that applied programming wanted the 660. Seems as though everyone said that that was a good basis for decision.'

'Once they made a decision, they moved fast compared to other companies,' said Charley Smith. 'Once the argument was over you picked up the other guy's answer and ran with it. You didn't stand around and sulk and lose days. This is a powerful force in IBM.'

This process remains relatively unchanged, no matter what the organization chart. Because the charts are a moving target, it is impossible to pinpoint responsibilities from outside with any ongoing reliability – a factor which enhances IBM's privacy. In 1973, before Tom Junior left the company, the MRC consisted of Tom Junior, IBM's new chairman Frank Cary, and World Trade chairman Jones. The MC at that time was chaired by Jones, with senior vice presidents Bob Hubner and Warren Hume. The MOC, new in 1973 and still somewhat the junior committee, consisted of World Trade president Maisonrouge plus vice presidents Dick Warren and Bert Witham. Different members of this eight-man top management group are 'contact points' for different parts of IBM. Jones in 1973 was also a member of the three-man Corporate Office – the day-to-day management of IBM – where he was contact point for World Trade and part of Domestic while Cary was contact point for the rest of Domestic; Tom Junior let his two MRC partners do most of the contacting.

At each layer within each organization, there is similar complexity, with 'functional' lines (the people who tell you what to do) and 'administrative' lines (the people who tell you what to charge it to and otherwise handle the 'housekeeping'), not to mention a plethora of dotted lines, task forces, temporary assignments and coordination points. With plenty of practice in reorganizing and a history of secure employment, most IBMers take these 'n-dimensional matrices' of management lines in their stride. As one graduate said: 'IBM gets away with murder organizationally, because of this magnificent, unanimous commitment and dedication to service and sales. With all those dotted lines and multiple bosses, everybody's on the same side. Thus you get cause for debate but not real disagreement because the ultimate goal is the same. I've never seen this in any other company.'

The primary divisions — what might be called the thickest lines on the moving-picture of an organization chart — in the Domestic organization are related to produce lines, while those of World Trade are geographical. In addition to OP (typewriters, copiers, dictaphones and so on — which are sold rather than leased) and military systems, the main computer group has breakdowns into what amounts to hardware, software, and tape/disk storage product divisions. The basic research group is separate from all these, but each has its own development labs. The DP group used to have a separate manufacturing organization but this evaporated into the separate product divisions in 1972, as manufacturing got cheaper and less important, and other jobs needed to be found for surplus manufacturing people. Another mysterious disappearance in that reorganization was any grouping related to terminals (a growing part of the computer business); presumably these were considered too important to be left in an exposed and visible position while everyone was discussing how to break up IBM, so they dissipated into separate clusters within industry-related groups in other divisions.

Activities pinpointed to particular groups of customers, such as airlines, hospitals, or insurance, are getting more important in IBM. The labs are tending to specialize towards certain industries or 'applications', as are certain big-city sales offices. Each target industry also has Domestic and World Trade 'centres of competence, for advance applications, usually on a Cooperative basis with a large pioneering customer.

The stresses within this confusing and changing (but exceedingly orderly) organization are myriad. There are stresses between OP and DP. OP is less glamourous than DP, both in sales and manufacturing, but somehow seems more 'Watsonian' in spirit. OP people. tend to be younger. When an OP man makes a sale, 'he gets his points on the board tomorrow and his commission cheque next month,' while his DP counterpart may have to wait six months before he knows whether he's made a sale or not. OP people tend to object that the profits from the products they sell bring in instant cash to support expensive research for the computers the DP people lease. Their facilities are seldom as elegant as those of DP. Sweden, for example, hosts a fancy DP training centre with 30 employees on a handsome site. But the OP people there have their training centre in the cellar of the Stockholm headquarters, staffed with three men and a girl.

There are delicate differences in status between salesmen, systems engineers (SEs) and customer engineers (CEs) too. Salesmen and SEs are closely allied. The SE tends to be a little younger and a little more technical. If you come in straight from university you become an SE first, and then you may become a salesman later. The two have a similar level of seniority; if the salesman makes exactly 100 percent of his quota he makes slightly more than the SE, who has neither commission nor quota though he is attached to the branch office and paid as part of the marketing budget. The SE, on the other hand, has less risk, and considers himself more intelligent than the salesman. He is also the salesman's conscience figure. The salesman's tendency once he has closed a sale would be to rush off and sell another; the SE is much more concerned with the hardware and intimate software he has sold to the customer, and how to get it to do what the salesman said it would do.

Both the salesman and the SE look down on the CE, whose job it is to oversee installation, maintenance and the actual working of the computer. The CE is not even part of marketing, but reports to a CE manager at the district level. However, the CEs hold their own with a rich diet of jokes (conferring membership in their own subculture) at the expense of the salesmen. For instance, they tell about the SE, CE and salesman who had been stranded in the blizzard for a week, in a forest full of wild bears. Finally the salesman, a natural leader, took control. 'OK lads,' he said. 'The only thing to eat is one of those bears. Let's each take one of these logs as a club. You two stand in the hut, either side of the door. I'll go and taunt a bear and get him to chase me into the hut, where we'll knock his brains out.'

The SE and CE stood shivering in the hut for half an hour, until they heard a tremendous trampling and roaring. The door burst open and the salesman rushed in, closely followed by an enormous bear. Quick as a flash the salesman nipped out again and called exuberantly from behind the closed door: 'Great! You chaps sort this one out; I'll go and get another.'

Obviously there is stress between World Trade and Domestic people, but the organization does everything it can to allay it. Since the 360 announcement in 1964 there has been a steady evolution towards a 'one-world product line', so the wall has become less important and there is less chance that the two halves of the company will clash head-on. In this approach to organization, the geographical sales organization is responsible for the revenues from a product — how well it meets the sales quotas (which are different for planning and motivating purposes). The costs for a product are the responsibility of manufacturing, which is organized roughly on a continental basis (though this, too, is growing in a one-world direction). World Trade manufactures for itself most of the IBM product line, except for a few low-volume items. The profit a particular product generates is the responsibility of the single laboratory that has global 'control' of the product — an arrangement that came into being after some major clashes between Domestic and World Trade labs.

The stress was worst in the early sixties, when World Trade proposed to develop its own product line. At that time even equipment conversions to Europe's 50-cycle electricity had to be handled by special request to New York. Although Tom wanted a single, unified product line, Dick passionately maintained that Europe was different. World Trade had to compete with Bull, Olivetti, Powers, and half a dozen British computer manufacturers. Dick tried to set up his own group for R&D inside World Trade, starting with an inexpensive business computer, the Model 3000, that worked on small punched cards (a precursor to the modern IBM System 3 computer). After World Trade had taken quite a few orders and Dick was actively pushing the machine for US markets, Tom Junior questioned the programme; Dick began to question it too. It became clear that World Trade was not geared to carry out as much independent manufacturing as Dick had envisaged. This led to cancellation of the project, which gave Domestic engineering people the chance to say quietly to their own management: 'See, World Trade can't do it.' The World Trade R&D people continued to come up with odd things like a Chinese typewriter, but R&D was gradually absorbed into the world-wide activity after introduction of the 360 line.

Tom Junior seemed happy to allow a wall between the sales organizations, traditionally the most important and competitive part of the company. But manufacturing and R&D were another matter. He insisted that the manufacturing people have frequent contact with their foreign counterparts, and there were many points of contact between the two organizations in every other function, even while their sales people were battling for supremacy. The near-conflict between the brothers over the 3000 may have had some influence on Tom Junior's eventual decision to have a one-world product line; further conflict was to be avoided at all costs.

54

'Africa and Israel are part of Northern Europe'

World Trade and Domestic can never be completely intermingled. They are structurally and psychologically different. The men who have international careers, going from one country to another, insist that their jobs give them more room to be resourceful and creative than those of their more stable Domestic brothers. A man going through five countries in five weeks had to be able to solve problems as he found them and to make decisions on the spot, rather than simply to gather information for someone else's decision-making. To the local IBMers he *was* headquarters. For the nationals who run the various country organizations there is more autonomy too. They are separated from (or buffered from) the various headquarters layers by national cultures, languages, laws and government or economic situations in a way that no American IBM office could envisage.

The World Trade men sometimes made mistakes, but each segment was small enough that a wrong decision in Manila did not have a major effect on the overall results from the Tokyo-based area. The countries were folded into areas and regions. As the organization grew, the IBM map took on strange shapes. British Africa was part of the Northern Europe region, but not a subsidiary of IBM UK, while the former French possessions were part of the IBM France organization. Israel was first run from the United States, then it joined the Northern Europe region (along with Iceland, Scandinavia, the UK and others.) The French African countries joined France and its former possessions in Southern Europe. Greece, Turkey, the Arab countries, Iran and Pakistan were lumped with Switzerland, Austria etc. as 'Central Europe'. Area and region lines were drawn and re-drawn to suit the convenience, personalities, or political situations on the spot.

Two-thirds of World Trade's income traditionally comes from 'Europe', and the lion's share of that has always been from Germany. However, France was originally the flagship of the World Trade fleet and is again pushing close to Germany in net contribution. IBM Europe is headquartered in Paris.

In a financial sense World Trade could do business in only five countries (Germany, France, Britain, Canada and Japan, in roughly that order) without appreciable loss of income. But that was not the Old Man's concept of IBM, nor Dick's. World Trade has not five but 45 'big' countries, and more than 80 'little' ones. These little country organizations where IBM 'shows the flag' are just as important to the corporation as their political counterparts are to the United Nations. They battle for degrees of autonomy — a little extra money for education, or a few more assignees. Fierce fights for resources have nothing to do with international politics; the Arab and Israeli IBM men show no discomfort when they sit down in the same IBM classroom.

The organization has traditionally had two major segments — 'Europe' (in its expanded definition) and the rest of the non-Domestic world. Military orders (including Vietnam) are handled from the Federal Systems Division in Washington. As foreign business increases and Domestic business levels out by comparison (in a market that is much closer to saturation), IBM envisages a new organization, playing down World Trade or even eliminating it as a separate corporation,* and growing up four separate 'companies': Domestic, Europe, Asia/Pacific and Latin America. This is probably the only way the Watson wall can be completely obliterated.

As the seventies approached, two things affected the wall. First, World Trade's real and visible growth was so rapid that it threatened to outstrip Domestic. Second, Dick left to become US ambassador to France. The World Trade growth seems to have surprised IBM, though as early as February 1963 *Business Week* said: 'If as a mathematical exercise you project IBM's current growth rates for foreign and domestic revenues, the two sales curves cross in 1973 at about $6 billion each.' (At the end of 1973 IBM reported sales of $5,850 million for Domestic and $5,143 million for World Trade, but the profits were $722 million and $853 million respectively.) Later in the sixties an IBM financial man predicted that World Trade would pass Domestic in sales by the mid-seventies. 'They all told me I was out of my mind,' he recalled. He prepared the classic flipcharts, with all his assumptions and conclusions, and presented them to his boss. They then took the presentation to Dick, who didn't believe it either, but mentioned the prediction to Tom Junior. He, in turn, asked his lieutenant Learson to comment; Learson came in with a thorough presentation showing all the reasons why it could never happen.

Like Tom Junior, Dick avoided head-on confrontation. In the early sixties Tom Junior decided to move IBM headquarters out of

*The two segments were formalized in 1974 when 'World Trade' was overtaken by two US-chartered offspring: IBM Europe/Middle East/Africa Corp. (E/ME/A or Emma for short) under Maisonrouge and IBM Americas/Far East (A/FE or 'Ah-fee' for short) under Gordon Williamson.

New York City to Armonk. There was pressure on Dick to move World Trade headquarters too, but he didn't want to be seen to be abandoning the city or the United Nations. Rather than take a stand, Dick took a survey. The results were predictable. The managers generally wanted to move north, where most of them already had their homes. The administrative employees, on the other hand, came from the five boroughs of the city, and they wanted World Trade to stay where it was. In IBM the feelings of the lower employees take precedence, so World Trade stayed at the UN Plaza location for another decade.

Once Dick left the company, Jones set about erasing the last vestiges of the Watson wall. Jones was already straddling it with both corporate and World Trade positions; as Maisonrouge showed his ability not only to represent the non-American view in World Trade but to head the organization in fact as well as in voice, Jones moved to the more remote recesses of Armonk. He negotiated more autonomy for World Trade at the same time he started dismantling the single New York headquarters and pushing more decisions and visibility into its Ah-fee and Emma components. From indications in the MRC minutes of 1971 and 1972, Maisonrouge was pushing for maximum independence, especially for IBM Europe in Paris, while most of the American vice presidents were reluctant to lose any more control. Jones deftly manoeuvred a gradual change whereby the role of World Trade headquarters in New York became less autocratic or 'fatherly' — and a little less important. Instead, headquarters became a little more supportive, practical, almost 'motherly'. The changes did not carry words like these on organization charts or memoranda,* but that's how they were understood within the IBM Family. In March 1972 IBM Europe became an 'operating group', which denoted the change in management philosophy. It could decide its own announcement dates, and country-by-country plans, which were formerly negotiated with New York separately, were combined, coordinated and negotiated by the men in Paris, who then submitted a single plan to New York for coordination with the plans of Ah-fee.

'Budget-setting and quota-setting are different things'

Most of the things IBM does exceptionally well are simple. Financial planning is one of them. The Old Man used to have a

*Until April 1974.

plaque on his wall that said: 'Businesses are built on *net* profits!'
Net profits happen this year, not ten years hence; they are measured
in terms of earnings per share, which must be a steadily rising line on
the graph. Prudent management, in his terms, meant the ability to
maintain the shareholders' earnings and still find enough profit to
plough back into the business to build future net profit.

IBM does not like discontinuities on its charts, either up or down.
Tom Junior learned this lesson early. In September 1952 when he
was already distressed ('resigning for the 18th time') because everything he proposed to do was getting revised out of recognition, Al
Williams came in with 'bad news' — an 18 percent increase in gross.
But the spending was out of proportion to the income, so there
would be no increase in net profit. 'Where's the control?' he asked.
'How can that happen?' He was worried about how he could explain
it at the subsequent annual meeting, but fortunately nobody asked,
partly because stringent economy helped him eke out a 2 percent
profit in the remaining months of the year. He didn't ever want to
be surprised again. He wanted to decide, rather than have it happen.
Carl Olson was then brought in as IBM's first director of budgets,
to institute precise control.

World Trade's plans were always remarkably accurate — much
more so than Domestic's, as many World Traders pointed out. One
key finance man said: 'This wasn't because we were bigger geniuses
than Domestic. But we had a hundred different planning offices,
where they had only a few. We were closer to our markets.' Both
halves of the company were and are extraordinary compared to
most companies. By the time the seven-year planning process was
seven years old it was possible to see amazing correlations between
the first projections and the actual results — though this 100 percent
accuracy may be a kind of self-fulfilling prophecy.

In addition to pinpoint planning, the IBM finance mechanisms
were full of characteristic protections. Contingency plans, special
funds, everything it took to ensure that there were very few surprises.
'Of course there are all sorts of reservoir accounts on the balance
sheets,' said a former finance man. 'These were our "extra bucket".
There were no surprises. We didn't use shadow corporations or things
like that — just good, clean, honest business intelligence, with
plenty of rainy-day accounts.'

When it comes to the corporation's total revenues, the sum is
smaller than the parts. This is a basic principle of consolidation in
accounting, but dealings in more than a hundred countries have
developed it to a fine art at IBM.

All the revenues and profits calculated on business between the various national IBM companies must be cancelled out before their results are put together in the corporation's annual reports or monthly print-outs. Because each country has slightly different reporting rules and accounting principles, this is a major task. One thing that has kept it orderly is the point system — IBM's international monetary unit of account. One point is equal to $1 per month revenue. The salesman's quota is expressed in points; as are the two-year plan, the 'greybook' plan for each product, and the account in each country. In 1972 an eminent American said: 'We have been fortunate being tied to the dollar. Converting pesos to pounds, or coping with the inflation with French francs was a terrible problem. At one point the French would devalue every nine months! Every IBMer can convert points into local currency, annualize them, figure commissions on them (if they are quota points). Yet the books are kept in pounds in Britain, in francs in France and so on — a multinational kind of double-entry book keeping.

There are really three processes here, not just one. These are budget-setting, quota-setting, and planning. The budget-setting determines this year's expenditure, with a rolling second year that is more changeable. The budget is how much an organization will spend. The plan is how much it expects to bring in, on a product-by-product basis. (The two-year 'operating plan' which is a World Trade manager's bible has no country-by-country breakdowns — only numbers and project descriptions on a function-by-function basis such as 'DP Manufacturing' or 'World Trade Personnel'.) The quota is the geographical breakdown of the plan to the country, district, branch and individual salesman.

Quota-setting is the basic element in the planning process. Each geographical organization proposes upwards; World Trade's major thrust is at the country level, with varying degrees of 'assistance' from headquarters people, who try to guide the process so the countries come in with what is expected of them. The budget derives naturally from the quota, with less interference. 'It was a bottoms-up process, with oodles of guidance from headquarters, but it was still their plan; they made it and they were responsible for meeting it,' said a former budget director from World Trade. Most of the guidance dealt with product allocations rather than country totals.

Each layer of the plan, expressed in the usual bulky roll of flipcharts, is reviewed with the area manager and several staff people. They look most closely at the quota — the number of points growth (NIRI or Net Installed Revenue Increase, or installed points) the country expects for the first year of the plan, followed by the increased sales (NSRI or Net Sales Revenue Increase, or sales points), which aren't likely to be income until the subsequent year, and are not quite as important in budget-setting as a result. IBM counts no chickens before they hatch, even though it keeps close watch on these fertile eggs and protects them fiercely if a competitor threatens them.

From the country manager's viewpoint, the cultural ideal was to set difficult, aggressive targets, then meet them. Israel gained a particularly good reputation for this; European countries tend to be conservative. Sales offices know they will be rewarded for meeting quotas and punished or expelled from membership for not meeting them, so they turn in conservative plans. The process of negotiating them up — until the 1970-1 recessions — usually resulted in a plan that dovetailed closely with the actual results. A different situation exists for manufacturing plants, which have to support real estate, expensive machinery and production workers. Manufacturing managers tend to turn in high goals, which mean they will get more men and machines to meet them, so divisional managers traditionally disagree, negotiating for lower targets and less expenditure.

Because IBM acknowledges that plans exist to be changed, they can help the company or a unit within it to react with a surprising degree of flexibility for such a large firm, rather than freezing it into a single set course with unchangeable assumptions and expectations. When the recessions hit and it became clear that it was not just one bad month, or two, or seven, the quotas were negotiated downwards to preserve morale and the integrity of the planning process — and the budgets were cut as well. This ability to react is exemplary; however, the extreme measure of homework IBM puts into planning, with contingency plans and fallback positions for every conceivable disaster, may have forced the company into a defensive posture of reacting to external change rather than initiating it, particularly in World Trade. The planning goes to almost ludicrous lengths to cover things that everybody knows cannot happen. One graduate suggested this lifted rather than imposed restrictions: 'One secret of success is that nobody pays much attention to the work done by the overabundance of talented staff people. The major decisions are made on "judgment", not facts. The men who have to make the decisions *know* the staff people have done their homework, so they can go on to the things that take intuition.'

Every country uses the same forms, same layout, with everything expressed in points. All the standard planning forms have computed ratios, which derive automatically as the forms are filled in, so managers at every level in every country have standard measures of performance. They can tell at a glance whether the ratios for productivity, expenses or service are in balance. Thus many decisions can be made almost automatically. However, the standard ratios can also cause problems. The 'balanced growth' approach Al Williams created when IBM was still hungry for cash may not be appropriate for a company that now has an embarrassment of riches and too few permissible ways to invest them. And this approach is not suited to today's developing country organizations, which can afford to invest faster than they produce revenue — providing headquarters has high confidence in their planning abilities and political stability. Some are now allowed to absorb more cash than they generate, the first sign of erosion of the balanced-growth principle. These countries are small, so the policy so far has had little effect on financial results. But the seemingly minor change, which began in the early seventies, marks a major change of attitudes at the centre of World Trade.

'People in motion are the oil in IBM's machinery'

All the specialists — CEs, personnel people, education, lab people, finance — have their own specialist reporting lines as well as product and/or geographical lines. Which lines are solid and which dotted on the changing chart is supposed to be determined by the situation. Sometimes the official situation and the real one are different. 'When the dotted lines are stronger than the solid ones,' one graduate observed, 'it's usually a function of the people rather than the chart.'

'A lot of tensions and conflicts in World Trade are attributed to nationality,' another headquarters graduate commented. 'They say "Those damn Yanks". But some of the tensions may actually be due to the solid versus the dotted lines on the org chart. The British or French professionals resented interference from Corporate just exactly like the people in Endicott resented it. It was just easier for the foreigners to rationalize that the problem was due to nationality.'

In addition to the dotted lines on the charts, there are the invisible lines. The IBM people are constantly meeting, briefing each other, task-forcing, travelling or telephoning. As one European put it: 'Every other minute we had visits from head-quarters people or our counterparts in marketing, personnel or finance. Or we'd go down to Paris and see them. Then there were all the phone calls between countries — that's money! That's *big* money! When I started with IBM I was amazed when I saw every-body casually picking up their phones to call Paris or New York. Even when they cut down our budget, they never cut the budget for phone calls.'

Combined with all the assignments, transfers, education activities and Family Dinners, this phoning and visiting gives people a chance to develop informal networks, groups of people they know and trust. Those are the channels for many important communications and innovations. The corporation tacitly encourages them (to a point). As an American graduate put it: 'Top management has a good feeling for the way things really work. They are aware that things are done outside the formal organization, through friends in the company. They want to keep those paths open.'

9
Sales
&
training

Except for the lowly but lucrative typewriters, most of what IBM calls sales is really rental. In the Old Man's time all of IBM's equipment business was rental; since 1956 the balance between sales and rental has had a profound effect on the company's culture as well as its balance sheet. In the annual accounts, a slight shift from rental towards sales can have a sharp effect on the profit, causing embarrassing ups and downs that somehow have to be smoothed. On the behavioural side, salesmen develop a totally different attitude when the company retains ownership of about 80 percent of its products.

The leasing basis amounts to a self-enforced guarantee to the customer. The computer industry is one of the few businesses in which the company that makes the product actually continues to take care of it. It is also one of the few in which a firm can go bankrupt simply because a product was much more successful than the firm or its financial backers anticipated. Hence IBM's traditional insistence on 'balanced growth'. Each machine leased to a customer uses up more capital, until the pipeline fills up with income from previous years and/or the rate of 'sales' slows down.

IBM computers are not the least expensive.* Nor are they the most technically advanced. The very size of IBM's customer base also means they must be 'generalized', all things to all users, rather than specialized for a particular type of industry or task — a problem which brought many specialist competitors into the market. How then does IBM go on dominating the computer industry, to the extent that about 60 percent of Europe's computers (and as much as 70 percent world-wide) come from IBM? The Old Man's emphasis on 'service to the customer', stressed again and again until it became an overriding tenet of the culture, seems to be the only possible answer. IBM's service may not be perfect, but it is best — a point on which customers and competitors agree.

'IBM is a lousy loser'

Historically, IBM's strongest point has been its salesmen. They embody the combination of arrogance, image, pretentiousness and service that gives IBM its present eminence. During the depression after 1929, when others were cutting back their inventory and employee levels, the Old Man went on expanding. A colleague mentioned this to him one day and he answered:[1] 'Well, Bill, you know when a man gets about my age he always does something foolish. Some men play too much poker, and others bet on horse races, and one thing and another. My hobby is hiring salesmen.'

After he hired them he trained them, twice as long as any other company in the business (a ratio that still holds in the computer industry). The IBM salesman doesn't go out on full quota for 12 or 18 months after he enters the company. Then, once he is in the field, he is bombarded with communications, contests, conventions, all designed to keep up his spirits and reinforce the IBM ethic. According to Tom Junior[2] the early conventions were spectaculars. 'Salesmen on awakening would find newspapers under their doors carrying a complete account of the previous day's events. Our overseas salesmen attended our conventions at that time, and when they got to their seats, they found small headphones with which

---

* There are many variations on the theme that IBM prices are astronomical. A helpful SE graduate recalls the cartoon of the customer's managing director fainting during an IBM presentation. The salesman turns to his boss and says: 'Do you think I ought to tell him when he comes round that that was only the maintenance charge?'

they could hear the speeches in their native tongues.' However, this early use of earphones rebounded when IBMers discovered in the fifties that they could hear the proceedings from the swimming pool area of the convention hotel. After a few sparsely attended meetings the convention organizers caught on and lightly clad people with earphones were herded back to the hall.

IBM realizes that a handful of its biggest customers (like its largest countries) account for the majority of its income. It seems to have a dual reaction to this phenomenon. On the one hand, IBM seems to fear these large customers — holding off for several years a product that might offend AT&T in the United States, for example. On the other hand, it uses them capably when it needs intercession with governments. In the late sixties it was only after a customer survey and some mobilization of customer executives to plead IBM's case with the government that IBM decided to tell Japan it would pull out of the country rather than allow the Japanese to hold more than half the shares of IBM Japan.

Banks are among IBM's biggest customers, and IBM is in turn an excellent customer for the banks. Its accounts are spread out so that a number of banks in each country have impressive IBM holdings. The company's sales people are not always above implying that the two could be connected, but most of the banks ignore such suggestions and IBM management discourages them. Since 1968 IBM has cut down its debt in the United States and borrowed money abroad to finance much of its equipment leasing, making it a very good customer indeed for its banks. One European banker said: 'We earn a lot of interest from IBM, and we give them a big line of credit. But it's a mutual relationship. I figured out that they were earning more from us than we were from them.'

In each country as an IBM organization was set up, a target list of customers was compiled — big companies or institutions in that country where the size or prestige of the account made it important to IBM's standing or revenue. The list is maintained and improved as time goes on. Some large computer users have held out against IBM, list or no list. One target company resisted IBM's blandishments for 20 years, and only succumbed by merger.

Even though it fights fiercely to keep the large accounts, IBM has resisted the temptation to concentrate all resources on this part of the market. IBM shows the flag to small shopkeepers with the same enthusiasm it pursues Unilever or General Motors. In sales, as in everything else, IBM does its homework. Task forces are formed to look into each question — what to do about development of a new kind of large customer system, or whether to handle 'turnkey' contracts. Sometimes the task forces just last a few days, some-times months or years.

The IBM sales organization sets up a kind of permanent task force for each major customer (or SIA — Selected International Account). In 1972, for example, 77 companies accounted for more than 10 percent of World Trade's sales. Each of these has its own international team, spread around the world wherever the client is and headquartered wherever the client's nerve centre is. 'The one thing that separates them from the rest (of IBM's clients) is strong headquarters control,' an IBM manager commented. Thus Shell, for example, is handled by a team of four in the Hague who liaise with another special group in London and keep in touch with all the other World Traders who deal with Shell companies. For this single account the communications programme includes a newsletter and seminars as well as teletype, telephone and letter contacts.

Multinational clients have commented that they sometimes find out about their own company's decisions from their IBM salesmen before they are notified by their own management. The SIA response time is phenomenal. One year Univac thought it had a chance to get into a Chrysler installation in Europe. However, 48 hours after the opportunity seemed possible IBM's SIA man from the United States who headed the Chrysler account 'just happened to be in Geneva'. The SIA teams also give top client and IBM management annual progress reports and executive briefings. (Christopher Tugerdhat[3] has suggested that reports like these should be given to governments too.) The funds for this kind of marketing come on a cross-industry and cross-organization basis. World Trade and Domestic usually share the cost and the resulting information. World Trade also monitors about 2,100 smaller international accounts, to make sure that out-of-territory commission claims are shared out fairly.

An earlier institution to improve coordination was the 'centre of competence'. In 1962 World Trade began to wonder whether it might not be helpful to bring Europeans to the United States to work on advanced applications. (In those days anything that had a terminal involved was an 'advanced application'; airline reservation systems were the *ne plus ultra*.) World Trade shipped 30 of its best Europeans to Poughkeepsie, and in return asked for some free assistance from Americans who were already experienced in advanced applications. A centre to handle 'real-time' work such as the airline systems, process control and teleprocessing was set up in Corbeil-Essonnes near Paris. However, there were almost no French people

66

in the new group (though it included a collection of other nationalities as the Europeans began returning from Poughkeepsie).
Eventually the little group decided it would get a warmer reception
and more dependable phone lines in Britain, and moved to the
Hursley laboratory where the competence centre idea finally took
root. The laboratory appreciated the contact with real-world real-
time applications, and the new centre appreciated the good technical
people who rotated in and out.

The first real-time centre was so successful that World Trade
began setting up others, usually in tandem with large customers,
just as the first centre gained impetus from American Airlines,
then Swissair, SAS and BOAC in Europe. The medical industry
centre was set up in 1965 in Sweden, working with the Karolinska
hospital. Amsterdam, conveniently close to Shell headquarters,
hosted the chemical and petroleum industry centre. Düsseldorf and
Hoesch enjoyed the iron and steel centre. The banking centre
started slowly in London in 1964, with Lloyds as a primary partner.
Eventually Vienna won a law enforcement centre, and France
achieved competence centre status for advanced retail applications,
working initially with Nouvelles Galeries (which later changed to
Univac).

The process of deciding to set up a centre was not only democratic
but pragmatic. World Trade headquarters would canvass the European
country organizations saying: 'We have a chance to set up a centre
for retail in France. Will you use it? If so, indicate your budget
commitment.' If they said they needed it, they put up the money
while the enthusiasm was hot. If not, no centre. One headquarters
veteran also noted that because the competence centres were not a
Watson idea, the concept was allowed to start slowly. Thus initial
suspicion within World Trade could be overcome at a natural pace.
After a few success stories got around the enthusiasm also grew at
a natural pace.

IBM product these days tends to displace old products. Then
there are different patterns of product acceptance. 'When a product
is announced in the United States customers are willing to order it
right away,' said Maisonrouge. 'Europeans are much more conservative and cautious. Perhaps inspired by St Thomas, they wait
to see it before they order it. So there's always a bulge of new
orders in the United States right after an announcement, while
we get a much smoother line in Europe.'[4]

In the sixties every large sale had to be approved by World Trade
headquarters in New York, which wanted to know why the user

wanted the installation, how self-supporting it would be, and whether it replaced existing IBM equipment; this seems contradictory, since it has been official policy to treat all customers equally. IBM says this was a protective mechanism, to prevent 'overselling', but some salesmen in Europe saw it differently, worrying that concessions or special features might not be given if it was going to be a 'nuisance' sale — or bring in less income than the preceding system (particularly after the 370 announcement) — no matter how good the customer might be in the long term.

Another control was the point system for salesmen, which could be adjusted by special bonuses or contests. The sum of points set for their quotas was often greater than the total points in the country plans. The salesman's commission would then be based on a percentage of his points, with a guarantee of about 80 percent (later 90 percent) of his quota and a rising percentage of commission as he neared or exceeded quota. Replacing a competitor's machine is obviously more remunerative to IBM than replacing an IBM system, so there were bonuses for 'new sales' (NSRI), as well as special competitions now and then to keep sales thriving and motivate the salesmen to learn about new products. 'In every office you'd find a sales-plan lawyer,' said one graduate. 'He's the one who can read between the lines or figure out the system. You'd get your plan in January and a modification in July, but the lawyer is the one who notices that if he turns in the Bloggs renewal in April instead of March it puts him into a special category with more points.'

The life of the branch manager has even more excitement than that of the salesman. Most branch managers (especially *former* branch managers) realize that theirs is one of the nicest jobs in IBM. One general manager in a small country knew he was only a branch manager in IBM terms. He said: 'I like it. You enjoy a lot of freedom and independence out here.' To be 'Mr IBM-Akron' or 'Mr IBM-Nigeria' is a happy experience, close enough to where the action is to be involved in every problem or achievement, and far enough from headquarters that VIP visits are rare. The branch manager is master of his own fate and career to a greater extent than almost any other type of IBM employee; he is normally six steps down the management ladder from the president in Domestic — add two for World Trade — in a hierarchy that has remained relatively stable through all the reorganizations.

Naturally there is stress between the hinterlands and headquarters, but the men in the hinterlands can ignore it most easily.

One man who spent time in World Trade headquarters, area management, and then country management put it in perspective: 'When I was in New York, I was convinced that the areas knew little and the countries knew nothing. When I got to the area headquarters I began to wonder if New York wasn't too remote, and felt that the countries needed help. When I got to the country organization I felt the area knew something about our problems, but New York was never-never land.' Cultural differences seldom filtered through to headquarters. One Asia/Pasific veteran told of a visitor from headquarters who asked:

'How do you like the training stuff we're sending out from New York these days?'

'Some of it is OK.'

'What do you mean, "some"? We're putting a lot of work and money into that stuff. Don't you appreciate it? How about our September selection of aids for the Fall Kickoff Meeting?'

'First of all,' said the weary country man, 'the word in the English-speaking countries out here would be "autumn", not "fall". And below the equator it's coming up to spring, not autumn. Finally, the word "kickoff" relates to a uniquely American sport. So we weren't able to use much of the material.'

IBM's sales efforts look quite different if you turn around and view them from the customer's side. There you find a love/hate relationship, a strange mixture of fear — of the unknown and of IBM's power — and respect — for IBM's consummate service and ability to deploy its resources.

The fear or concern among IBM customers is natural. Once they have selected IBM equipment, they know their most important information is dependent on an outside company. More important, before they make a selection that company is going to be pressing, hard, to make sure they decide in favour of IBM.

Some customers complain that IBM is 'too remote'. Others worry that somewhere the company is building CIA-like dossiers about them, just in case they should think about giving up the true faith. A number of managers have complained with some justice about IBM's habit of going over their heads to criticize them to their supervisors.

These worries are a mixture of fact and fiction. IBM is a lousy loser. So are IBM salesmen. Trained within an inch of their lives, they hang on with dogged determination. Sometimes they exceed the bounds of tact, if not propriety, by bringing in top IBM people to lunch quietly with top customer people, just in case a little

extra 'understanding' of IBM or the company's proposed use of
IBM might help. Fairly often these conversations include
unflattering allusions to the customer's "technical people".
Customers sometimes point out that this kind of pressure is not
always in IBM's best interests. At Cambridge University, for example,
the university's computer professionals worked from mid-68 to late-
71 to push through a requisition for an IBM machine, against strong
political pressure to buy a British computer from ICL. 'We had to
stop IBM from helping us,' one senior man commented. 'If they
had been any more involved in the decision they'd have messed it
up in three easy steps. No matter how often they asked, we simply
refused to tell them how the university's decision processes
worked.'

Unlike the little discussions, the dossiers are more fiction than
fact. They are standard 'call notes', just like those kept by any other
well-organized salesman in any other field, noting subjects discussed
and any useful likes, dislikes or future needs. A more important
aspect of the IBM information retrieval is use of personal observations by *customers*, not IBM. Too often a user's last check on a
would-be DP manager is a phone call to the friendly neighbour-
hood IBM office — giving the corporation informal influence
it shouldn't have and doesn't necessarily want.

From the sales viewpoint, the most common IBM abuse of its
own competitive ethic is this tendency for the salesman to go over
his customer's head when there is any danger that a decision might
go to a competitor. In essence he (or more often his boss) implies
to the customer's boss (or a convenient board member) that the
DP man in question seems to be getting a little old fashioned, or
that the system specification is not quite adequate. IBM would of
course be happy to do a little study to bring it or him into the
twentieth century. In 1973 several state governments in the United
States complained that legislators were suddenly turning up with
surprisingly knowledgeable protests whenever non-IBM systems
were proposed. 'You have to have a boss or a client with guts if
you are going to recommend non-IBM equipment,' said DP
consultant Philip Dorn.

One IBM graduate in Denmark had recommended to his boss
that the company for which he left IBM choose a non-IBM computer. 'As soon as they know we've decided against IBM, the
salesman will be in your office with his boss, and they'll begin to
let you know how I was one of the people who couldn't make the
grade at IBM,' he asserted. His boss couldn't believe it, so they bet

a beer on the outcome. Several days later his boss phoned. 'Come up and get your beer. The IBM men are in my office, and they've just said exactly what you predicted!'

Losing an account is the salesman's misfortune. But even worse than losing one is doing so without preparing the way with IBM management. 'One of the worst things in IBM is a surprise,' said an American. 'If you're going to lose an account, you'd better be sure your manager knows the reasons it is being lost and who's going to get it. If you lose an account that could have been saved by bringing in more IBM resources — someone from a competence centre, or a top manager for more discussions — then you're in deep trouble.'

In October 1973 Cary wrote a long letter-to-the-editor to *Newsweek* discussing an article about IBM's competitive practices and describing the 'business conduct guidelines'. He pointed out that IBM's salesmen make about 25,000 customer contacts every working day. With competitors, customers, the government and press constantly on the lookout for offences, the examples that had turned up were few indeed, and when they occurred, he said, 'appropriate disciplinary action is taken.' A few months earlier Delaware observers had an example of this, when IBM's two top men in Dover were 'fired for trying to block state use of competitive equipment', according to the *Wilmington Journal*. The IBM term for this sin is 'overselling'. The vice president who asked the state government to accept IBM's apology said firmly: 'That's not the way we do business.'

The sensible thing to do when overselling occurs — which is not infrequent — is to use the same technique to 'educate' the IBM salesman (and his boss if necessary) to his or their own best career interests. A well-prepared would-be victim can tattle on the IBM predators, to their own bosses. If the customer manager and his top management can take the initiative and write to the chief IBM executive in the area (with carbon copies to Maisonrouge, Jones, Cary, Tom Junior, or in extreme cases *Datamation*) expressing their concern, then the salesman or branch manager will quickly receive a little education himself. To make a complaint effectively — as IBMers themselves learn to do — one documents excesses of zeal to use this Open Back Door.

'ICL exists by the grace of IBM'

Before he went to World Trade in the early sixties, Jones proclaimed to a Hundred Percent Club meeting: 'I want our competitors to survive.' Then in a stage whisper he added: '... barely!' He couldn't give the same speech today. With increased anti-trust pressure domestically and political pressure abroad, IBM is grateful for every healthy, thriving competitor it can point to with pride. At the same time, IBMers harbour a slight sense of supercilious pity for the people who choose to work for other computer companies. They also compete fiercely, at every level from the strategic decision-making committees of Armonk to the branch offices of the remotest outposts.

There are a number of ways that IBM can inconvenience its competition at a strategic level. There is the old walnut-and-pea game, for instance. In this case the pea is the controller for a disk system, and the walnuts are the various boxes of equipment in the computer configuration. In the olden days each disk system had its own controller, located along with one of the disks. Then one day, when the independent disk manufacturers had been making inroads on that market, the newest IBM system was announced — with the disk controller built into the central computer somewhere. The cost of the computer was higher (of course it was a newer, faster, better computer) but the disk costs dropped considerably. Then the independent disk manufacturers had to go hunting around the various boxes for the controller and trying to find new ways of plugging their equipment into the new configurations. They never quite managed again to get their prices 25 or 30 percent below IBM's.

This game came to a halt when Telex, one of the 'plug compatible manufacturers' (PCMs in computer industry jargon), sued IBM for monopolistic practices. Given the size of Telex's claim (hundreds of millions of dollars) and the number of other PCMs waiting in the wings, IBM could not afford to settle out of court. After a complicated lawsuit in which 40,000 pages of intimate IBM documents were displayed for the titillation (and occasional edification) of outsiders, Judge A. Sherman Christensen came up with a judgment in favour of Telex, with a set of injunctions forbidding IBM to practise certain types of 'predatory' behaviour, as well as a huge fine which focused public attention on the money rather than the injunctions. Noting that IBM had attained its position by means of 'skill, industry and foresight' rather than robber baron tactics, the Judge nonetheless decided that IBM was too big to have complete freedom of action. As *Fortune* expressed it:

What the competitors are complaining about is not how IBM clawed its way to the top, but what it did once it got there. Long after it had attained dominance, Judge Christensen observed, the company sought to entrench itself by calculating the economic 'viability' of its competitors and setting out on 'a sophisticated, refined, highly organized, and methodically processed' campaign to discipline some of them.

IBM appealed of course, and he gave way quickly on the $352 million fine; while the appeals were in process IBM quietly but voluntarily suspended some of the practices mentioned in the injunctions.

On the other hand, IBM is a source of supply for competitors — supply of people and products too. In a cross-suit IBM filed against Telex, Judge Christensen found the PCM guilty of 'misappropriating' IBM trade secrets, largely by hiring people who worked on identical products for IBM — in one case with the promise of a $500,000 bonus if the Telex imitation could be delivered at almost the same time as the original IBM disk system. The new people were then given such tight delivery dates that they were essentially forced to fall back on detailed knowledge gained at IBM, rather than doing original work. Telex and other PCMs raided IBM development labs for several years before the Judge insisted the head-hunting must stop, enjoining Telex not to use IBM graduates on similar projects for at least two years after they had left IBM. He underscored the message with a fine of almost $22 million, which may have deterred other PCMs from filing their own monopoly suits against IBM.

IBM traditionally maintained a kind of benign umbrella over the rest of the computer industry, keeping its prices high enough that there was room for other companies to develop new products profitably or build competitive peripheral equipment for slightly less. While Tom Junior was chairman this approach held to a large extent. However, he had a heart attack in late 1970, and resigned from the chief executive position in mid-71, in favour of Learson, who was a year older. Tom Junior had planned to retire in 1974, when he reached sixty, using an early retirement for top executives to clear the 'pack' at the top — Learson, Jones and several others were very close to Tom Junior in age — in favour of Cary, who was virtually unknown outside IBM in 1970. Learson's 18-month tenure was marked by almost overt aggression towards the PCMs. I have conjectured that this might have been in part a strategy to draw attention away from the more important curbs on the third-party leasing industry, or to give IBM an aggressive posture from which it could draw back in consent decree negotiations — a situation that existed naturally in 1956, when the

Old Man wanted to fight and his son preferred to settle. It also gave IBM time to expose Cary (who took over as chief executive at the beginning of 1973) to the public as a more conciliatory type than Learson.

Even in Tom Junior's day, any significant new market penetration or achievement by the traditional rivals at Univac brought instant attention. Univac usually tried to sell advanced computers before the market was ready, while IBM confined itself to its more conservative market base as long as possible. Being the market leader means you have more to lose if the expectations of your customers change. Learson had won Tom Junior's admiration in the early days of computers by conducting an effective holding operation with customers for a year after one Univac announcement, until IBM's own model 650 computer could reach the market. 'It was plain old salesmanship, plus Learson's whipcracking, that broke Univac's huge advantage into little pieces,' said a graduate. Univac's marketing staff said their biggest problem at the time was not so much IBM itself, but IBM's consummate salesmanship and the 'customer anxiety syndrome' it created; every DP manager or customer executive knew that if he chose IBM and something went wrong, no blame could be attached to his decision.

Inside the computer industry it used to be said that ICL existed by the grace of IBM — that stronger competitive moves by IBM at any time in the years since 1950 could have swamped the fledgling British computer industry. (The British companies could have been swamped, but not Britain's technical contributions, which have been important to almost every computer company in the world including IBM itself.) There seemed to be cultural reasons as well as strategic ones for this almost parental politeness to the prodigal son. According to one veteran: 'The idea was to cripple but not to kill ICT (which was still dominated by its BTM component), so they would come back into IBM of their own volition.' Without referring to 'seeing the error of one's ways', the Old Man actually said once to Cecil Mead, then head of ICL's predecessor company: 'We would be willing to welcome you back to the fold.' In later years it was sometimes said that the policy to ICL was to 'keep it alive, but only just'. As more than one UK graduate understood the policy, though, it was simply to compete fiercely and fairly, but a little more fiercely when the competition was Univac or later Honeywell.

In the four countries that constitute IBM's largest overseas markets (Germany, France, Britain and Japan) holding out against

IBM's blandishments is often considered a patriotic duty. All have their own computer companies, subsidized by their governments.

One of the entries on IBM's UK target list in 1950 was British European Airways, the short-haul airline that served most of Europe. BEA had IBM punched-card equipment, but went to EMI (one of ICL's precursors) for its first mechanized accounting system, then to Univac for a pioneering real-time reservation system. IBM, perhaps feeling that this was insult added to injury, went around the stubborn in-house computer specialist. IBM UK's leader Tom Hudson (who later became chairman of ICL) visited the boardroom of BEA to put IBM's case, but it is said that he called the chairman 'milord' once too often. Whatever the cause (conceivably faith in a good computer man), BEA remained with Univac, DEC and ICL — the only major airline never to buy an IBM computer. As the years passed IBM sold BOAC, the other main British airline, a large system that grew even larger. In 1972 the government merged the two airlines, putting a BOAC man in charge of computers; in 1973 it was announced that the mixed non-IBM equipment at BEA (by then noted for its efficiency) would be replaced by a huge IBM system.

For most of the world's computer users, the question is not so much one of holding out against IBM, but how to wring from the giant corporation as many concessions as possible. To get the ultimate in IBM service it helps to have a large voice; but it is more important to know which organizational buttons to push. The Open Back Door works pretty well if there is a genuine case to plead. Another useful technique is to hire a former IBM salesman or SE to run or advise a user's computer group. These are the people who know how to negotiate, how much the company will *really* do to keep the account (or keep it happy) and what the various nuances of the IBM language of negotiation really mean. Several graduates believed this ability alone more than justified their high salaries in the outside world.

Yet another technique for the user or competitor who feels badly treated by IBM is the lawsuit — but it can be risky and expensive. IBM has a huge corps of legal people, as professional and well trained as its sales corps. Even so, a well-publicized 'order to show cause' can often bring top management attention if the Open Back Door shows no sign of working. IBM's willingness to negotiate usually increases under legal and/or public relations pressure — again, provided the other party has a reasonable and well-documented complaint.

I believe the greatest problem for IBM with respect to its competitive behaviour is not one of determining external strategy, but instead one of resolving an internal dichotomy. For the individual IBMer, particularly the salesman, there is tremendous stress between the ethics his training and his culture have instilled, and the extremely competitive approach — the 'will to win', the '100 percent success' — that is just as deeply ingrained. But the computer industry is not as simple as the punched card industry — and there are no more Watsons around to exemplify the twin qualities IBM values so highly.

'If you're playing with a good team, you look good'

From the other side of the negotiating table, the IBM salesman has a rich view of IBM marketing — a complete (and élite) subculture within the IBM culture.

To the average IBM salesman, the most important institution in this sales subculture, evolved over 60 years, is the Hundred Percent Club. This is the three-day gathering, a cross between a party, an old-time revival and a sales conference, which is held to honour those salesmen who achieved 100 percent of their quotas for the preceding calendar year. Quotas are usually set with the intention that about 80 percent of the salesmen would make the Club — a mechanism designed more to weed out the inept and emphasize membership than to reward the super-stars. IBM's excellent reporting system means that results are in within days of the end of the year. Then the Clubs are held around the world in the months from February to April (making Armonk a ghost town as executives fly out to deliver inspirational messages to the elect). The IBMers who arrange and run the Clubs are special people — political appointees in a sense. For most of the lucky members next year's quota will be about 25 percent higher, of course.

All over the IBM world the number of Clubs a man has achieved is a measure of his status with his fellows; the figure is usually mentioned in promotion or transfer announcements. Eventually so many salesmen had achieved so many Clubs that the corporation instituted a super-Club, called the Golden Circle, for those who reached their tenth successive Hundred Percent Club. The Golden Circle, needless to say, outdoes the traditional Hundred Percent Club in every respect.

Attitudes towards the ancient idea of Hundred Percent Clubs

vary from country to country. In America some IBMers tend to be a trifle embarrassed at the collegiate atmosphere and inspirational overtones; mentions of them in the company's internal journals are less frequent than they were in the fifties or sixties. In smaller World Trade country organizations, they are still a primary motivator. All Africa is proud of Julius Fummey, the first black African to achieve membership.

It has normally been an unwritten understanding within IBM that if you failed to make your quota for three years in succession, you shouldn't be in sales. Though IBM people are not fired without reason, men who are unable to make their quotas yet want to continue in sales generally must leave the company; non-sales jobs are often found for those who are willing to take different career paths. This is never a one-sided decision. The man is consulted and counselled throughout his sales career. Only since the end of the sixties have entire organizations failed to make quotas with any regularity; the 1970 recession was the first one to bite in the computer industry, and IBM was hit particularly hard because its customers tend to be the big companies who can defer their computer plans easily. IBM is adept at adjusting quotas if things seem to be going drastically wrong, but the number of Hundred Percent Club memberships in some countries was considerably less in 1971 to the extent that the MRC considered cancelling the Clubs. (Instead they delayed meetings and adjusted the salary/commission balances for the demoralized salesmen.)

The IBM salesman views himself as resourceful, self-starting, ethical, dedicated, obedient, competitive (and 'thrifty, brave and reverent'). One favourite story among the international salesmen deals with Ed Somppi, a Canadian World Trader with a Finnish name who spent most of his career in Africa. His colleagues particularly respected his understanding of the African mentality and his resourcefulness in cultural situations. Apocryphally, Somppi got off a plane at Khartoum in the Sudan after the usual gruelling flight and went down to IBM's favoured hostelry there.
He was sleepy, hungry and ready to collapse. When he walked up to the desk the clerk didn't look up.

'My name is Somppi. I have a reservation.'

The clerk scanned his list and said politely: 'I'm sorry. We don't have any reservation for you.' Somppi scanned the list for himself and found at the bottom the name 'Zomppi'.

'Ah, there it is, ' he said with pleasure.

'No sir. I'm sorry. We haven't any reservation for you Mr Somppi.'

Rather than argue, Somppi simply picked up his briefcase and walked around the block. Then he came up to the desk.

'Good evening. I am Mr Zomppi. I have a reservation.'

'Ah, yes sir,' said the clerk, and called the bellhop.

(In Somppi's own version of the story, he simply went out on the verandah and watched the Nile flow by until the clerk had dozed off again.)

IBM's team phenomenon, with all its raging enthusiasm and fiery competition, builds big expectations. 'If you are playing with a good team, you can look good whether you *are* good or not,' said one graduate. 'Whether I knew a subject or not, I could become director of it; the team was so good it wouldn't let me down. I'd have time to learn to be good at it. But outside of IBM in the real world, you have a sales meeting and you say "We're going to do this, fellows!", and everybody nods. But nobody does anything.'

The men's expectations from IBM are matched by the company's expectations from them. One frequently told story concerns Jones giving the opening address to a class of new entrants. The door opened and one neophyte had the misfortune to walk in late. Without a break Jones said: 'Just keep on walking, son.'

Sales dedication in World Trade was exhibited in its ultimate form in Operation Close in 1962. A graduate described its birth one night in New York as a top-level task force struggled over a set of flipcharts. Around 8 p.m. Jones came in and looked over the results. He asked Basil Morrissett, then director of marketing:

'Do you mean to say you're going to tell Dick we're not going to make quota?'

'Yes, I'll have to,' admitted the unhappy Morrissett, looking at a chart which showed World Trade missing quota by an estimated 10 or 12 percent. It was already September and they were only at 50 percent of quota.

'But do you realize what this will do to us? All the development programmes that won't get done?...' Jones worried.

'I know,' came the weary answer. 'It will knock the pins out from under everything we have in the Plan.'

The next day's meeting progressed in a predictable manner. They reached about the fourth chart before Dick interrupted: 'This is unacceptable! If you are here to tell me you aren't going to make quota, that's not acceptable.'

The word went out to every manager in World Trade — what were they going to do to make quota? 'Then it really got warm,' said a bystander. 'They wanted an action programme. The whole thing was developed over one week. Then they had another meeting and decided to call it "Operation Close". The idea was to get every executive out of New York and on the road, helping in the countries. Even Eddie Goldfuss came in with a plane ticket one day and told us we had thirty minutes to make a salesman out of him. Naturally the headquarters people didn't help much, but the gesture stressed the importance of the project to the guys in the field, and a look at the real world didn't do the headquarters lads any harm.'

Charley Smith stayed in New York running a world-wide hot-line, working straight through Thanksgiving and Christmas days in traditional IBM style. 'We could have a banking expert in South Africa day after tomorrow,' said Smith, 'or invent a special device overnight. We tapped into Domestic or other countries to find whatever our men needed. This brought in a fantastic amount of business. We were shunting specialists all over the world like railroad cars. Jones was in the field a lot of the time; it was lonely at home, with only Dick and me back at the centre.' Operation Close made the entire headquarters a four-month floating task force.

With all these visible manifestations of IBM's sales drive, out-siders are apt to underestimate the ethical underpinnings on which the sales organization is built. From the Old Man's earliest days at C-T-R he was determined to have a blameless reputation for himself and his company. The visible portion of that company is its sales force. Even sixty years later, each salesman understands and respects the commandments. One general manager in a developing country told me: 'I can lose a million dollars worth of business and just get a slap on the wrist, but I cannot afford to use sales techniques that may be normal here but are against IBM's ethics.'

One of those commandments is 'Thou shalt not criticize the competition.' IBM men not only avoid criticizing competitors, they sometimes commend them. 'You establish your credibility this way,' said one cheerful Machiavelli. 'Out here the customers look at us like we used to look at our family doctors. We find that saying good things about competitors inspires even more confidence in us.' However, many IBM people simply don't know about the competition. They say they are too busy learning about their own equipment.

This remoteness from overtly competitive behaviour was strongly reinforced by Tom Junior. In March 1961 he made a speech about anti-trust responsibility to a meeting of IBM executives. This was subsequently printed in a booklet which every IBM employee must read and sign annually. In this booklet Tom Junior outlined clearly and forcibly the acts which were then illegal (though the six year limit on the 1956 consent decree had almost expired then and is ancient history now). He also listed those which, though not illegal, were nonetheless forbidden (such as discussing a new product before it is announced in order to thwart a competitor, or disparaging his products), and a third category which involves no violation but might nonetheless provoke monopolistic complaints and thus the dreaded anti-trust action. Tom Junior said: 'We must avoid the type of action — even lawful action — which irritates, antagonizes and finally goads a competitor to action. We simply cannot shoulder people around or give the appearance of doing so.'

All IBMers know that another commandment is 'Thou shalt not unhook.' Unhooking, in IBM language, is getting a customer to change his mind and order IBM equipment after he has given his order to a competitor. It fits into this last category of actions which Tom Junior characterized as lawful but irritating. It causes great gloom to salesmen to see an opportunity and be unable to grasp it. In complicated computer procurements, as in courtship, a period of self-doubt or disillusion often sets in when commitment has been made but the other party (in this case a competing computer manufacturer) begins qualifying his promises, or making doubtful noises about delivery dates or service promises. For a company like IBM with its excellent reputation for service, this is often an excellent opportunity for the high-level executive chat — but the high-level executives and the lower-level salesmen who might derive the points from the sale are supposed to resist the temptation once the letters of intent have gone out.

This dichotomy between the low profile and the hard sell must somehow be resolved by each salesman. It means no delivery concessions, no price concessions, no extra help on programming — or that is what it is supposed to mean. (A competitor pointed out that on some seemingly minor points 'they seem to change the rules daily' — but a phone call to an unhelpful CE's manager would usually bring the required document or service quickly.)

The competitors are not under anti-trust scrutiny to the same extent IBM is (a fact of which they are well and sometimes gleefully aware). Except for entire categories (such as universities or an overall government contract), nobody is supposed to get cut-rate computers from IBM, no matter how enticing the special deals the competitors are able to offer. A number of competitors and graduates said that IBM gave only lip service to the one-price policy; cases of oblique discounts have certainly been documented. But as one former IBM executive put it: 'It was certainly *harder* to get a different price for IBM than anyone else.' The amount of service on the other hand could be adjusted in the old days. Competitors sometimes complained that IBM furnished so much service to a particular treasured client that they never had a chance.

Another commandment is 'Thou shalt not bribe.' An executive commented: 'IBM never paid for business under the table. This used to be a constant sales strategy problem in World Trade. If there was hanky-panky, people got fired.' The IBM men know this, and it helps keep hanky-panky to a minimum. In some countries IBM has a reputation as 'that American company that doesn't pay bribes.' An IBM country manager in such a culture commented: 'It is most unprofitable to bribe. You destroy your image completely. If you ever heard government people talking among themselves about the companies that bribe them you'd see how self-defeating it really is. Furthermore,' he added with IBM practicality, 'it comes right straight from profit!'

Gordon Smith is a World Trade star who went on to work for Univac and later Singer. He said candidly: 'In some countries of the world, the Univac lads used to come in regularly, claiming that IBM people must have paid off handsomely, in baksheesh or whatever the local form was, to have snatched this or that job. I kept an eye open, partly because after my years in IBM the claims surprised me. In years of looking for it, I never saw any indications of it. But the boys continued to be certain of it every time they lost a job. They just couldn't conceive that a company could not pay bribes and still win.'

IBM didn't need bribes, with its mastery of more effective forms of influence. The competitive salesmen may not have realized that the IBM manager's wife was probably having tea with the pertinent minister's wife. That is another matter — one which may help account for the number of wellborn young men (and wives) in World Trade's smaller country organizations. Several graduates suggested that because of IBM, the computer industry (unlike construction and others) is singularly free of corruption.

The IBM sales managers have to watch their footwork among all these commandments because they sometimes conflict. One of the important ones is 'Thou shalt not sacrifice thy employees for profits.' IBM simply doesn't think that being nice and being profitable are mutually exclusive. Thus when bureaux had to be closed in northern Scandinavia, a few IBM people were actually laid off — profit goals demanded it — but they were given an extraordinary amount of advance notice and IBM helped most of them find jobs with IBM customers in the area.

The most rigidly observed commandment of all is an internal one: 'Thou shalt not book bad business.' This means, in IBM's own vocabulary, reporting results that have not yet been achieved, or listing likely prospects as actual sales. At one time in the early sixties this aspect of the IBM culture came into conflict with the face-saving aspect of the Japanese culture. Pushed from above to 'sell, sell, sell!', a Japanese sales manager dutifully exhorted his people, saying again and again in Watsonian terms: 'That is unacceptable!' or 'There is no alternative; you *will* sell so many points by November.' His subordinates may have argued at first, but eventually they simply turned in papers that seemed to meet the quota demand (thereby inflating World Trade's own quota expectations). This naturally (for IBM) led to larger demands, until someone during a World Trade board meeting in Tokyo figured out that the actual situation didn't bear much resemblance to the rosy reports that were coming in. Furthermore, this dishonesty amounted to lying, not just in terms of the statistics, but about the always-critical relationship with the Japanese government.

World Trade shipped out an airborne task force from New York immediately. The problem was compounded by the fact that the responsible sales manager was believed to have been in training as a kamikaze pilot at the end of the war. Some of the earnest New Yorkers were unnecessarily but naturally afraid that he might embarrass IBM by volunteering to commit hari-kiri to save the corporation's face. The Japanese manager was gently but rapidly extracted from the embarrassing situation and escorted back to New York to World Trade's main 'Penalty Box', as its institutions for punishment and redemption are called.

This was World Trade's Watergate. As soon as he discovered the Japanese mess Dick took a brilliant step. All managers in the chain of command responsible for the Japanese situation went into varying degrees of purdah — or 'Penalty Boxes' — and he allowed people to herald the internal scandal by word of mouth throughout the entire company. One former World Trader said: 'The Japanese situation had a lot to do with the eventual success of World Trade.

It taught us all a lesson. It put people on notice that they couldn't mess around.'

IBM and World Trade abound with stories of the purgatory experiences of those poor souls who broke the commandments of the sales subculture. These all seem to be part of the self-policing mechanism that keeps IBM ahead of those who would impose regulation or break up'the corporation arbitrarily. Until the 1973 Telex trial and its subsequent injunctions, they were also the only assurances the outside world had that IBM would behave as a relatively benign competitor.

'Even Gil Jones spent some time in a Penalty Box'

Like most cultures, the IBM culture demands a scapegoat whenever a crime against the culture has been committed (or more important, seen to have been committed). A single human being is a much better and more visible symbol than a group. Thus in the Japanese affair, it was the kamikaze-trained sales manager who was sent to the Penalty Box, though several others suffered a diminishing of the bright light of power for a while. Jones's lieutenant, Gordon Williamson, took some of the blame at headquarters, and another World Trade executive was banished from the marketing group for a while. All these punishments of Americans also helped ease the loss of face to the Japanese company. The ex-kamikaze manager eventually ended up on a hilltop in Japan, quietly running IBM's new management training 'hotel' for the Far East; both the position and the school were built while he was cooling off for a couple of years in New York.

The official Penalty Box in New York City was called the International Sales Centre. From the outside it was a perfectly normal part of the company, chiefly responsible for wining and dining important clients from abroad. A very important personage from IBM Philippines is a magnificent host to customers arriving from the Asia/Pacific area, and so on. From the inside, International Sales was *the* Penalty Box, where the big league sinners were sent for punishment and rehabilitation. This also gave time for local scandals to die down, and gave the company time to find new and useful positions for the detained ones.

One didn't necessarily have to be a sinner to be sent to the Penalty Box. One brilliant man who was relatively abrasive made no real mis-steps, but caused certain discomfort to powerful colleagues. He spent time in the Penalty Box while IBM tried to find a better place to sequester his undoubted talents. In another case the Penalty Box was used to help resolve political difficulties in IBM de Mexico. The general manager there was having trouble getting along with the American who was area general manager (and as agent of the shareholders', his boss in some respects). Each thought the solution to the problem was to fire the other. After high-level surveys another American (this one Spanish-speaking) was sent in, ostensibly as assistant general manager, to be a buffer between the two strong personalities. Eventually the Mexican general manager went into the Penalty Box while the situation cooled off.

There are other Penalty Boxes too, both physical and organizational. Each country organization seems to have some quiet corner which serves this purpose. Certain jobs can become Penalty Boxes, depending on who holds them. An announcement goes up on the bulletin board that the man who has been director of marketing for an entire continent is getting a rather fluffy-sounding transfer (usually worded: 'has accepted a position as . . .') to become director of spare parts in a small and unimportant country organization. IBMers understand. Several years later he might be given some interesting assignment a little closer to the mainstream of corporate life. That told the rest of IBM that he was back in their real world. Five years later, if he had demonstrated not only penitence but an ability to go on learning, he might be found in charge of manufacturing for a major segment of the company.

Dr Reginald Revans, an iconoclastic expert in corporate behaviour, suggests that IBM's Penalty Box has historical utility, reflecting Toynbee's anthropological myth of withdrawal and return. Jesus spent 40 days and 40 nights in the wilderness. Moses went up to the mountain. John Bunyan wrote *Pilgrim's Progress* in Bedford Prison. (Hitler wrote *Mein Kampf* in prison for that matter.) Nixon, de Gaulle, Gladstone, Churchill, Lenin, Marx — all had their times in the wilderness and came back from exile or rejection to new power.

So did Jones, who later became chairman of IBM World Trade and essentially IBM's number two man. The events which led to his incarceration in the Penalty Box are best described by Tom Junior:[5]

In one instance our CEs were spread too thinly across customer installations. This was good for profit, but the

morale of the overworked CEs began to sag. Our high
standards of service were certainly in jeopardy. Corners
had been cut on two beliefs — respect for the individual
and service to the customers. We quickly righted the imbalance
and looked for other ways to hold the cost line.

Jones was head of Domestic DP group at that time In 1960
one of his subordinates, sent out to cut down maintenance costs,
made a major error in judgment and did the job too well — to
the extent that the service people threatened to form a union.
(They didn't go so far as to sign petitions or hold organizational
meetings. They didn't need to. Delicate inferences to ultra-
sensitive IBM top management were sufficient.) Incurring a
unionization threat is a cardinal sin in IBM terms.   The
subordinate was sent into permanent purdah (or Siberia') and
Jones, who had backed him to the hilt, went into a Penalty Box.
He had a tiny office and few visible duties. Colleagues recall
being greeted with unaccustomed enthusiasm when they walked
by. After less than a year (a very short time in IBM's Penalty
Box) Jones was assigned to the obligatory transitional job, a sign
to his colleagues that he was returning to a state of grace. In
early 1962 he moved to World Trade, entering as executive vice
president under Dick.
    This roller-coaster effect — the knowledge that one can be way
down, and still become chairman of World Trade — serves a
useful purpose throughout the corporation. It reinforces the
concept of redemption as well as the punishment of sin, and it
keeps motivation high. The fact that so many IBMers know about
Jones's own Penalty Box experience, or Gordon Williamson's
restoration to grace (and power) after the Japanese crisis, shows its
significance as a symbol to others.
    Worse than the Penalty Box is 'Siberia' — the state of expulsion
in which a man gets no mail, no attention, no hope. This
phenomenon is a somewhat unpleasant backlash of IBM's pleasant
personnel policies. The corporate view is that once the company
has selected a man and trained him, it has assumed a responsibility
for him. Somewhere in the company an appropriate job must exist.
The trouble is that humans must implement this superhuman policy.
It is sometimes easier to put a man in a backwater where he can
cause no trouble and then forget him. Eventually the man in
Siberia is expected to retire or be paid off to leave — but he is
never directly ill-treated.

Expulsion to Siberia is most likely to occur if one has offended against the corporate ethics or one of its chief viziers. While Tom's tempers were mercurial, Dick's tended to last longer. One man who had displayed some form of behaviour Dick considered 'disloyal' said he could see there would be no more promotions, no more interesting assignments, no more 'membership' when Dick was around. The man left World Trade rather than go to a Siberia.

'You can't sell machines until you have trained people to run them'

Everybody goes to school at IBM — over and over and over. The selling is all based on schooling, and most of the schooling is pointed towards selling.

There are differences between how it works in Domestic and how it works in World Trade. Take the seven-day executive course, for example, when the 360 computer was announced in 1964. In Domestic the IBM executives dutifully came along to the 'hands-on' course because it was expected of them and all the other important executives were going. The process was not quite so simple in World Trade. The course started on a Sunday, with rather short advance notice. (This is no problem in Domestic, where the corporation has clear priority on an executive's time.) However in IBM Europe France's Baron Christian de Waldner had to be called back from a hunting expedition in Spain; others were similarly inconvenienced. Even so, almost all the European chiefs were there: Louis Castaldi from Italy; Joe van de Kamp from Holland; Tom Hudson from the UK; Walter Boesenberg from Germany, and so on. The only missing chief was the Dane, Henrik Lykke-Hansen. He had the only valid 'excuse for the teacher' — an appointment with royalty.

The emphasis on education for everyone in every country from the top down, both inside and outside the company, came directly from the Old Man, who believed salesmen were not born but taught. He once commented that the Great Depression came about because of lack of education. Making sure that no such disaster could ever touch his own monument to posterity, he began to set up courses as soon as he took over C-T-R. Salesmen went into the factories and learned how to distract attention and cover up when their equipment broke down. They took lessons in public speaking, and learned the company songs during their breaks.

In 1922 the Old Man sent two top American salesmen to France to sell his newest accounting machines. They came back empty-handed. He immediately sent for the top salesman from the French company and trained him in America on the use of the new machines. The Frenchman's subsequent success set the pattern for introducing new products in other countries — and started the growth of World Trade's own educational establishment.

When he was setting up World Trade in 1949, the Old Man made another decision which still affects IBM training. He clearly laid down lines between those matters which were to remain in American hands, and those which could be left to local option. Although the flexible factors included advertising, selling, customer relations and many other important functions, the American way was to dominate in employee relations, training and customer education. Mature IBM country organizations challenge this dominance today, but the cultural pattern remains strong.

IBM Domestic has a strong tradition and a strong organization for internal training. Executive training for all top IBM executives (including World Trade's country general managers) takes place at Sands Point, Long Island — an institution that has no World Trade parallel. The original facility for training customer and IBM managers in the United States was the 'homestead' at Endicott, New York, where C-T-R had its first home. To this day the hotel-like training facilities around the IBM world are called 'home-steads'. The corporation also has a technical 'graduate school', called the Systems Research Institute, which occupied an inelegant old laundry building next door to the World Trade headquarters in New York. Now somewhat better housed this institution has a unique academic reputation both inside and outside IBM.

The organizations for education are also different in Domestic and World Trade. The Domestic organization is strongly centralized, with a corporate director of education. Under him each major division has a director of education who has charge of the educational real estate. This 'Marketing Education', organization is a line function; the existence of so much property devoted to education gives it an aura of permanence and importance in corporate councils. (However, Tom Junior once reminded the education professionals: 'The only reason we are in the education business is to help sell products.')

World Trade's education organization tends to be a bit more haphazard, with only two or three managers as a staff function at the centre, and the education officers attached to the marketing departments of the various country organizations. Within the constraints of his father's vision of the two halves of the company, Dick wanted separate but equal institutions for training of World Traders.

For middle managers and customers, World Trade has a number of selfcontained homesteads. The Nordic Education Centre in Sweden takes care of most of Scandinavia's needs, while people from the rest of Europe went to the centre at Blaricum, near Amsterdam, until the new Brussels centre was finished in 1974. Japan hosts a homestead for Asia, on a hilltop at Imajō. Another hilltop, in Cuernavaca, Mexico, takes care of Latin America. Some of the larger countries also have their own centres, though they continue sending their people through the international centres too.

The Executive Development Centre (know to World Traders as 'Blaricum' until it moved to Brussels) hosts IBM's International Management School, a four-week course that is essential to World Traders on their way up. 'Blaricum was just another example of the little brother trying to throw the baseball just like big brother,' said one American graduate. However, the Europeans tended to view it as something uniquely their own; Canada (which could choose between Domestic and World Trade facilities) flattered the European companies by sending most of its managers through Blaricum. There was usually an American World Trader in each class too.

One of the founding fathers of this institution described Dick's personal involvement in the Blaricum programme: 'What Tom Junior had done for Domestic Dick wanted to do for all the World Trade countries. Although we did it with much less organization and structure, in many ways the internal programme at Blaricum was Dick's finest hour. More than any other American executive, he participated in that programme. He was dedicated; he showed interest; he wanted to be there with his people. One Friday, when he was due to come up from Paris, Schipol airport had been closed by weather for 36 hours. The first plane to come in after the storm was the IBM company plane, piloted by Dick himself. This was a tremendous symbolic gesture.'

By the early seventies more than 1,300 managers from 50 countries had poured through Blaricum. With minor modifications, the content remained fairly standard. Each class of 21 becomes three groups of seven. Using case material, they are expected to learn more from each other than from the teacher. An internal journal[6] described one exercise, where each seven-man team took over 'management' of a 'company' with strong potential but a poor financial situation. The way one member described the growth of the various teams as they pursued the case told something about IBM management values. One group, he noted, became competitive and aggressive. Another was introspective, its members more concerned with personal dynamics and learning about each other. The third, he said, was 'business-like, unemotional but very effective, and won the game because it maximized the financial performance.'

The real backbone of IBM education is the training its salesmen and SEs get — about twice as much as competitors give. The difference seems to be in cultural rather than technical content.

Hiring is done at the branch level. The typical entrant is fresh from university and eager to learn IBM's way of doing things. IBM does not mind a few years of seasoning in the business world. However, until the seventies very few entrants were over 30. One British graduate commented: 'When I joined IBM at 26 I had been in business for four years. It was very easy to change my habits, to do it their way instead of my way or somebody else's way. It's real indoctrination, not just sales school. It's brainwashing in the IBM ways. What they do is put you into an absolutely standard style, both a selling style and a management style.' (Other ex-IBMers who are now selling against IBM made similar comments.)

The indoctrination seems to impose a standard vocabulary. During the interviews for this book one IBM marketing executive was interrupted by his telephone: 'Hi,' he said, and continued in another language, his conversation peppered with IBM jargon: '...task force...team effort... excess resources problem... project risk... briefing Wednesday night... amend the operating plan... Cassani project flipcharts... training resources... OK... G'bye.' He turned and apologized. 'We learn to repeat the main points in English too, just to make sure everybody understands.'

The classes for salesmen and SEs are highly competitive. One Domestic graduate said: 'You wouldn't believe the politicking that went on for Class Secretary. Those positions are important to the branch managers who hire the guys. When you've heard your branch manager bragging about so-and-so who was elected vice president and song leader of his class, you try a little harder to live up to his expectations.' (A World Trader pointed out: 'We never did any singing, so we never elected song leaders.')

'There is no saturation point in education,' the Old Man used to say. Training for IBM people goes far beyond the initial courses. There is clerical training, job development training, industry training (where the bank salesmen are taught by bankers), negotiation school (and advanced negotiation school), an Advanced Marketing Institute, and courses for everyone involved whenever a new product is coming on the market. Then there are the hidden costs — management and planning for all these activities, supplies, manuals, translations, surveys, travel, and coordination with plant sites, to name only a few.

Separate budgets — generally the marketing budgets of the local IBM companies — cover customer education, which can range from cozy top-executive seminars to mundane operator or keypunch courses to brisk and businesslike meetings on specific products. A typical product-related meeting was held at the Intercontinental Hotel in Geneva for three days in 1971. It was attended by about 100 people from customer companies who were using (or thinking about using) IBM's production control programs. Each customer or cluster of customers was shepherded by its own IBM sheep-dog, a salesman taking care of all their administration, translation, introductions, and hosting at their lunch and dinner tables. Two business journalists were included in the outing with a press-office shepherd of their own. Veterans of many conferences, they were astonished at the dedication to duty not only of the IBM people but also of the customers. Although the hosting included an innocuous nightclub (the kind with a magician — IBM nightclubs in Europe always seem to have magicians), hangovers were noticeable by their absence. At 8 a.m. the Germans, Italians, English, Dutch, Swiss, Swedes filed into the lush auditorium with expressions of anxious enthusiasm to hear about COPS, CLASS BOMP, KRAUS or PICS.

IBM takes (and can afford to take) a long view regarding customer education or potential-customer education. In 1962 World Trade started with six students in a summer-job programme that built up to 54 students in 1967 and became an institution. The students, aged 18 to 30, went to World Trade headquarters in New York where they were given assignments that varied from market research to systems analysis. Tod Groo, who was a World Trade vice president at the time, told a business journal:[7] 'The summer programme is part of our overall effort to know the people who will make up our future markets.' The investment in transport and expenses was viewed in IBM's characteristic telescopic sights. Even if the students didn't return to IBM as employees, Groo pointed out: 'We'll have made friends with a group of students, many of whom will be industry and government leaders in their respective countries in a dozen years.'

Until 1970 customer executive training for much of Europe took place at Blaricum. Technical training for customer DP people usually takes place in the country's educational centre. There is also ad hoc training within customer installations. Keeping the high-level customer education at Blaricum created stresses after the mid-sixties, when several countries built their own centres. Like the company plane and the on-line information system in Britain, the cost allocation for customer education at Blaricum was originally on a straight pro-rata basis according to the revenue of the country organizations, rather than the traffic they furnished. Thus Germany, with a perfectly adequate centre of its own, was paying the lion's share of Blaricum customer education. On the other hand, the small countries alone could scarcely afford to carry the entire burden — yet they had a potentially higher growth rate. World Traders at headquarters for a long time agreed that the best solution would have been to eliminate customer education from Blaricum — it could have been done in hotels — but it had been Dick's idea. 'Nobody had the guts to go tell Dick we wanted to wipe out Blaricum,' said one veteran. Dick left IBM to become US ambassador in Paris in 1970; in the same year, customer executive education also moved to Paris. This eased the strain on Blaricum facilities (and the ego of the French company), but the charging anomalies remained.

This is a classic example of a common business problem — the make-or-buy decision — that grows particularly delicate in multinational companies. Once the decision has been taken to 'make' one's own training facilities, for example, it is much more difficult to change the resulting institution than it would be if there were no physical property (and thus no national, corporate or organizational ego) involved.

IBM, never a company to overlook a marketing or diversification opportunity, has also made money from its training. World Trade brags that it had schools for a fee long before Domestic, starting in Mexico in 1965. The idea had always been tempting and demands from students were increasing, but Tom Junior maintained that if the company were going to charge customers to go to IBM courses, they had to be a type that could not be duplicated in any of the free courses already offered by the company. Finally the education innovators turned this restriction inside out and rewrote IBM's own internal sales and sales training curriculum, cutting out all the 'sales pizzazz', then offered it outside for 16 weeks for $5,800 (plus hotels).

There are other formal and informal kinds of education activities in World Trade. The larger country organizations, for example, often send their promising young men for advanced degrees. This led to a difficult situation in the UK in the mid-sixties, when a young man named Miles Broadbent read in his policy manual that IBM supported further education when it was related to a man's professional development — a policy that was generously worded. He applied for a place at the Harvard Business School; when he was accepted in 1964 he went to the UK management and asked that they consider supporting him under this policy. He was a good salesman; they sponsored him enthusiastically, then wrote a story about him in the UK house journal.

Another salesman, Ridley Rhind, read about Broadbent's Harvard training and said to himself: 'Why not me?' They sent him in 1965. Then, IBM fashion, they made it into a competition and a number of people applied in 1966. George Hughes won the IBM UK support that year but several others attended unsupported. Meanwhild Clive Mellor from the UK was already at the Harvard Business School, and was able to get a grant for his 1965-6 school year. The corporation looked benignly upon all these upstanding British scholars in America.

Today, not one of those men is with IBM UK. Few of them even came back to Britain after their Harvard experience, and the only one who remained in IBM stayed with Domestic. Some of the problem may have been a lack of re-entry plans, but much of it is built into the very training IBM wanted them to gain. As one of them described it: 'Harvard has a strong effect on a man. You get arrogant. You have very high expectations. At that time we were besieged by recruiters, most of them willing to put large cheques in our hands. We looked at IBM in Britain and saw that it was a sales company. But Harvard trains you to think you are a general manager. It's Wall-Street-oriented and consultant-oriented. Nobody from the top of the class was going to large corporations then.'

Broadbent left IBM UK within a year of his return to work
for a brewery. Rhind went straight from Harvard to McKinsey.
George Hughes became an investment banker in London. Only
Clive Mellor, who originally went unsupported, remained with
IBM — and he stayed in New York, where the action was. The
UK company stopped writing articles about its Harvard men,
and quietly amended its policy to encourage training closer
to home. Even so, they were losing people who went through
a masters degree programme in the UK in the seventies. One
wonders if perhaps outside education — and the concomitant
exposure to outside cultures and values — is innately counter
to the IBM culture. Certainly the people who take the
trouble to go through such programmes tend to be independent
types with more entrepreneurial leanings; many of these
'wild ducks' regard the cohesive IBM culture as constricting
once they have been given a chance to try their wings
outside.

In spite of corporate attention, World Trade's attempt to
create its own post-graduate technical institution was not
notably successful. The 'European Systems Research Institute'
(know internally as ESRI) finally started in 1967 in Geneva,
patterned after the original SRI or 'internal graduate school'
in New York City. However, there were major differences,
most of them stemming from the innate structural differences
between a single monolithic organization and a more loosely-
knit confederation of national companies. In finance and
planning, the shorter distance to the country manager often
gives World Trade an advantage over Domestic. In education,
the monolith has a better chance to get its programme
launched.

Like Blaricum, the Geneva budget for ESRI had to come
from the country budgets, on a per-country basis rather than
a per-student basis. The New York SRI had jelled; good
managers were found and they tended to stay for a few years,
while the instructors who were wooed by IBM labs tended to
move on after two or three years. Working on Tom Junior's
concept that you could only have a high-level university-type
environment if you did research, the SRI in New York was
able to attract eminent insiders with research interests;
because they were graded by the students they had to be
good teachers too.

In Europe the situation was different. The competitive
country organizations often resented having to give money,

teachers and students to a central institution for high technology that seemed less useful to sales companies than it did to the more integrated US organization. Thus ESRI had a much lower budget than SRI; thus it had almost no research, which made it less attractive to European technologists. In addition, undercurrents of international rivalry contributed to rapid management turnover and sluggish instructor turnover. The institute was started by a small group from the United States; then an eminent Italian took over. He was rapidly replaced by an American, at which point the French students took umbrage and went home en masse. Maisonrouge sent them right back again. As one instructor put it at the worst of the crisis: 'The managers changed so fast here nobody knew who ran it any more.'

While managers spurted through Geneva too fast, the reverse situation set in among the faculty, which began to suffer hardening of the institutional arteries. Countries were unwilling to send their best SEs to teach there; instead they tended to send more difficult people. ('It's a Siberia,' said a New Yorker. 'If a country had an unmanageable prima-donna who was a nuisance and doing harm with customers, they'd send him to Geneva.') Lacking New York's internal reputation, the European institute became more of a dead-end for careers. Job offers for the instructors were few, and re-entry to the small country organizations would be difficult at best after the luxurious park-like atmosphere in Geneva. The labs looked elsewhere for good technical people. Thus the teachers stayed on too long, getting farther behind the state of the art, thereby making the courses less appealing to the students. The country organizations, who were assessed a fixed fee to support ESRI, grew so reluctant to send students that a kind of 'reverse quota' was imposed.

This précis is unfair to some excellent men who have taught at Geneva. A few took their chances on re-entry to country companies that were essentially sales organizations, in order to do work that was more technically challenging for a while. Some were able to exit into the labs. Nonetheless, most of them grant that Geneva never developed the momentum that monolithic backing was able to give the American sibling.

Polite solutions to some of the European stresses are in the planning stages. The elegant new European education centre in a forest near Brussels will eventually handle 7,000 students every year.

The new centre houses the ESRI from Geneva, the Executive Development School from Blaricum, the Customer Executive School from Paris (and before that Blaricum), plus the CE Management Training School from London and the Advanced Marketing Institute and International Administration Education Facility from Brussels. Staff from the new educational smorgasbord includes some of World Trade's interesting 'technical mavericks', who may finally be able to achieve a first-class postgraduate school for IBM Europe. In addition to its critical mass of good instructors and this breadth of activities, the centre now charges on a per-student basis instead of the old per-country basis, alleviating some of the stresses that beset Blaricum, Paris, Geneva and other institutions.

Along with centralization of centres, there is more decentralization of the education process. In 1972 Jones wrote in *Think International*: 'The key decisions are made in the marketplace — how we are going to handle the customer, what resources we are going to put at the customer's disposal, how we are going to train our people — these types of decisions are delegated as near to the customer as possible.' Whether this is already policy or just an indication of direction, it affects IBM education, primarily because it was Jones who said it.

Problems notwithstanding, IBM manages to educate thousands of its own employees and those of its customers every year. As Nate Newkirk once expressed it: 'There's an old Mexican proverb — "In the land of the blind, the one-eyed man is king." If you look at it in perspective, IBM is far better in education than most companies — and all other computer companies.'

IBM is also better in education than many countries. It trains most of the world's computer salesmen and users. Whether this came about because IBM has the majority of the world's computer market or vice versa, the fact has important implications. It means that sales techniques, ethics and computer training (like computer languages and attitudes) are to some extent *de facto* standards imposed by IBM on competitors, users and governments. It also means that developing countries must depend on a foreign firm for what they are beginning to consider a basic resource: their trained technical people. And all these people are trained in IBM techniques and attitudes, whether they like it or not.

5
Manufacturing

Most people think the salesman is king at IBM — and to a large extent he is. But close behind him in top-level reverence, and considerably more immune from top-level abrasion, is the factory worker. One of the Basic Beliefs in IBM is the dignity of the individual. There is a diminishing of this dignity as men go up the management ladder; no one could call the sales meetings or motivators 'dignified', and just because the salesmen are so crucial to IBM's success they are subjected to pressures that would be intolerable if they were not highly motivated salesmen. The specialists and administrators often feel left out, poor cousins in the IBM hierarchy. Scientists complain that they are walled off from the real world. That leaves one group of happy, dignified individuals — the people who work in IBM's factories.[1]

Numerically they are a diminishing proportion of the IBM workforce. Like every other aspect of business, manufacturing would be much easier if there were not crotchety, undependable human beings involved. Like every other company, IBM spends an inordinate amount of management time and attention making sure the workers are happy. Thus, like every other commodity today, computers tend to be made more and more automatically. Much of the thrust of IBM research has been to reduce the human content in manufacturing — and thus the opportunity for human error. Instead of single bits of storage, a computer now has thousands of circuits on a single semi-conductor 'chip'. Expensive machines, manned by a few expert workers, do what many workers used to accomplish by hand. But no matter how much the workplace changes or the factory work-force shrinks, those are 'the individuals' for whom the Basic Beliefs were first laid out, and to whom management bows five times daily.

In this context, it is easy to understand why IBM was one of the first (and most sincere) companies to try 'job enrichment' in all its colourful permutations. Unlike most companies, IBM's moves in this tended to come more from cultural conviction than fear (unless you count an almost morbid fear of a 'union situation' that permeates the IBM culture).

Most companies find that the primary non-technical barrier to job enrichment is a natural distrust on the part of the employees, who are convinced (usually from a long experience) that the company is never altruistic, and is thus only trying to 'enrich' their jobs to enrich itself in some way. Thus they tend to respond with new demands to enrich their pay packets, saying in essence: 'If I do more I must be paid more.' In most companies, such attitudes are based on a 'pluralistic' attitude — us and them. But IBM is not 'most companies'. This is where the Old Man's beliefs have their most visible payoff. All those years with higher than average pay, stock purchase rights for all workers, and no unnecessary layoffs have created a different ambiance for manufacturing people, who have a more 'unitary' attitude — 'we're a team'.

The results of this cultural conviction have been spectacular, especially when they are compared to industry at large. Viewed from inside, IBMers find it harder to realize the importance of the company's achievements; almost every factory manager has his crises. Every group has its gripes. But IBM has never lost a day of work in any of its factories due to a strike (unless you count the general unrest of the 1968 Paris general strike, and even then the IBM factory voted to go back to work).

IBM tends to have fairly small factories, well scattered but sited conveniently near labs or other IBM facilities. Europe, for instance, has 12 manufacturing plants (two of them making typewriter products) and 28 smaller plants making punch cards.

Each of these was a grand achievement to its host IBM
company when it was created. Each factory is today a
fairly independent entity, free to make engineering changes
inside its products, so long as it keeps the rest of the corporation
informed through well-specified channels.

'Job enrichment is being sold like soap'

It is important to look at IBM's entire job enrichment
philosophy. Long before the subject was popular, IBM
had hired some of the world's most capable behavioural
scientists for 'personnel research'. Many of their activities were
global attitude surveys, or fire-fighting whenever there was a
tricky management situation or potential union crisis. Notable
among these men are Saul Gellerman and David Sirota in the United
States and Geert Hofstede in Europe.[2] (All three eventually left IBM.)

The job enrichment experts stayed flexible, dealing with one
job or work group at a time, using insiders rather than
outside consultants (and keeping their own hands off much of
the time).

One of the best job enrichment activities in World Trade
happened at the Amsterdam typewriter factory. Dr Sirota's
Domestic work may have had subtle influence in Amsterdam
but the managers there insist their own job enrichment
experience was completely home-grown, a 'happening' rather
than an IBM programme.

The three 'fathers' of this project were A. C. Bakker,
J. Lievestro and Wim Smits. With full employee consultation
they broke up several 60-man assembly lines into groups of
20 — and several of these 'mini-groups' in turn broke
themselves down into 9- or 10-man 'micro-groups'.

In April 1970 in response to employee suggestions, they started
a pilot mini-line and encountered their first real resistance. The foremen
were already dubious about the sweeping changes their managers
and assemblers were proposing. When they were asked to send
'average' employees to the pilot group, most of them (naturally)
treated it instead like a garbage dump.

A second mini-line went up in September 1970 and a third in
January 1971 as demands on the factory grew. By this time the
foremen were more accustomed to the mini-line idea, and they
were running out of problem-workers to send over, so the general
quality improved. At the same time, Lievestro started a full year

training for the entire typewriter assembly workforce, at a cost of about £20,000. In the original assembly lines each operator did a single task that took about three minutes. In the mini-lines, the work was organized in ten-minute segments (give or take a minute) so each worker had to learn at least two more operations in addition to the one he already knew. Some employees who were already doing highly rated tasks objected to learning lower-class tasks — in essence they felt their jobs were being enriched *downwards*.

Although they knew the assemblers were deeply involved from the first, the managers were nonetheless taking a huge risk when they made the total changeover in June 1971, during the annual three-week holiday. The first pilot mini-line was still below the average productivity for the traditional assembly line. The cost of training had already been high. Some tools had to be duplicated for nine mini-groups instead of two assembly lines. Most important, word had come filtering down through the World Trade hierarchy that they *had* to have the entire operation up to its previous production level within three months.

They took the brave step anyway. Within the first month they were surprised and delighted. Productivity per man in the new mini-groups had already reached its former norm, even though the original pilot group was still below par. As they got used to working together, the groups began to take on more administrative tasks that had previously been done outside the assembly lines.

The managers encouraged changes, mostly by interfering with them as little as possible. They helped streamline the paperwork. Instead of the former maze of forms, reports, codes and cards, each group could send in a single piece of paper each week. As Bakker expressed it: 'Part of the improvement in productivity came from eliminating all the checks and monitoring systems that were brought in over the years to measure productivity.'

The results were spectacular. The productivity (measured quite simply — the number of typewriters shipped compared to the number of employees it took to make them) was up by 50 percent at the end of 1973.

This is only one of many IBM factories. But one can assume that there have been fiascos and problems in job enrichment, even in IBM. Problems notwithstanding, the impression remains that IBM factories are usually brisk, productive places where people seem to enjoy their work. Credit for this situation belongs not only to the modern job enrichment men but to the Watsons with their Basic Beliefs — notably Respect for the Individual, particularly when the Individual is an IBM production worker.

6
Research
&
development

arketing at IBM is organized on a national basis. Manufacturing is more or less continental. The one global activity in the company is research and development. R&D — which is mostly D — has a budget that is bigger than the defence budgets of most medium-sized countries: $726 million in 1972 and still rising. Why then, with a budget this size, is IBM so seldom the source of major innovations?

One answer — important in IBM's terms — is that the basic purpose of most of the R&D money is not technical achievement but profit achievement. A 'development' will often turn out to be a way of manufacturing computers or components less expensively, or an expensive piece of machinery that cuts down maintenance cost. IBM makes money every time it builds a computer, and it goes on making money for the lifetime of that computer; the direct thrust of R&D is therefore pointed at making money.

Another purpose for R&D at IBM is to *absorb* money — which (as $726 million would indicate) it does effectively. In this sense R&D can be a comfortable internal 'cushion', one of several contingency funds available to keep the financial lines smooth — although this is a point that IBM's competitive R&D people would debate hotly. Nonetheless, R&D spending goes

up when profits would otherwise be embarrassingly high. It has
sometimes dropped sharply when there was likely to be trouble
meeting high profit levels from a previous year — a problem Tom
Junior encountered in the late sixties when the shift from leasing
to 'third-party leasing' gave artificially high profits.

As one graduate put it: 'IBM is in many ways a creature of US
government policy. There's a kind of accordion effect; they're
squeezed in upon themselves. They can't cut prices — that would
be bad for competitors. They can't acquire companies, even in
other industries. What are they going to do with all that
money and all those people? This accordion forces them to do
R&D.' The spending ability used to depend on the company's
place in the five- or six-year product cycle, but in the past few
years even a major product line like the 370 series has not been
able to change the cash situation much; work towards the major
product line due for announcement in about 1976 is already under-
way, being written off in an orderly manner as current expenses
in the year in which it occurs, so even that activity is not expected
to make a large dent. IBM's cash and (conservatively valued)
negotiable securities amounted to $1,875 million at the end of
1971; a year later the total was $2,576 million, and at the end
of 1973 it was $3,322 million.

IBM's first research laboratory was created at Endicott in 1933.
Already the Old Man was building his ties with the academic
community, and lab people were encouraged to teach or learn
outside. Endicott took root and flourished, sending up sprouts in
other locations, until the company had a world-wide network
of 32 labs for research, development and engineering. Sixteen
of the largest labs work on hardware and software for IBM's
computers. Six of these are in Europe and the newest one is in
Japan. Hursley, centred on the elegant old Hursley House estate
near Winchester in southern England, is one of the largest of the
European labs. Others are located at Boeblingen (near Stuttgart),
La Gaude (near Nice — a site chosen at the peak of de Gaulle's
hostility to foreign companies), Uithoorn (pronounced oot-
horn) in the Netherlands, Vienna, and Lidingö, near Stockholm.
Most of the sites were chosen for political as well as personnel
reasons; all are located in major markets.

'Wild ducks fly in formation'

It was Tom Junior who first stressed the need for 'wild ducks' in
IBM — independent, entrepreneurial people who were not afraid

to risk their jobs if they needed to disagree with policy or push for new activities. This is particularly important in R&D. One of Tom Junior's first important acts in 1956, as IBM began to change from a punched card company into a computer company, was to hire Dr Emmanuel Piore, who had been the US Navy's chief scientist. Assigned to head IBM's R&D activities, Dr Piore immediately increased the emphasis on basic research and initiated a research division. In IBM's lexicon today, 'research' is the (Piore-stimulated) pure research carried on by that division at a handful of small laboratories — looking at how much energy it takes to move a level in a laser, for example. The research division has labs at Yorktown Heights and San Jose in the United States. Only one overseas group, in Zurich, works on this level.

Most of IBM's budget for R&D is spent on what the company calls 'applied research' — bringing these principles down to the product level. This is done by a number of somewhat larger laboratories under control of IBM's product-oriented divisions. The applied research is really 'product development', making the principles work, at reasonable cost, in marketable products. Of IBM's 20,000 people in R&D around the world, more than 15,000 are in product development, which also gobbles up about 93 percent of the huge R&D budget. In 1972 the company spent $676 million (more than ten times the combined R&D budgets of all its competitors) on product development; 'only' $50 million went into basic research.

In addition to the basic research division and product development labs, there is a third little institution inside IBM that contributes to the flow of new ideas — the Scientific Research Centre (or SRC). The SRCs tend to be 20- or 30-man groups, funded by the external affairs (PR) budgets of the host countries. One journalist who called them 'mini-think-tanks'[1] pointed out that while the basic research labs were doing 'bench-research', the SRCs were doing 'desk-research'. Most of them concentrate on current or near-future problems with significant social impact, which justifies their inclusion in the public relations budgets. A few receive support from World Trade as well.

France started the first mini-think-tank in 1962; the group studying human linguistics and non-linear programming there had produced about 1,000 monographs by 1973. The German SRC in Heidelberg works with the local cancer research institute, using computers to improve screening techniques and plan treatment for tumours. Italy hosts a group at Pisa working on econometry and hydraulics, one at Bari working on computer-aided instruction, and another at Venice trying to help refloat the sinking city with computer calculations. The SRC in Tokyo is not too surprisingly involved in shipbuilding. The Spanish SRC has projects on air, noise and water pollution. Mexico City is studying the educational problems in developing countries (which would have pleased the Old Man). Tel Aviv has a team working on medical monitoring. Brazil hosts an econometry group at São Paulo. Great Britain's SRC at Peterlee deals with a large databases for such activities as local government planning, or modelling the thermal pollution in the Baltic for ten years before and after the installation of new nuclear power stations. Almost all the projects are done in a joint venture manner with people from outside educational institutions or government. About 300 people work in mini-think-tanks in World Trade.

All together the European labs employed about 4,000 of IBM's 20,000 R&D people in 1973. They also played a major part in world-wide development activities. Each lab has been assigned certain 'missions' to coordinate all technical activities for a product or range of products, which it oversees on a world-wide basis. Even more serious than a mission is 'control' of a product. If a product doesn't come up to expectations technically or economically, it is the manager in the 'laboratory for control' (or LFC) who gets into trouble. If capstans are breaking on tape drives, service people rush their reports to the LFC, which studies the problem, hopefully solves it, then sends out new documentation, manufacturing or maintenance plans to every plant making the drive or every office maintaining it. No plant can make a change (such as machining a part instead of casting it in plastic) without coordinating the change through the LFC. One graduate called this 'a vitally important IBM management concept — one of the greatest manufacturing miracles I've ever known.'

The degree of automation this dispersed control system permits for technical development is impressive. Computer-generated directions for numerically controlled machine tools, for example, not only control the machines that make the parts, but also the other machines that make the wiring diagrams or other documents that go with the parts. These individual blueprints for every machine are then bound into big blue books that go with the equipment.

This is an elegant structure, of which IBM is justly proud. The company says this kind of incredibly close control would be impossible without the 'one-world product line'. It was not always so tidy. When World Trade was younger it tended to create its own product line, either by selecting only certain of the Domestic products to emphasize abroad, or by developing major products of its own. At this stage squabbles between Domestic and World Trade Labs were frequent and irritating (as well as expensive). It was Bob Evans in Domestic who managed to bring the ravelled edges of the lab organizations together during the 360 development and knit them together so firmly that they couldn't split apart any more. Once the 360 was in the marketplace, it was not possible to reverse the trend again; no customer would ever want to buy a 'foreign-designed' model of an IBM computer if they could get the 'real' one. The one-world product line freed IBM from geography. Foreign LFCs after 1964 could control products made in the United States without any trouble. Once the company had the system set up it didn't matter where the LFC or the plant was located. Communication between various locations is instant, with a network of computers, phone lines and telexes sending voices, magnetic tapes or management reports back and forth nonchalantly by satellite or cable.

Mission and control are easy to confuse from outside, but IBMers know the difference. Hursley,[2] for example, once had the mission for World Trade's middle-sized computers (models 135 and 145), the PL/1 programming language, and small disk systems. This set the tone at Hursley, where three separate groups (1,500 people, about 1,200 of them 'professionals') mingled pleasantly on the campus-like grounds and in the local pub (for which the Dolphin disk was named). At the same time, Hursley had *control*, world-wide, for the 370/135 computer as well as the Dolphin disk and PL/1. Then, as the language cycle evolved and PL/1 was no longer a pioneering language but a full-grown one that had to be blended more closely into the fraternity of computer languages, the control passed on to a New York group which took over all major language developments. The 135 computer also reached maturity and it, too, moved on (back to Endicott, which already had the 145 control). It should be noted that this much change in control is not normal. Most products remain with the maternal LFC for their entire lives, but in this case in 1973 IBM was tidying up after a major Domestic reorganization.

Hursley then received new control functions and missions, for what IBM called 'industry systems'. These are computer systems for specific industries, dressed up with special terminals and software. This form of reorganization tended to protect the terminal and software activities for the target industries from potential anti-trust threat (at a most threatening time), as well as welding together at a practical level the hardware and software product activities that had been splintered in the 1972 Domestic re-organization. Assigning the new industry-systems mission and control to Hursley also put the lab under the wing of the new Domestic hardware division, after six months of organizational malaise.

The emphasis in all of Hursley's new industry-systems work was to help computers do useful work for clerks, managers and other non-technical employees in the target industries. Hursley got world-wide control in insurance and utilities, World Trade mission in rail transport and government (particularly local government), and a joint mission in airlines and aviation, working with the nearby airline competence centre at Feltham.

The UK group already had experience with British Aircraft Corp. on Concorde and with the Boadicea reservation system at BOAC (now British Airways). The banking control was still in a state of flux, though a Hursley-developed and Greenock-manufactured banking terminal for Lloyd's bank was getting corporate scrutiny. As one Hursley executive described the 'typical' process: 'Obviously you hope your bank terminal will work in more than one country, so you put through an RPQ (Request for Price Quotation) to Paris. Then you get back an order to build 50 of them, as modifications to existing terminals. If that precursor is a success, you tune it up. If the market studies show a likely market in the world-wide banking industry, it will eventually go into some lab (probably Raleigh, North Carolina, whose mission was terminals). If it looks like the UK terminal is only suited to UK banks, we'll keep it here as a special product out of our own special engineering group. The important thing is the transition from the special systems category to inclusion in the product plan, world-wide.'

Hursley is a lively, independent place. It has its own product and industry responsibilities, a positive attitude that is character-istic of Britain in general and technical people in particular; it also has delicate lines to walk between independence and subservience to the parent corporation. The lab depends on the UK company for administration and housekeeping. Thus when IBM UK Ltd suffered the hiring freeze of 1970-2, so did Hursley. In the midst of the freeze, Hursley had to meet the product demands laid down by three new divisional parents (processors, programming, and storage products), then get used to the new bosses, negotiate new budgets with each of them, keep up employee morale, maintain a flow of new ideas from the orderly wild ducks, and somehow continue competing for new missions and resources.

'You get things done in IBM through your friends'

In most companies, the result would be chaos in three dimensions. Somehow, at Hursley, it worked. Some kind of basic stability permeates the place. People know what they are supposed to be doing there, and they do it, without much worry about the solid and dotted lines on the organization charts. The organizational insecurities affected their managers, but IBM and the managers agree that they are getting paid well enough to accept insecurities. Most important to Hursley's resilience was a 'real' organization, based on communication at every level (not only meetings and presentations, but after-work gatherings at the famous Dolphin).

One example of the result of informal communications, particularly among IBM's technical people, is the product line itself. 'Many of the hardware and software products come from what are really moonlight projects', said one graduate. 'In the old days we actually had a phenomenon called the "Moonlight System". In the 7000 series era at Poughkeepsie a couple of guys wrote a programming system so you could use a smaller computer as a connection to a larger one. This increased the effective work both machines could do. But (perhaps for that reason) they couldn't sell the idea to the company. They kept working quietly, and told most of their friends about it. Eventually one of the friends brought a NASA man through the plant and he "accidentally" learned about it. He ended up buying a baker's dozen 7000 computers equipped this way. That gave IBM a little extra time to bring in the 360 project.' Moonlight was a direct precursor of IBM's modern multi-computer.

Managers at various levels often look the other way when a bootleg project is in its delicate early stages. 'They don't want to put out 'Plan B' or make any commitment to it,' said a graduate. 'But if it grows organically, they let it grow.' One of the case histories used at Sands Point for executive training deals with a stalwart of the old product line — the 1401 computer — which originally 'came out of left field as a printer controller'. By enshrining the case in the Sands Point folklore, IBM lets it become part of the executive litany that says clever planning from the top down is not the only source of good products and services.

Later, in the 360 era, the 360/67 computer (IBM's first 'time-sharing' model) was a decidedly un-standard product. One group had been working on this kind of machine for the government's SAGE project, to monitor air defence in 'real time', but attempts to push the new techniques into commercial computing had been fruitless; most members of the team had dispersed to other companies when SAGE was finished. Then the Massachusetts Institute of Technology (an institution which had always been IBM territory) began to buy time-sharing computers from General Electric. IBM took immediate notice, then reacted with a $60 million budget for the '67 project'. Those who remained from the old SAGE team simply called all their friends who had left the company and invited them back. The result was the 360/67 precursor to the virtual memory announced in the seventies.

Management has to walk a fine line with respect to moonlight projects — to minimize the variety of products but somehow allow the good ones to filter upwards, even when they aren't planned. The process is sometimes related more to the energy of the progenitor than the merit of the product, but on the whole the laissez-faire management approach works. Top management seems particularly pleased when products come out of World Trade this way, partly because it enhances IBM's image in the host country, and partly because it keeps the Domestic innovators on their toes.

In one instance, though, a World Trade development met firm resistance. American management at first opposed the 'Carnation project', a French-designed system to handle telephone communications with a computer, so voice and data communications could be mixed on the same system. 'They were afraid of making Bell nervous' said Ted Merrill, an American IBM graduate, who reports on computers and data communications for *Business Week*. The giant Bell telephone system in the United States is one of the few organizations larger and more powerful than IBM. It is also subject to government regulation — a situation IBM does not wish to invite. 'I don't know where the guys in France got the budget to carry Carnation on,' Merrill said. 'We certainly didn't approve the project over here. They probably used built-in slush funds from the local chief at La Gaude.' In truth, the first Carnation models were built for the La Gaude lab's own telephone exchange. Even though it was a moonlight project, Carnation grew into the trendy 2750 and 3750 products that took IBM into a new and expanding field.

Often a bootleg project doesn't take funds at all, just an exchange of people. Some of the 'centres of competence' grew up this way in Europe. 'That was all bootleg,' said an ex World Trade man. 'The guy heading the SAS project for an airline reservation system would go out to his friends in the major countries and say: 'You know this kind of system is coming; send me one of your bright guys, on your budget, and we'll get him trained for you.' It was a low-level effort at first, and it kept a low profile, but before they knew it upstairs there was a first rate group of guys working together on airline reservation systems around Europe.

'Technically, when you do this, you are taking a revenue-producing resource — the bright guy — from one country and using him to produce revenue in another,' the graduate continued. 'There is some question of tax exposure here. The legal guys in IBM begin to clamp down when the practice gets too visible. With a lot of cells growing up they had to formalize the competence centre phenomenon in the long run. They formed new companies and charged the countries more formally for the work the centres did for them. Nonetheless, the centres of competence were allowed to get going organically, within the network of marketing people in Europe. When their activities spread beyond marketing alone it got to be an issue, and the new institutions were the result.'

While Hursley was undergoing all its changes of mission and control in 1972 and 1973, it was also learning to live with a new boss, Dick Bevier, a brisk, outspoken American with enough World Trade experience to be viewed as a Bevier rather than an American when he made a decision. Bevier's main concern in 1973 was to negotiate the resources (money and people) he needed to change Hursley's activities at the pace the corporation demanded. There were some discretionary funds available to him (fortunately there always are in the IBM labs), but the budget was tight.

'Everything is a trade-off at IBM,' he commented. 'Except for pure research organizations, I don't know any big company or government institution where you can go get big chunks of uncommitted funds — sandbox money. Slush funds for independent research are the first thing you cut in most places when times are tight. But it's like your own bank account. You have to keep putting some away for a rainy day.'

Bevier's economies amounted to keeping administration over-heads down. He tried to keep track of the number of Atlantic crossings — about half a dozen of his people were in the United States every week — but beyond that he was fatalistic about the cost of coordination. 'If you're anywhere near the forefront of technology in a widely spaced company like this, if you clamped down on travel and telephoning you'd kill yourself. We really *don't* duplicate effort or carry parallel developments to the extent most people think. We try to avoid unnecessary duplication by staying in technical communication with all these phone calls and trips. If you cut that off, then you *do* reinvent the wheel. Technical journals aren't enough to prevent this.'

This idea that IBM does 'brute-force' research, with two, three or four parallel developments for each kind of device or technology has been prevalent for years (and an inconvenience to lab managers). It stems from three phenomena: the industry's traditional secrecy about its new developments, IBM's own closed approach to public relations, and the fact that IBM *does* carry parallel projects — to a point.

One day an article mentions that IBM has three different teams working to develop fast line printers. Then two of them have their projects killed at what journalists (and IBM team members that day) would consider the 'last moment'. Unhappy team members or their associates spread the word to the press that IBM has killed yet another parallel development, and the impression builds up that the corporation is trying to corner the market on technical wild ducks by keeping them locked up in labs, paid superbly for doing work that will never emerge. As one journal draws this conclusion (and IBM says nothing), another rewrites the story from a slightly different angle, emphasizing the charge that IBM is cornering the people market to keep the local computer company from getting good technical people. (A fallacy; all of Europe's computer companies have equally good technical people, some better than IBM's.) By the time the first journal is quoting the seventh, another myth has grown up.

IBM does have parallel developments, but they tend to be parallel at an early, inexpensive stage. Only one out of 80 suggested products actually reaches the market place though IBM can afford to carry many to an advanced stage of development before deciding among them. The product cycle that results seems to be effective from a profit viewpoint. Each phase in the cycle has its own technical and management reviews, its own start-points and check-points, its own budget negotiations.

Entire new product lines (or 'generations') happen every few years. However, the days of giant, all-new developments are past in the computer industry. The 370 range of computers announced in 1970 was from the user's viewpoint an evolutionary outgrowth of the 360 range (announced in 1964), though there were revolutionary changes in the manufacture, reliability and technology. Different labs with control for different 370 models were able to build them around different kinds of memory technology, for example, without upsetting the 'upwards-compatibility' that lets users run programs written for one model on another (more expensive) model. In fact, the technical people were so successful at making their new technology 'transparent' to the user that an alarming number of 360 users were able to 'upgrade' to *less* expensive 370 systems.

In this sense, IBM is easily its own biggest competitor. Any major improvement in price-performance for the user hurts IBM just as much as it hurts competitors. There is evidence that IBM delays announcements of computer improvements until competitors threaten to gain market share with their own innovations, or until demand from users is so loud it cannot be ignored. In this sense, IBM retards progress.

The 360 series was probably the last and certainly the greatest revolution to affect customers. The internal processes and stresses that went into Tom Junior's 360 decision were documented in 1966 by *Fortune*,[3] in a manner that embarrassed the corporation by its candour and accuracy (and shut publicity doors even more firmly thenceforth). Reporter Tom Wise spent months exploring the ways in which technical decisions were made for the 360. Calling it the riskiest business judgment of recent times, Wise quoted Bob Evans, then 360 chief, as saying (only half in jest): 'We called this project "You bet your company." '

From its 1962 inception, the 360 had swallowed up over half a billion dollars in R&D alone by 1966. Yet in perspective, that is less than a single year's R&D budget in the seventies — and all the money for later R&D came from the success of the 360. By that one great risk, Tom Junior may have proved that IBM was at last too large for any technical decision ever again to be a major risk. The very fact that IBM makes a decision to go in one direction or another now makes that direction the one true way to the majority of customers and competitors. In addition, the profits from that 360 risk now support some parallel projects that take the risk out of current 370 or 380 decisions.

The 360 gamble paid off, but no company can afford 'creative tension' on this scale as a rule. Development in the seventies comes from a well-understood process within a more disciplined IBM. Only conception is left to chance. Entire product lines may be conceived anywhere in the IBM world. Often a product originates with a special customer request. Or someone in an industry marketing group requests a certain type of gadget, and someone else sees a broader market. Or an engineer in a lab sees a possible change to a product he is working on, and asks whether it would be useful to the marketing people. In this informal way, within the constraints of the one-world product plan, people determine the 'requirement' and agree a specification for the eventual product, with occasional little differences of opinion that mirror the great debates of the early sixties but underscore the differences in scale. The 'spec' is then parcelled out formally to the selected lab (which may have been supporting the project on a moonlight basis), with a budget attached. This is the essential portion of the conception phase ('phase one') of a product's development cycle.

Then a design is worked out to meet the specification (they call it 'phase two') and a prototype is built and tested ('phase three'). All these phases take place before the announcement is made. A product can be killed at any point in the process, with no embarrassment and low investment.

Often there are parallel developments. Two types of terminals, for instance, might be developed in Poughkeepsie and Greenock for bank customers. They probably both reach the prototype stage and undergo what IBM calls 'A-test' by a separate testing group in each lab, before final choice must be made between them. In the case of the bank terminals, they are both likely to reach fruition, because a single large bank order in any country — particularly the UK — justifies considerable R&D expenditure. It is not too expensive to carry several different approaches for a single unit along this path to the prototype; the R&D people work in small (and thus low-cost) groups. When one approach is chosen over another, a few development engineers in the losing lab may be disappointed, but they understand the process and are usually given other interesting work quickly to keep the slump to a minimum. Wise competitors try to pounce at this point with job offers; quite a few succeed. Foolish ones often try to hire away the men from the winning project team; Judge Christensen set the cost of this at $21.9 million in the 1973 Telex trial.

Once IBM commits to a product at the end of phase three, announcement plans begin and it can no longer be killed easily, though a few have quietly slipped into oblivion if they didn't make the grade in later phases. In phase four a production-type machine is built. This means the designers and production engineers are not just looking at how to do the job, or whether it can be done, but how the device (or even software) can be built and maintained at minimum expense. Then they 'B-test' the product and if it passes the reliability and performance specifica-

tions they release it to the plant for large-scale production.
Phase five is building and testing the first production models,
followed by the first customer delivery (FCD, 'phase six')
and thorough testing under customer conditions (called the
'C-test'). Several customers have turned down the honour of being
C-test guinea-pigs for new computers, despite the high degree
of support IBM offers the chosen few at this stage. 'Too many
IBM people underfoot,' one of them growled.

When the product has passed all these tests, control goes from
the development engineering group to the production engineering
group at the LFC, usually for the rest of the product's life, though
the shifting missions at Hursley demonstrated that nothing is
immutable in IBM. LFC people continue to review the product as
it gains field experience, and improve it as the technology improves.
Thus a 360/20 computer built in 1973 is a different machine from
the first 360/20 to come out of Boeblingen in the mid-sixties.

The lab manager has slush funds that can come into play anywhere in the early stages of the product cycle. Bevier referred to
his as 'ad-tech money' (for 'advanced technology'), but other
funds at other labs may have other names. They are usually used
for independent or minority ideas that would not otherwise find
funding in the cycle — 'wild duck' ideas.

In the case of the Dolphin disk at Hursley, one manager
believed that a particular technique for better production could
be developed in 12 weeks. However, one of his subordinates thought
that with ten weeks' work he could develop a better technique to
to the same job. In most companies they would have done it the
manager's way. Not so in IBM. The two (who were good friends
and remained so) went to Bevier and asked him to resolve their
impasse. He called in the experts, and after a few flipcharts he
agreed to fund the subordinate, in parallel with his boss, for
12 weeks. The man did the job, proving within ten weeks that his
technique worked. The difference was one of degree between
the manager's way (which worked) and the subordinate's way
(which wasn't quite as good as he had expected, but nonetheless
appreciably better than his boss's). The difference in production
cost for a high-volume product like the Dolphin will show up in
Hursley's records as well as IBM's overall profits.

Size is not as important as disposition of the ad-tech money.
'Its purpose is to take a lad who has a good idea and let him do
something with it,' said Bevier. 'But it's on a scale of carrying him
for six months to the next check-point, not carrying a monster
team for three years. At least 75 percent of the time the

researcher comes back at the end of the six months and says
his idea doesn't quite work the way he expected. If you have smart
people they are bound to have different ideas. You hired them
to be creative and inventive. But very seldom, anywhere, have I
seen that one guy's idea is so much better that everybody falls
into line.

'Generally the funds are used for projects where a guy has an
idea out of his own area,' Bevier continued. 'If it fits within his
own area, his manager is likely to find money in his own budget
to explore it. If it doesn't, he comes to this office because his
manager has no interest in his brainstorm and won't fund him.
If the thing looks good, we put in a little money. Everybody
in IBM knows it's available. It has different names and more or
less formal means of acquisition and distribution in different
labs, but it's all the same thing: a small fund, looking to creative
ideas, especially interdisciplinary ideas or minority ideas. It's a
mechanism to keep them flowing.'

His defence against the charge of cornering the technical wild
duck market was simple: computer scientists are made, not hired.
In the IBM culture, you grow your own specialists rather than
buying them ready-made. He wasn't too interested in 'computer
scientists' at all, in spite of all the new degree courses in the
subject. Bevier said: 'We haven't had a people problem in the
computer industry since the mid-fifties, when systems
programmers were in short supply. If I had the go-ahead, I
could double the size of the lab fairly easily. There are plenty of
useful people out there: physicists, chemists, electrical engineers,
mathematicians, biologists. It's people who are out of their own
fields who are the inventors. Those are the people we want, and
that's where we use our R&D slush funds.'

Politically, the labs pose a problem to host countries outside
the United States In many countries the advantage or prestige
of doing advanced technical work is offset by the feeling of
impotence; local scientists have no local voice in deciding what
work to do. This discomfort bubbles to the surface more often
in Europe than it used to. It is contributing to the growing
pressures for an IBM Europe that can stand on its own R&D
feet. IBM would face enormous stress, both emotionally and
organizationally, from this kind of shift back from the well-
organized one-world product line to continental product lines.
Even so, the markets are sufficiently important that the change
will have to be considered.

7
Personnel policies & practices

IBM wants happy employees. The company's morale, which has to a large extent been a result of consistent personnel policies with this objective, is the one thing above all others that IBM's competitors envy most. It is also the one thing which brings a management crisis to a head faster than anything else in IBM. Let the attitude survey results slip a point or two, or the complaints on a subject increase, and the corporation's top committees dispatch whole task forces to cope with the problem. IBM does its homework in personnel to an almost absurd extent, but this approach seems to pay off.

When the Old Man came to C-T-R from NCR he brought with him John Patterson's advanced views about the well-being of employees. Tom Junior in his lectures at Columbia University in 1962 described the way the Old Man's beliefs grew into IBM beliefs.[1] His father held to his values so strongly, said the son, that he was 'sometimes exasperating'. Tom Junior described his father's funny combination of fundamentals: 'The important values, as he learned them, were to do every job well, to treat all people with dignity and respect, to appear neatly dressed, to be clean and forthright, to be eternally optimistic, and above all loyal. '

These values grew into a set of personnel policies that included good pay and benefits, equal opportunity employment, a policy that employees would not be laid off for lack of work, and more two-way communications channels than most companies IBM's size maintain. A paternalistic flavour remains, underlying many of IBM's actions and reactions with respect to its employees, but like the attitudes to competition, it is subtle and sophisticated. The company is virtually union-free, and the policies are acceptable to the employees because for 60 years IBM has demonstrated to them that it keeps its promises.

IBM is a strict parent (especially for managers) but a good provider. The policy with respect to pay is to be about 7 percent above the national norm for similar workers — in most countries. In a few places where IBM pay is determined by industry-wide union negotiations, IBM tends to pay the going rate except for key groups of employees where extra motivation can make a major difference. In addition to the excellent pay there are bonuses, prizes, awards, surprises. 'There are no real extremes in the bonus programme,' one ex World Trader commented, 'but people get cheques out of the blue for significant achievement. These are not necessarily from the department budgets. IBM has little kitties here and there to sweeten people's cheques. They'll give a guy $500 or $5,000 when he doesn't expect it. This develops terrific loyalty — a direct reward for the work he's done — and at the same time they move his goals up. It's five times as effective as a raise, and he only gets it once.'

The world-wide stock purchase programme is not out of line with the rest of industry, but like the salaries just a trifle better than most. Its real merit is the IBM shares themselves, which for many years performed far better than most. An employee can spend up to 10 percent of his salary to buy IBM shares at about 85 percent of the market price on the previous 1 July or of the present price, whichever is lower. There are other fringe benefits such as the £10,000 interest-free loans available to some UK employees. (One graduate noted that this 'company store' inducement 'locks people into IBM because it is repayable when or if you leave the company. They have traded their belief in opportunity for material gain and security, but the real achievers aren't motivated that way.') The stock option plan, available to only a few hundred top executives, is a separate programme, closely allied to IBM's large bonus programme for these people.

The Old Man was fond of giving shares to employees in the early days, in the same one-time surprise way the awards shower down more systematically on today's high performers. However, although the population of IBM millionaires is high, very few of them live in Europe. They weren't around to receive this Watsonian largesse in the early days, and didn't become part of the stock purchase programme until the mid-sixties.

National differences have always had to be considered in formulating IBM's pay and security policies. Saul Gellerman reported on several hundred mid-sixties employee interviews in the Orient in one article.[2] Compensation there, he pointed out, has traditionally been regarded in a parental way, as an obligatory payment by an employer responsible for the employee's welfare. Thus, even with IBM's clear-cut policy to pay more than the local rates, the employees tended to consider themselves underpaid. Viewing the almost limitless resources of the employer, they felt its ability to elevate their economic station should also be limitless (a problem that was not confined to IBM). Furthermore, they mistrusted the individual performance evaluations that were taken for granted by American managers.

In Japan, Gellerman found that a postwar image of power and omnipotence had created paradoxes when Western managers failed to protect the prerogatives of office, were too informal with their employees, or wore shirtsleeves in the office. When it came to the evaluations, communications difficulties made the task even harder. Moreover, a less-than-perfect evaluation for a Japanese employee carried with it the risk of exposing the employee to shame.

In the Philippines, outwardly Westernized, Gellerman found an even more formidable barrier to evaluation or merit pay in the 'compadre' system, which makes each man's pay a matter of open knowledge to his friends. The Americans there were regarded with concern because they seemed to value other things (like efficiency) above friendship.

India, on the other hand, suffered in Gellerman's view from extreme levels of competition between employees, most of them over-educated and under-employed; the spectre of unemployment was constantly present. Even IBM with its full-employment policies could not counteract the everyday sight of so many less fortunate people. The result was what Gellerman called 'competition run rampant', with internal jockeying for position, dissension and factionalism (not to mention regionalism), manifested in anonymous letters to management, attempts to bring personal grievances to the attention of visiting executives, and numerous denunciations, exposés and revelations. Attempts at evaluation there ran head-on into the high level of formal education, which was sometimes unrelated to the job that had been obtained. The 'qualification' to the Indian was his university degree, not his job classification.

By hiring young graduates world-wide, IBM is able to alleviate *some* of these traditional difficulties. Gellerman believed the situation would improve as Western businesses became more common in the Orient. Nonetheless, he expected no rapid change in the basic cultures, so the two-way culture shock would continue in some measure.

'Some people are more equal than others'

In addition to national differences and stresses, there are many others. Any large organization includes dozens of different sub-groups — women, blacks, people over fifty, foreigners, and so on. The more downtrodden the subgroups feel they have been historically, the more uproar they seem to cause as they grow visible and cohesive. IBM has its share of subgroups, plus a long history of male American dominance. In the Old Man's day it was rare for a woman, a black, even a Catholic, to be selected for an IBM job if there were a young male white-anglo-saxon-protestant (WASP) available. World War II cut down the number of young male WASPs in the job market, and the rise of technology brought Jews into the scientific corners of the company. Once IBM recognized the changes, it did a good job of assimilating minorities, to the extent that there is only one subgroup still likely to cause uproar — the foreigners.

Women began to invade the company in noticeable numbers during the war years. Until the late sixties they remained in subsidiary positions with one exception — the highly paid System Service Girls. This group was set up in the late fifties to alleviate recruitment and training problems; the well-trained, personable service girls turned out to be successful at soothing irate customers, and fixing machines; eventually they amounted to about half the Domestic customer service force until computers made customer service a more technical job. Attempts to promote the idea in World Trade seldom fit local tradition, so the number of girls in World Trade customer service remained low.

In the forties the Old Man had appointed Ruth Leach, a customer training specialist, to a vice presidency. She left after a

few years to get married, and no woman again achieved this
pinnacle until Women's Lib 1972, when Jane Cahill became vice
president, Communications. Dorothy Chappel was the first female
executive in World Trade in the early sixties. By 1972 the IBM
annual report was unctuously proclaiming that the number of
women managers in IBM had increased by almost a third — to a
little over 600, out of about 30,000 managers. Five of them headed
sales offices of the DP division.

The position of blacks and other minorities has been improving
for some years. IBM was one of the first major companies to be
aware of the need for minority managers — to pay more than lip
service to equal opportunity hiring. Company publications for
the past five years have been comfortably full of black success
stories. A dynamic Ghanian, Julius Fummey, became the first
black African to head an IBM country organization. Though men of
Jewish extraction felt cut off from the main stream (and Jewish
salesmen are still rare) this prejudice too seemed to diminish under
Tom Junior's liberal guidance. The 1971 appointment of Patricia
R. Harris — an eminent Washington attorney who also happened to
be black and female — to the main IBM board was another
important symbol to IBM minorities. Shortly thereafter Maersk
McKinney Moller, a Dane, made his appearance on the main board,
to the pleasure of foreign 'minorities'.

Like the OP people, IBM's technical people sometimes feel
downtrodden in a company so clearly dominated by DP salesman.
In the getting-ahead ethos it is clear that IBM managers are inter-
changeable parts of the system; a good SE manager could become
an international bureau manager, and so on. Success is based not on
technical achievement but on IBM's 'management principles'.
However, DP salesmen themselves have been more technically
oriented since the late fifties, when IBM did a little study of all
previous promotions in sales and found out that 35 percent of
those promoted had technical backgrounds, although only 8 percent of the sales force were thus endowed. The company then
began recruiting its salesmen in technical schools as much as
possible.

One IBM country manager said: 'If a man is good it doesn't
matter what his speciality is.' But where does this leave the real
technical specialists? They have professional paths of their own
up to a point — and a specialist can reach a salary level higher than
his own manager. But those career paths flatten out fairly quickly
— especially in the smaller World Trade countries. One Englishman

who fought for years to get on the Domestic payroll said: 'IBM UK had no place for a top-level technical man; it was just a rather shallow sales organization.' Hursley, like other overseas labs, belongs to the US divisions for which it has primary missions. Even if he goes into general management at IBM, the technical man is faced with a dilemma. Either he gives up his association with technical decisions, or he stays low in the organization. 'Technical guys are foreigners at Armonk,' one of them said rather wistfully.

IBM recognized this problem. Dr Piore was the first chief scientist in Domestic (also the first Jewish vice president). In 1973 World Trade appointed Dr K. Ganzhorn from the Boeblingen labs to a comparable position with IBM Europe, to extend the identification and aspirations of the technical people — a suggestion that had first been made by technical people interviewed during Project HEAR in 1969.

This aspect of IBM equality must be viewed from another direction. The dominance of the sales people at IBM over the technical people may be one of the company's secrets of success (a point made more often by outsiders than insiders). The other computer companies — some of whom started with similar technology and resources — tend to be dominated by technical people. One graduate differentiated between the competitors who thought a computer was a thing used by scientists using interesting electronics (notably RCA, English Electric, General Electric/US) and those who thought computers were for commercial DP (IBM, as well as ICT and Burroughs). RCA and GE are now out of the computer business and English Electric was absorbed by ICT (now ICL).

Then there are downtrodden projects, and the people associated with them who tend to feel inferior in the IBM status structure. The importance of an IBM project tends to be related directly to the status of the leader who is supporting it. 'We used to code projects according to their sources,' said a World Trader, mentioning that anything that had to do with yacht-racing was a Tom-project in Domestic, just as there were Dick-projects, Gil-projects and Jacques-projects in World Trade.

Another minority group is the management. IBM executives are assumed by the corporation to be 'fair game'. 'They're being paid well enough to take a little flak,' said an eminent graduate. 'The general employee is usually happy with the company and quite secure, but there's much more insecurity among managers — more of it the higher you go.' Another commented: 'The nearer you get to the centre of IBM, the more you have to conform. More of your attitudes are determined for you up there.' (It is my own belief that the two men who are the best example of this phenomenon are Tom Junior and Dick.) On the other hand, further down the ladder the high performer, particularly in sales, has quite a bit of leeway with respect to the small rules. Sometimes managers are shifted sideways or eased out simply because they do not exude a tough enough image, no matter how capable they are as managers. A 'soft' label can be deadly. This may be one reason there are so few personnel or education professionals near the top. It may also be no coincidence that Jane Cahill has a reputation among the company's communications people for being 'tough'.

The last real hot-spot in IBM's campaign to stamp out minority flare-ups seems to be the foreigners, and solving that will take time. Like many Americans abroad, the Old Man's view of other people's nationalities was both over- and under-impressed. At one Paris convention in 1929 he apologized for not speaking French, but continued: 'However, I feel perfectly at home here, because all IBM men look alike to me.' Yet after the war, from the same podium, he told IBM's French people: 'In this organization we must keep in mind that France is first and IBM is second.'

Even though the company has always done an excellent job of having its foreign organizations staffed and managed by nationals, there is a scarcity of foreigners in the Armonk boardroom — a problem IBM shares with other American multinationals. Maisonrouge experienced a spectacular rise to become chief executive of IBM World Trade and a member of the World Trade board. Even so, if you listed the 200 most important managers in IBM from the top down, it would be hard to find many other foreign names on the list. A few are being groomed for higher altitudes — a number of them Swiss, like Kap Cassani, Otto Weideli and Hans Luethy (to the extent that several Americans referred to 'the Swiss Mafia' infiltrating World Trade headquarters).

As the seventies advance and Watsons are less active in IBM, the wall between World Trade and Domestic is eroding. IBM wants foreigners at Armonk, in World Trade headquarters, on the main board, and in every other place where they could be a symbol of equality to the foreign employees of the company, not to mention its ranks of foreign customers, governments, and a few overseas shareholders. The problem has traditionally been one of loyalty — whether a man was primarily a German or Swede, or primarily an IBM man. In the Old Man's day, being an IBM man meant being a US citizen.

One European graduate who achieved eminence in his own country after he left IBM was quite fierce about the decisions that faced him in the early sixties. 'When you look at IBM from a realistic point of view, all the theories about the equality of men evaporate and you see that some people in IBM are more equal than others. Look at the top managers: you find only Maisonrouge who is not a US citizen. He is the only symbol they can point to with pride.'

Maisonrouge himself, with his pleasant French accent, sounds more like an idealist (and a conscious symbol) when he explains his devotion to IBM. Citing IBM's policies and principles, he said in one interview:[3] 'That is what makes us foreigners like this company, even though it is sometimes hard for a foreigner to be in love with an American company. Our great success is that we are almost all foreigners. We have 115,000 non-Americans out of 115,300.' (The 300, it might be added, are not clustered at the bottom of the World Trade hierarchy.)

To bring more Europeans into IBM's top ranks will take many years. 'You have to move them across boundaries early in their careers,' said a European. 'Later their attitudes get too complicated. You can't wait too late because they would have no place to go back to — the re-entry doors would be closed. In my day, if I had decided to take an international position in World Trade, I would have had to take the consequences and become American.'

Until recently IBM discouraged the young men who wanted international positions. Many of the international aspirants who finally made it into IBM's international management were only able to convince the company of their earnestness (or get permanent US working papers) by applying for US citizenship. This also entitled them to US-level salaries, even when they were on European assignments. Otherwise, a non-American returning to his home country on a US salary would be the subject of violent resentment.

Because of early unhappy experiences, World Trade promulgated the myth that the Europeans didn't *want* to move. Yet unpublished results of European opinion surveys show that the number who would be willing to take international assignments or international careers is surprisingly high. In the mid-sixties such revelations may have been unwelcome. In the seventies they have spurred on a search for European managers for Paris and New York positions. Although there is no one within reach of Maisonrouge yet, there is much more movement a level or two down.

In addition to discouraging speeches in the sixties, the international aspirants suffered discriminatory policies. There was plenty of help for Americans moving to Paris, but very little for foreigners coming to New York. The foreigners had to volunteer over and over again before they were selected. Domestic men who wanted World Trade assignments usually found it easy, with American salaries, allowances and excellent tax benefits (IBM reimbursed them in the rare instances where local taxes exceeded US levels), so that many were able to save large sums while living pleasantly abroad. The foreigners who actually achieved US assignments, though they had some help in travel allowances, remained on their home country payrolls, at the lower overseas salaries. Unless they were Swedes they also served *without* guaranteed re-entry, although Domestic always gave its World Trade assignees such promises. One reason for the imbalance was that it was more difficult for a European to get a work permit in the United States than vice versa.

Frank Smith's experiences illustrate the problems of the would-be international man in the sixties. He was an energetic, self-starting young man who won the Watson Trophy as World Trade's number one salesman in 1959. (This drive may have contributed to Frank Smith's early death of a heart attack in 1973, when he was only 42.) Though he carried a British passport his accent carried traces of the Canadian army, and he spoke fluent German. ('I am truly international,' he once said; 'my parents and grandparents came from different countries all over Europe.') He was one of the best sales training men IBM had ever encountered. This skill earned him positions in Paris and later at Blaricum. But in spite of his sales and training achievements and his obvious desire to become one of IBM's international men, he couldn't escape the shackles of the UK's pay scale, which was then low in IBM terms. World Trade managers in Paris and New York preferred to ignore the Frank Smith problem — citing as usual the re-entry issue if he ever wanted to come back to the UK. After Jones and Maisonrouge went through this litany in Paris, Frank Smith flew to New York at his own expense, the traditional Open Door action. Even though he assured IBM he was quite happy to waive the question of re-entry, the answer was still no. 'If I had taken up US nationality it would have been fine,' he commented in 1972. 'I didn't see why I should have people working for me on much better terms. You can't have re-entry problems until you can *enter*. At that time they simply couldn't accept in their American company a truly multinational person.'

Turned down in the last Open Door stages, Frank Smith left the company. When he resigned he was subjected to the usual A-List succession of interviews with Maisonrouge, Jones and so on, all well aware why their high-performer was departing. Frank Smith then set up his own sales training company in the UK. IBM hired a leading authority on personnel in multinational companies to do a two-year study telling them why they were losing so many high performers.

Another Englishman was able to get into Domestic in 1958 as a $300 a month clerk, but they wouldn't let him into sales because of his accent. When they sent him to the UK with the 1401 computer he was able to make the transfer (with a salary cut from £1,750 to £1,000 per year) in 1962. In 1963 he made £6,000, 350 percent of his quota.

There are more Europeans in New York and Paris now. But the process is slow, and the foreigners are likely to feel like a down-trodden minority for some time to come.

The most equal people in IBM, then, if you take out the foreigners, women, blacks, Jews, OP people, technical specialists and top managers, are of course the American DP salesmen — who happen to be IBM's historic mainstay, the Old Man's secret weapon. 'Successful DP men run the company' is the adage — and the truth.

'Most of their communications people are communicating inside'

The fluidity of IBM's people is one important reason for the extreme attention the company pays to internal communications.

Whenever a man changes his job, a staff memo goes on the bulletin board. Almost the only personnel press releases that go outside are the carefully worded two paragraphs to local papers when there is a new plant manager, when a national director is chosen in a foreign country, or when a major change takes place at corporate headquarters. But internally there is a snowstorm of postings. Each one is read carefully. If a notice says the man has been 'promoted' or 'elevated into a new position', then it is viewed as an increase in status. If it says he has been 'transferred', 'accepted a staff assignment as . . .' or 'has been appointed . . .', no matter how elegant the new title, IBMers will normally assume that these are euphemisms for moving laterally, or going into a holding pattern of some sort.

IBM has strict policies about the bulletin boards, which are considered a primary means of communication with employees. In many Domestic facilities they are used to post job openings. The practice is less well-established in World Trade, where line managers (equally reluctant to lose good people) have a larger say in communications policy. Internal watchdogs make sure the bulletin boards are not contaminated with the want-ads, bowling-club notices or group photos so common in most companies. These items go into well-organized publications instead.

In the United States every employee gets *Think* magazine, in its restyled form (for internal use only). In addition there are 14 different editions of *IBM News* and a further 20 publications produced entirely on a local basis.* World Trade countries produce about 30 national publications and many local ones. These facility newspapers are splendidly informal, with photos of the rugby team, not to mention 'Miss Cancer Drive' exhorting her fellow-workers to give generously, Bill Bloggs telling how he was motivated to win the OP Spring Sales Spree, and photos of the employees who won awards this year in the suggestion programme. There are also Speak-Up! responses that reveal a little about the employees in that plant and a lot about the central thrust of IBM internal communications.

The facilities also have technical brochures, describing their products or processes. Some of them have delightful non-business pamphlets. Hursley, for example, has one telling the history of the old building and its village back to medieval times. In the terminology of an IBM plan, most of the employee publications would 'inform and motivate [the employee population] by reporting news of the company and industry as completely and candidly as possible. They [would] portray IBM World Trade as a company responding in multinational terms to what is needed in the fields of industry, education and science.'

The managers have their own plethora of journals. All US managers, World Trade managers at headquarters and country general managers receive *Management Briefing,* a newsletter that was already going to 10,000 managers ('the majority of whom many companies would call foremen,' as Tom Junior put it) in 1962. The country general managers can distribute it further or have their own management newsletters. The quarterly management journal for World Traders used to have translated versions available in Germany, Italy, France, Japan, Brazil and Spain; the new one, *Dialogue,* goes out in English and Japanese. In the late sixties World Trade also started a top-management newsletter called *Outlook* for 450 English-speaking key men.

IBM UK News is sometimes called 'Izvestia' by its loyal readers.

In addition to all the formal papers there is a modern-day extension of the Old Man's 'telephone broadcasts' to his employees. Now they are videotaped, often with tailor-made messages of Watson-like congratulation to specific stars in each office. The central message only needs to be recorded once, and the special messages can be spliced onto the beginning or end, giving another boost to the 'small company' flavour the Old Man nurtured. One year Jones recorded a Christmas message to World Traders on the commercial equivalent of IBM's little 'floppy disk' for computers — a thin plastic 45 rpm record.

These are all 'downward communication' — ways for management to talk to employees. But the company gives equal attention to some mechanisms for upward communication too. One sometimes gets the feeling that these channels in the other direction have been instituted over the years to resolve the natural action-oriented, dynamic management tendency, which is *not* usually compatible with relaxed listening. In spite of the natural discomfort managers may experience when forced to listen, these mechanisms have been effective and play a large part in achieving and maintaining IBM's relatively serene employee relations.

'Dear Tom, When your father hired me ...'

The employee who feels he has been punished unfairly or treated badly in any other way has several communication paths open to him. The most common is the Open Door, a formal IBM institution. The employee goes to his boss with his complaint; if his own boss can't right the wrong (or is the grievance) the employee has the right (and sometimes the duty) to go directly up the line, to whomever he chooses, whether it be the next manager, the top local man, the country general manager, Maisonrouge, or the chairman himself. Usually the employee chooses the level that fits his idea of the seriousness of the conflict. Unless he started with the chairman, he can continue working up the line if he is not satisfied.

For old-timers in danger of losing their jobs or wounded in some other manner, there was for many years a top-level short-cut around the Open Door — the Dear-Tom letter. Invoked generally by the gentlemen who dated back to the early days of the company, this phenomenon usually began: 'Dear Tom, When you father hired me . . .' It struck inordinate fear into the hearts of IBM managers. Time after time graduates recounted tales of being sent to far-off places to sort out problems, only to have their solutions cancelled at a stroke by Dear-Tom letters. (For a few years after the Old Man's death a Dear-Jeannette letter was the ultimate weapon in this armoury of the oldtimers.)

In one instance, Jones went down to sort out a Mexican crisis. The traditional manager there had 'littered the streets with the bodies of his good men'. World Traders in New York were convinced the tyrant's success in the Mexican market was due more to good luck than good management. When Jones had reviewed the situation he fired the man, putting out the (obligatory) announcement that he had decided to go into business for himself (the classic Golden Handshake). But the deposed manager immediately flew to New York to see Dick — a real-time Dear-Dick letter, as it were. Six weeks later he was reinstated as director of education for IBM de Mexico.

The consternation a Dear-Tom letter could cause among managers was awesome. 'You heard in peculiar ways if a letter got to Armonk before you'd had a chance to read it,' said one senior graduate. 'Managers developed their own G-2 system to let each other know if something slipped through. Once it reached Tom Junior or Dick you went up to answer questions whether or not you knew what was in the letter.' Action was fast and personal. Once about 50 Belgian Congo company employees sent in a letter in such splendid calligraphy that it 'looked like the Magna Carta'. This elegant document in flawless French asked that the company put in a non-Belgian manager. Within three days World Trade had executives in the Belgian Congo. They immediately put the Belgian (the ubiquitous Emile Genon) on a plane back to Europe.

The ordinary Open Door complaint is supposed to be handled on a similarly personal and immediate basis. 'A lot of companies have Open Door policies,' said Charley Smith, who had to cope with many Open Doors. 'But I doubt if many have the hard attitude that the employee is right unless proven otherwise. Injustices were done, of course. Managers were not always prepared to defend a case; but it was basically good for the company.'

The handling of Open Door cases until quite recently favoured the employee over his manager whenever there was room for doubt. The corporate attitude seemed to be that the executives were being paid well enough to take a little insecurity; they were fair game. Headquarters was much more concerned to keep the general employees happy with the company and feeling secure. This was an important distinction, and had a moderating influence on managers as the company grew. As one manager commented: 'It's good. It puts the pressure where it belongs — on the manager. We used to spend a hell of a lot of time on situations that involved people. If a manager's time is taken up this way, so be it. People are more important than paper.' Tom Junior noted that by its existence the Open Door was a deterrent to abuses of management power.

Although it is clearly a useful tool to keep managers in line, the Open Door sometimes creaks at the hinges. One personnel expert pointed out that it doesn't really cover the kinds of shop-floor grievances that need airing. The employee can theoretically complain all the way to the top about having too much work to do, but most managers can handle this by saying it is 'too minor', and perhaps making tiny token adjustments that put workers off going any further but do not really solve the problems. On the other hand, the belief of the employee in the existence of the Open Door can give it real power — provided the employee has that belief. One UK graduate stated that the Open Door doesn't work unless your boss and his boss believe it works — and the further away from head-quarters an organization was the less assurance an employee had that his managers shared his faith in the institution. It was also harder to reach the effective top managers from geographically separate locations. The 1972 World Trade attitude survey of 30,000 employees[4] showed a marked drop in confidence in the Open Door procedure. Some voiced the opinion that using it could actually hurt their career progress rather than help it.

The Open Door is not exercised lightly. Cases are investigated thoroughly and at each step the manager must be thoroughly prepared. Any manager who proposes to fire or demote an employee learns to anticipate an immediate Open Door unless he has taken exceptional precautions to avoid it. If the employee is not doing satisfactory work, the manager is supposed to discuss it with him frankly and work out some kind of improvement programme. If the problem is the relationship between the two (as it often is), then the relationship itself gets an improvement programme. Thus, if things don't work out, the employee knows why. If he leaves it is usually with a fair settlement and a clear knowledge of why he is departing. If he doesn't think the resolution was fair, he goes immediately to higher authority. Thus the manager has had to keep meticulous records of the discussions, the improvement programmes, and all actions taken. The mere existence of this hard-line Open Door policy keeps many Open Door misunderstandings from occurring. In one instance a manager in Africa fired a salesman. 'He deserved to be fired,' said a headquarters man later, 'but the manager hadn't warned him properly. When it got up to us I had to recommend an apology and a larger settlement, though once he was gone we wouldn't hire him back.'

Outsiders can use the Open Door too. (I used it myself in going around the watchful press corps to contact Jones directly, after requests through all the proper channels had been ignored.) The German labour courts once used their own interpretation of the Open Door. IBM had regretfully let some people go, in a very gentle manner, with good settlements and full assistance in finding new jobs. But the labour courts sent some of them back, saying in essence: 'You are a big, prosperous (and foreign) company. Find some place else to use them.' IBM took them back, of course.

That is another important thing about the Open Door policy. It would not work the same way in a company that did not have room to move people around. When a manager and a subordinate finally get to the point of an Open Door case it is sometimes like a marriage that has reached the point of a property settlement. No matter who wins, there is seldom any way to retrieve the shattered relationship. The sensible thing to do (and the thing IBM usually does) is move one of them. This does not mean that all Open Door cases are based on broken relationships. Sometimes the employee is complaining about a policy and its interpretation, and the manager may give him tacit encouragement to take the matter higher, knowing it will get more attention if the complaint comes from a lower level. Budgets have been increased and manpower ceilings raised through such judicious use of Open Doors.

Over the years the managers have learned some tricks of their own to cope with the bias against management that IBM tends to exercise in Open Door controversies. They have learned to keep good records. (Management training courses now include a presentation on Open Door records.) Employees who try to use the Open Door as blackmail against their managers are often told: 'Fine. Would you like me to arrange it right now?' So the delicate balance is shifting; managers who used to be afraid to let troublesome employees go are more aware that it might be a greater sin to keep them on too long.

Sometimes there are cultural differences. In one totalitarian country both the managers and the employees had trouble getting used to the strange idea that they should bring differences to the surface, or that the lower employees could do so with impunity. Once the idea was accepted they went through several years when the managers were constantly badgered by employees who were enjoying the ability to turn the tables and criticize nuances in the style of management. Eventually the constant demonstrations of management willingness to listen and adapt helped simmer down the situation. 'I felt more like a social worker than a manager for a while,' said the relieved general manager when the trial period was over.

Another institution, to handle questions and clarify policy, is the Speak-Up! programme. In this phenomenon the employee with a general question or a 'why-don't-they' suggestion about procedures (as opposed to profit-related suggestions, which are handled in the separate suggestion programme) can send it to the Speak-Up! administrator who carefully preserves the employee's anonymity and sees the matter through to some sort of conclusion. It is also used as a grievance channel. One graduate said: 'You can't afford to ignore them, but they put the guy's manager in an unfair position — Kafkaesque — of not knowing his accuser or even precisely what the accusation is.' But the anonymity is important; like the Open Door, the Speak-Up! programme was instituted to eliminate or reduce the petty tyrannies that plague most firms.

IBM employees are surprisingly content compared to those of other companies. If numbers are any indication they seem much more concerned about the company's manufacturing efficiency than internal complaints. In the average month the entire corporation handles about 1,200 Speak-Up! enquiries compared to about 14,000 suggestions. (It must be kept in mind, though, that a winning suggestion brings its originator up to 10 percent of the savings in the first year — and the Speak-Up! programme lost credibility along with the Open Door in the 1972 attitude survey.)

The Dear-Tom letter is almost a thing of the past as Tom Junior heads into retirement along with the few men who knew him or his father well enough to write one. But the more institutionalized phenomena flourish. As my typewriter salesman once commented: 'One thing I like about this company is that they have plenty of room for disagreement. We know we can complain through official channels if something really bothers us. I don't think most companies are this open.'

'IBM does its homework in personnel'

One of the more controversial phenomena in IBM's personnel arsenal is the opinion survey. Some cite it as one more effective method of hearing what the employees have to say, in a systematic way, and making sure the results feed back to first-line managers. Others dismiss it as over-elaborate and academic. Certainly, though no IBMer claims the company originated opinion surveys, IBM is one of the acknowledged leaders in their use.

In his 1962 speeches,[5] Tom Junior said: 'Today our frequent attitude surveys show that the importance we attach to job security is one of the principal reasons why people like to work for IBM.' IBM's leadership then in personnel amounted to the pay and full-employment policies plus the benefits, awards and stock purchase plan that stayed ahead of most companies. As professional psychologists filtered into the company in the sixties, surveying increased.

Gellerman was one of the first professionals to bring psychological skills into IBM's surveying activities. But 'surveying the world' really began in 1967. Dr Sirota was World Trade's manager of personnel research in New York then, and Dr Hofstede held that position in Europe. All three published their results widely, yet none of their outside publications refer directly to IBM. The results described here have come from some of those published works[6] (usually referring to a 'large electronics company') and from a few people inside the company.

Dr Hofstede did the first international survey in the labs in the summer of 1967; Dr Sirota followed with the total non-European World Trade population in December 1967. In spring 1968 they combined forces to survey salesmen, SEs and CEs in Europe. Their first results[7] showed a surprising similarity between the goals of IBMers in the 25 countries they had then surveyed. There was a much wider spread of attitudes among managers, salesmen and technical people than among nationalities. The IBM culture is striking in its strength. Training, for example, was one of the five most important goals in 69 out of the 75 rankings; challenge was among the five most important 70 times.

Dr Hofstede carried this work into the clerical and unskilled worker levels in 55 countries in 1969-70 and found much more important differences showing up among the different 'classes' of workers when the entire spectrum was included.[8]

The intriguing thing about all this work was the relatively small differences from country to country. One IBM personnel man, who has to sit out in a country organization and administer the Opinion Surveys, pointed out that all the questions about consultative and authoritative management styles had less to do with reality than with the IBM culture, its mythology, and its latest fashions. Perhaps the name for an ongoing management style has changed more than the style itself. 'If we had done the survey ten years ago,' he said, 'we would have seen totally different results. People would have thought we expected different answers.'

One of the most important aspects of the surveys, from a practical viewpoint, was not the feedback to corporate management or the social science conclusions that could be drawn from such a comprehensive survey to such a large population in so many countries, but simply the feedback to the employees and their first-line managers. '(The company) considers it a question of decency towards employees to handle survey information with great openness,' Dr Hofstede commented in one article, with characteristic closeness about the identity of the company.[9] At IBM each manager receives a booklet made up from computer runs, summarizing the results for his group compared to the results for his plant or organization. Then results for each small unit are discussed at a meeting between the manager and his employees. (Whenever there are less than ten employees in a single group their results are aggregated with a related group to keep everyone anonymous.)

'That was a fascinating process,' one maintenance man commented. 'I didn't expect it to be anything but another set of papers to fill out. But when we got down to the meeting it turned out most of us had been critical of the pressure we've been under lately, and the less interesting work. Our manager was surprised at first, but when we got through discussing it he set up another meeting for all of us with his boss. The work hasn't really changed much yet, but they've hired two more people already, even though it wasn't in our budget.'

Surveys can be a two-edged sword. Handling survey information with openness is easy when the results are good. In 1972 it was harder. Both Domestic and World Trade showed changes for the worse. As the World Trade management magazine expressed it:[10]

The survey does not make for pleasurable reading. Most of its findings are negative, showing a decline — in some cases, slight; in others, severe — in employee attitudes. But it could have been worse, and it should improve if the messages are heeded and action taken.

In 1972 the company surveyed 30,000 people and found pronounced declines in attitude (most often from 'positive' to 'neutral'), especially among DP people and non-managers. In 1968, for example, 40 percent answered 'one of the best' to the question 'How would you rate IBM as a company to work for compared to other companies you know about?' By 1972 that 40 percent had dropped to 27 percent. Those 'very satisfied' with IBM dropped from 34 percent to 19 percent. Many were disappointed at the lack of change that came about from the earlier survey. In discussing management practices 67 percent noted that their managers insisted that rules and procedures be followed (versus 49 percent in 1968), and 47 percent said their managers built team spirit (versus 59 percent in 1968). Young people were less satisfied with the challenge of their jobs and there was less confidence in the grievance channels such as the Speak-Up! programme and the Open Door. *A clear majority agreed in 1972 that social responsibility should be a corporate concern, and that profitability should not be an all-pervading goal.*

'In some companies the chances for change after a survey reveals a problem are perhaps one in a thousand,' Dr Sirota commented. 'In IBM perhaps one out of three really do something about it — and that's pretty good.'

In general, opinion surveys seem to play a part in IBM's overall sense of connection with its employees — and vice versa. Even so, Dr Hofstede eventually evolved two slightly weary 'laws' regarding surveys. He postulated that 'survey information will be most easily asked for (and in the second law 'acted upon') by the management of those parts of an organization that least need it — and vice versa.'

Opinion surveys gobble up *enormous* amounts of time for the personnel officers in the various countries. So does the 'assessment centre programme' which began in Europe in 1970. The assessment session is a means to identify potential managers a little more scientifically, perhaps a little earlier. (One basic premise, shared by the corporation and the assessees, is that every young man *wants* to be a manager; rational analysis of the manager's role in IBM might lead some of the applicants to think again.)

A 'manager' in IBM terms is anybody with hire, fire and pay responsibility for two or more subordinates. The company classifies about 12 percent of its population as managers. With about a quarter of a million employees there is a constant demand for managers. Given IBM's policy to create them from within rather than hiring them outside, it becomes important to find them early. Even during the drastic hiring freezes and economies of 1971, the management development budget in at least one distressed country was nonetheless increased by 50 percent.

The typical programme naturally starts with intensive training for the assessors, followed by two days studying a group of 12 candidates (chosen by their own managers, or men who have volunteered), then two or three more days of 'developmental' work, going over the assessment activities with the men and pointing out individual strengths and weaknesses. After an assessment exercise many people must be told that the company does not consider them suitable for management positions. This is a difficult task. 'I wish I could spend more time with these people,' one fatherly personnel man in Europe said wistfully. 'That's when they're most exposed, when they most need help. What I'd like to be able to do at that point is counselling as well as assessing or feeding out canned self-improvement programmes.'

This highly packaged 'programme' is simply an expansion of management techniques that have been used in IBM for years. One senior manager who had been through the process dozens of times said: 'We act in the best interests of the employee and the company. I tell my boss what I want in my next job, trying to be realistic. Then we discuss the various possibilities. He can only say he agrees or disagrees with my personal objective. Once he agrees, he undertakes to help me move this way. We have agreement on a direction, not a commitment to a specific objective. Perhaps this is one of the strong points of IBM.'

As years passed this process, too, was packaged, as the 'A&C interview' — appraisal and counselling. By corporate policy, an A&C interview has to be held each year between every manager and each of his subordinates. One objective of the interview is this joint process of setting objectives. The employee's personal objectives are the focus of the interview; it is the manager's job to fit them into the possible matches with corporate or department objectives. But IBM's overall purpose in the assessment and appraisal is not just happy employees; they need to eliminate manager selection based on the 'BOGSAT' system (the classic Bunch Of Guys, Sitting Around a Table — filling jobs from random names and hunches).

As the appraisal process firmed up, standard forms appeared, demanding the signature of the appraisee after the interview. It started a lot of Open Doors at first, but it seemed to keep the air fairly clear. To make sure it worked, the company computer would send out cards: 'Joe Bloggs appraisal due'. If the signed appraisal form didn't enter the system on time, as a former executive told it: 'You got a brighter card. They were like flypaper. You couldn't get out from under this system. Otherwise people kept putting off the appraisal interviews, especially if it were a disagreeable task.'

'Project HEAR was great, but it was a great failure'

Like all other specialists in IBM, personnel people gather frequently to sort our mutual problems or be subjected to further education in their speciality. In Europe a great deal of attention in the late sixties was being focused on 'management development' — the process of turning junior men into senior managers. Most of this impetus was coming from the Blaricum management training centre, where management development people were encountering problems not only making it clear to Paris and New York that management development must have high priority but also getting the various country organizations to pay more attention to a subject that could improve their autonomy. Meetings on management development tended to be infrequent and passively attended — 'inspirational' gatherings usually followed by inaction, although a professional brotherhood was growing up among the personnel men. The country managers were suspicious about the whole subject. In addition, the topic always seemed to spur some political manoeuvring between various country managers and World Trade headquarters people — who would be developed, and for what?

Finally, at one seaside 'T-Group' type meeting of the beleaguered personnel professionals, one man sat up and said: 'What are we all doing here with our feet in the Mediterranean? We have to go back to our countries and do our work there.' This sparked off a discussion of their mutual problems with management support. Creative sparks flew, and they began to look for ways to educate and involve their country managers. When they went back to their countries phones continued to buzz and plans grew.

The management development men met again in Madrid in December 1968, armed with a charter for 'The Management Development Institute — IBM Europe' (MDI). This was just the kind of 'packaging' that appealed to top men in the United States and at European headquarters in Paris, so they received encouragement. One of the Institute's primary purposes was really to develop the members themselves — a self-help group to get more money for MD, keep in touch internationally, extend the faith to their leaders, and encourage each other. Almost overnight the periodic and lethargic get-togethers became a regular group that believed it had decision-making functions. Initiative shifted from Blaricum to the peripatetic group, and members began to sparkle with shared commitment. As one member recalled it: 'Instead of the traditional centralized headquarters control we wanted a horizontal structure with leaders elected rather than appointed, and common problems solved by horizontal task forces. Several of us invested quite a lot of time in the (MDI) activities, but what never got solved was the relationship of the horizontal MDI to the vertical reward-and-hierarchy structure of IBM, of which we were all a part. It existed as long as the formally responsible managers in headquarters were weak and laissez-faire. We never had a strong man supporting us. One day a new European personnel director arrived who wanted to look strong, and he soon killed it.'

Even so, some of the MDI people were involved in one task force personnel research activity — Project HEAR. In this project European managers were supposed to hear what employees had to say; to get objective views on whether the company's multinational policies were meeting national or individual needs. It was set up so line managers from the six largest European countries interviewed workers from other countries. A similar project had been held in Domestic in 1968, and at the beginning of 1969 the ukase came across the Atlantic that Europe should have it too. Senior managers were told to drop all work (even ski holidays) 'as if they were caught by a sudden illness'. On two weeks' notice, 24 of Europe's key managers were taken away from their jobs for six weeks.

After intensive training (particularly in the art, not common in top line management, of listening rather than arguing or explaining), 12 two-man teams went out into the six countries and began interviewing randomly selected groups of six to eight employees at the rate of two groups a day. By the time the two weeks of interviews were over the managers had collected complaints and comments from 1,536 World Trade employees, about 7 percent of the total population of IBM people in the six countries at the time.

When the managers gathered for two more weeks of summary and analysis they found almost no adverse comparisons with other companies. They were surprised to find that very few of the complaints dealt with conditions in the cafeteria or matters of pay. The employees in every country were positive about the company, but much more worried about their individual opportunities in it. If a man in the IBM culture doesn't feel he is getting ahead, he begins to worry that he's falling behind. Yet (like the international trade balances Maisonrouge is so fond of citing) it is impossible for everybody to be 'getting ahead' of everybody else inside a single organization, not matter how fast the organization itself is getting ahead. For every man that gets ahead of the average, another must be falling behind, whether or not the average itself moves up.

Various groups had specific complaints. Managers were expected to carry too heavy a workload, and suffered from unnecessary deadlines from Paris or New York. (Most groups out in the country organizations not surprisingly thought headquarters should view itself as a service to the field rather than its master.) The administrative people complained that DP sales people had better training opportunities than they did. The DP people, on the other hand, complained that they were under so much pressure they didn't have time to take advantage of all the education available to them. Women thought their career path interests were ignored. Generally, there were complaints about crowding, understaffing and career planning. The employees wanted more open personnel policies, more connection between their appraisal interviews and their assignments afterwards, more job rotation, more job openings and foreign assignments posted on bulletin boards. Some of them also asked IBM to consider a more autonomous IBM Europe, with public share-holdings. Most of the complaints could be considered signs of rapid growth; none had reached crisis proportions, but any one might flare up if no action were taken.

As an exercise in management development for the line managers who did the interviews, Project HEAR was brilliant. The face-to-face contact with foreign IBM employees made them more aware that problems in their own countries were not unique. One participant said: 'It is a good thing we didn't interview in our own countries; the point is not that the people wouldn't have been frank, but that we couldn't have kept our mouths shut.' However, one weakness was that it bypassed all intermediate levels of management; it went right from the bottom to the top. It was therefore only useful to resolve problems which could be dealt with at the top. In this respect, the one-shot HEAR was in contrast with the ongoing opinion surveys which tended to concentrate on feedback to the immediate manager and to the levels above him.

Each group warned in its summary report that action must be seen to come as a result of the interviews — that Project HEAR had raised grand expectations. 'The benefits to the individual task-force members will not justify Project HEAR when no results come out of it,' one member warned.

But most of the actions they proposed required major cultural or organizational changes — changes that can't be made overnight, even in IBM. Some of them cost money, just as budgets were shrinking. And some of the proposals were really expensive pet projects of local managers, who blamed HEAR (often unfairly) when they were cut under budget stress. Those changes that were made appeared quietly, with little back-reference to Project HEAR. In fact, HEAR was not heard from again.

Yet HEAR's failure was really a success. Change takes a long time in an organization as big as World Trade. By 1973 the HEAR list of recommendations had nearly all been implemented, but the intervening five years had erased the exciting but ephemeral project and its equally ephemeral Institute from the corporate memory. The 'Basic Beliefs' were re-emphasized, and the profit motive was toned down to some extent in Europe, so IBM could no longer be depicted as a voracious tiger, either inside or outside. The stop-and-go approaches to manpower and buildings didn't quite evaporate, but they improved as countries gradually gained more power over their own budgets. An on-line information system was set up to help the European salesmen, CEs and administrators. Very slowly there grew more openness about personnel policies and career paths, though even in 1973 very few European locations posted job openings on their bulletin boards. Marketing teams were formed; international assignments were viewed more carefully from the assignee's point of view; a skills inventory was created; and in 1973 they even came up with a 'chief scientist for Europe' — a suggestion first made in the HEAR report. The recommendation to set up a task force to study the possibility of an IBM Europe with European shareholders had been followed several times in the intervening years, but the policy is so diametrically opposed to the Old Man's experiences that most of them are formed for the purpose of staving off the act rather than encouraging it. Public pressure and employee pressure will eventually bring it to pass; when the time comes, very few will credit the men of Project HEAR.

'The full-employment policy used to mean no layoffs'

The hiring and firing policies are another important aspect of the employee philosophy. Until quite recently almost all IBM openings were filled from within, which meant that most of the intake of new employees was at the bottom. However, in 1973 one began to find ads for DP salesmen in the UK, for example, suggesting that experienced salesmen of all ages would be welcome. (They received the same long and intensive training as neophytes, no matter how much experience they already had.) The shift in emphasis from computer techniques to industry techniques also required IBM to hire more mature people with experience in those target industries.

The rapid ups and downs of the computer industry around 1970 impacted both the hiring and firing policies — and created malaise in many parts of the corporation that had always taken the limitless opportunity and full employment for granted. 'The full employment policy is a myth!' one unhappy personnel man in Europe exclaimed. 'The policy should say "now and then we have to let people go, but we try to give them a few months to get relocated." '

The 1970 recession (and IBM's own manufacturing efficiency) caused major problems in Domestic as well as World Trade. Domestic had to make drastic personnel cutbacks, and the full-employment policy was strained to its outer limits. In the Domestic DP division alone more than 14,000 people were eliminated, almost all of them by attrition. Referring often to 'full-attrite mode', the MRC reviewed the 'excess resources' problem at almost every meeting for more than a year.

Task forces swung into action, and IBM began an intense exploration of the question of how to shrink. In the short term they managed to shrink by 14,000 people in Domestic that year while World Trade remained steady. There was the 'window' for early retirement — that took care of about 2,000. Learson himself set the stage for top executive retirement at 60, after only 18 months as chairman, thereby giving subtle notice to older executives in many country organizations. A back-to-the-field movement slimmed the overloaded headquarters and manufacturing staffs by about 3,000 more, though the legal growth at headquarters helped keep that head count around 2,000. Several of World Trade's labs were shifted from R&D to marketing support and customer systems work — earning money instead of spending it. Social leaves were emphasized for employees who wanted to do community work. Retraining and moving increased, always on the 'full-employment' basis of one job alternative — only one — when one's own job disappeared. For many it meant new opportunities, but others took a more cynical view, questioning top management's sincerity in every other respect when they found flaws in this Basic Belief. In a few locations the measures led to small (but culturally important) moves towards employee associations or unions.

Rapid changes of task or location encouraged some to leave, and there may have been pressure from the top down to lower ratings and raise goals. One employee, Marihelen Jones, sued IBM in 1973 for $1,000 million in a class action lawsuit. After seven years as an IBM programmer in Maryland, with the highest possible performance ratings, she was reassigned to the Dallas office, where her ratings were less adequate. Two years later she was reassigned to Denver, where she received 'unsatisfactory' ratings, and left 'under duress'. She claimed the change in ratings was caused by IBM's full-attrite policy, not any change in her skills or performance, and pointed to a 'performance plan' which was patently impossible to achieve in the time provided.

Even the fabled 'A-list' — people IBM couldn't afford to lose — began to evaporate. Yet despite the stress to lose people gracefully, IBM didn't want any help from outside. At one point an eminent professional body needed more people, at the height of the recession when it was known that IBM would like to lose some. The ex World Trade man leading the organization phoned a colleague in IBM personnel and asked for the names of some 'rejects' — people for whom IBM might welcome outside offers. 'We could never do that,' the IBM personnel manager responded.

At the height of the subtle campaign to trim people from the payroll, IBM brought in a psychologist consultant — to study the growing loss of middle managers! The outsider challenged some of their motivation assumptions and referred in specialist language to 'an underlying and unhealthy mental situation throughout the corporation.' He seemed appalled by the hierarchical structure, the rewards and punishments, and an 'aggressively masculine' management style, saying these factors contributed to the situation. The consultant had not had previous contact with IBM, so he may not have been aware of the elements of tradition in this style, or the cohesiveness its little reminders of a 60-year success story seemed to bring to the members of the culture. Even so, for the first time IBM's MRC began to question whether some of its basic assumptions were out of date with respect to personnel.

8
The
IBMer

We have looked at the culture in which the IBMer lives, with its first-name informality and white-shirt respectability, its democratic cafeterias and hierarchical but fluid organizations, and its history of advanced personnel policies. But what happens to an individual inside this environment? How does a man reconcile the ambition IBM encourages, and the frequent moves that feed it, with his need for independent action and thought, or his family's need for stability?

'IBM stands for I've Been Moved'

Up to a certain point — often around the age of 40 — a man's need for change and challenge can be filled by kaleidoscopic movement. This is not just upward movement because the IBMers are taught to value lateral moves too. So there is constant motion from organization to organization and even country to country for the man who is doing well.

Moves come in many flavours at IBM. There are the US-based 'international careers' and foreign 'assignments', usually of two or three years' duration. Then there are the 'third-country nationals', people who are not Americans, stationed outside their own

countries in the World Trade empire. Swedes particularly like
foreign assignments to avoid their high taxes at home. Germans are
particularly welcome third-country nationals outside Europe,
while the Canadians are the most frequent, particularly in former
British colonies. Finally there are the 'national' careers, which
can still involve many moves, though changing a branch in a
European country seldom entails moving one's household.
Moving is as natural to IBM's professionals as breathing. Not just
American IBMers but all of them. Of 2,500 IBM people on
international assignment in 1973, only 25 percent were Americans.
Half the assignees are managers; the others are specialists — a group
of production people from the Essonnes plant surveying new
production techniques at Poughkeepsie for several months, or a
personnel man from Munich filling a position in Khartoum for
several years while he trains a local man to take his place.

When technical change accelerated at the end of the fifties,
Tom Junior often had to 'make' experts who were otherwise
unavailable. He did this by simply naming men to jobs — many of
them jobs that had never existed before. Armed with his 'beliefs',
they muddled through quite well, although he worried as early as
1961 about the saying that IBM stood for 'I've Been Moved', and
insisted that moves should be made not for the convenience of the
company but rather for the benefit of the employee. Even in the
sixties most of the presentable young men pouring into IBM
accepted or welcomed the idea that a new post would be the
reward for mastering the present one.

The benefits to the individual of all the moving are obvious.
If he is the outgoing, intelligent, resourceful kind of person IBM
tends to hire, his horizons are likely to be extended by exposure to
new cultures and new countries. If he doesn't extend his own
horizons fast enough, IBM sometimes does it for him. Technical
men from all over Europe are sent to Churchill College at Cambridge
for several months for example, to learn about non-technical
subjects such as literature, languages or sociology. This is done
simply because someone upstairs in IBM felt that they were
viewed as representatives of the company in their communities
and outside activities. Therefore they should be seen to be concerned about (and well-educated in) subjects beyond computer
science.

As men go through this succession of jobs, broadening their
horizons and gaining confidence in their ability to solve new
problems, they seem to develop an almost religious faith in their

organization. One young manager in a developing country
assignment put it this way: 'There's a sense of one-ness. You
learn from each other and there is a way of storing problem
solutions without writing down the wisdom.'

'Would you want your daughter to marry one?'

For IBM and the IBM man moving around within the IBM Family
was generally a fruitful experience. For the IBMer's family it was
not always so good. Many wives were unable to cope with the
dedication that IBM demanded from its men, or the constant
search for new homes, new schools, new shops, new roots.

Although divorces were like drink — not openly acceptable to the
corporation — inevitably a few marriages broke under the strain. In
IBM's earlier days many broken or functionally nonexistent
marriages were bandaged together simply by fear that the company
would disapprove of their dissolution. One European who left
his wife in the early sixties later said: 'They tried to convince me
I shouldn't leave my family. The general manager invited me for
dinner and had a long night's talk with me. He tried to persuade
me to go back to my wife. I had the feeling that Paris was
involved, but wanted him to fire me, and he was trying to save my
job.'

Traditional love and marriage are another matter in the IBM
morality. One journalist interviewed a burbling IBM wife in
Westchester County:[2]

'I used to work for IBM, as a secretary, and I still call myself
an IBM girl,' the lady of the house said. 'I love IBM,
everything about it. Neither of us would work anywhere else.
Yes, we're an IBM family. We admit that we're gung-ho, and
that's that. I always wanted to marry an IBM man. When I
was at division headquarters, the men were always so handsome. My husband and I met and fell in love because of the
company. When we were first married we'd ride home in
the car together, and all the way we'd talk about IBM. Right
through dinner, too, and afterwards. Talk, talk, talk. We're
good friends with another couple, both computer
programmers, and whenever the four of us get together,
that's all we talk about. And every morning, I'm proud to
see my husband go off to work in his suit, with his briefcase.
It just gives me a very good feeling.'

Except for one or two outposts in their early, independent days, IBM was never a sexy company. It hires attractive, energetic young men and women, but expects them to leave each other completely alone. One man left his wife to live with a girl he met at work. The girl was dismissed and he resigned rapidly.

Times change, and even conservative corporate mores change with them. Some of the younger IBMers in Europe are able to 'live in sin' now, so long as they do it discreetly. The divorce rate in IBM rose sharply in the seventies, not necessarily because stresses on families were any worse, but because the corporation's attitude seemed to grow slightly more liberal. Even so, at higher levels the man who leaves his wife and children still knows that he is certainly deferring any advancement for several years, and may be creating a high-water mark in the tide of his IBM career. Some able men have left IBM at this point to keep up career momentum in corporations less concerned about their marital status.

Among men who had left IBM, a number were candid that family stress played a significant part in their decisions. One ex-IBM wife said flatly: 'I'd leave him if he ever went back there. Too many times the dinner overcooked while he coped with one last crisis, or we had to cancel an evening with friends or a Sunday outing because the blessed IBM Company couldn't get along without his presence at some special meeting. The poor man was a wreck, with the company telling him the way to succeed was to carry three men's jobs at once, and me telling him the way to succeed was to tell them to go to hell on Sundays.'

The stress is probably greater on the IBM man with a good marriage (or an outspoken wife like this) than it is on the man with a mediocre marriage or a sick one. For him the IBM culture provided many chances to be a workaholic. This is a situation that is certainly not unique to IBM.

No matter what the state of the marriage, IBM does more than most companies to alleviate at least the surface stresses on a family in motion. For World Traders abroad the company gives both financial and cultural assistance. In Paris, for example, one girl in the personnel department helps wives find housing, then arranges for such practical matters as turning on the power or dealing with the local authority. A young English wife is flown to the United States to help her husband house-hunt for a two-year assignment. A man in the Tokyo office handles domestic administration problems for wives when their husbands are away on business trips.

One French-language class in Paris included a Dutch girl, two from
Germany, two Canadians and three Americans — all IBM wives.
Their husbands were getting their French lessons at work. Here
the parallel to army life is strong. 'You must become independent
and self-sufficient to be a World Trade wife,' said one woman who
has done an excellent job of it. 'At one point I saw him ten days
in three months. With three babies and no family nearby, it was
pretty hard to cope.'

Culture shock hits the wives and children harder than the
husbands when they move from one country to another. For the
man, the IBM office in Beirut looks like the one in Berlin or
Boston. They will cash his cheques, make his travel arrangements,
and most important, talk his language. For his wife it can be
more difficult. In Japan the women had to learn completely new
ways of transacting the everyday business of a family. Because of
the language barriers, Japanese-speaking household help is a
necessity, but this takes a great deal of adjustment for women who
were used to doing their own housework. They also lost the
community activities that filled gaps in time and energy in other
countries when their husbands travelled frequently.

The household help was sometimes a blessing. In the Orient IBM
encourages wives to go along on some of the business trips. The
policy says that if a man travels 45 or 50 days, he can take his
wife on the next trip. 'These weren't overnight trips to London or
Paris, but two or three weeks at a time,' said a graduate.
'The area spread from Sydney to Auckland to Delhi to Manila. This
policy was necessary. It also helped the wives — gave them something
to look forward to.' American assignees in Europe, like British
adminstrators in the Empire, get home leave for the entire family
once a year.

The wives had to learn to cope with political emergencies too. At
one time the IBM man in Indonesia cabled his headquarters for
six German flags — two large ones for the house, two medium ones
for the gate, and two small ones for the car. He had to establish the
fact that his family wasn't Dutch during the touchy times there.
The 1968 riots in Paris not only put up the cost-of-living portion
of IBM's payroll (by 4.3 percent) but also affected the lives of
many IBM families living there. Paris banks and petrol stations
were closed during the riots, so IBM made arrangements to have its
people bring in money from Switzerland. 'We could cash $50
every day,' said one wife. 'IBM took care of us. They had plans to

pick up people without cars and whisk them out of the country
if things got worse. They set up car pools, and even had a makeshift
mail service through Belgium for the three weeks of the strike.'

Many IBM families thrived on the culture changes, even the
crises. For Americans who have never been abroad, a couple of
years in Paris or Vienna can be intoxicating. European managers
often have to cope with crying wives, begging for longer
assignments for their husbands. One wife who has survived a dozen
moves with IBM warned: 'You must put down roots, for your
children and for your husband, but you can't put them down too
deeply. You need stability, but not to be too upset during the
next transition.'

'Out of sight, out of mind'

Coming back from a foreign assignment is a major problem for the
men as well as their wives. First of all, there is an artificial situation
when an individual ends his fixed-term assignment. IBM has to find
him a job, but there may not be an appropriate opening when he
finishes his term. A second real problem is that people forget him;
he doesn't feel necessary when he comes back to his old office or
is sent to a new one. ('Out of sight, out of mind,' as one World
Trade article expressed it.[3]) A third problem is that some of the
people sent overseas are not the most effective people. Like
universities, the various organizations in IBM try to hang on to
their most successful stars and ship out the visiting professors they
can get along without. In some locations those are the ones who
enjoy the benefits of being big fish in smaller ponds. In 1970
World Trade task-forced the problems with a group who had
experienced re-entry. They came up with several solutions. First,
each country organization 'certifies' an assignment candidate as
worthy of a better job, and documents the expected re-entry date.
Then a sponsor or 'career manager' is nominated for the man —
his primary contact and the manager who remains responsible for
his pay, appraisal, counselling and buffering him through re-entry.

National pride constitutes another problem for IBM in moving its
people around. One European commented: 'If you don't want to
make your life in Paris or New York as a staff man, or be a
wanderer with two years here and two years there, you have a
problem. I have children, and they're getting too big to move.
I don't *like* New York or Paris. I know I have to move but I want

to stay in my own country from now on. I don't want to be a US citizen. I don't want my son to have to join the US army because of his father's ambition.'An English graduate grumbled: 'We used to think the European offices were too often staffed with Americans on two-year assignments, who had a pretty nice time by and large. They would pay an American a lot of money to preserve his Chicago standards in Paris, while a guy from Spain or Britain down the hall, doing a similar job, was pretty unusual if he was getting one-third the money'. In June 1971 another task force revamped the 'COM-9' allowances policy, which had been based on US government statistics relating all overseas allowances to the cost of living in Washington DC in 1966. Instead they created 'COM-14', which gave less emphasis to US scales and more attention to inter-country differences between other countries. COM-14's main contributions were to cut down the overpayments to US assignees and make provision for new changes in currency values.

Another resentment comes from the feeling that the Americans have an advantage when it comes to assignments. In the early sixties an irate Englishman asked Maisonrouge why Europeans didn't have the same chance at the top jobs. The Frenchman answered smoothly that IBM surveys showed the Europeans were less willing to move around from one place to another. The company had already paid to repatriate a few who suffered family pressures and returned home. On the other hand, a former manager said: 'They always had the question 'would you move?' on the survey forms. But I always took it to mean moving around within my country. I was honestly disappointed when I didn't get a Paris assignment.'

IBM finally changed its survey questions, and discovered that despite their aversion to intra-country moves, 88 percent of the Europeans surveyed said they would willingly change countries, and 50 percent were willing to consider permanent assignment abroad. Dr Sirota suggested that the bosses of good European people helped perpetuate the non-moving myth over the years by saying 'Louis doesn't want to move', when in truth Louis had not always heard about the foreign opportunity.

'Some of the best IBMers are the ex-IBMers'

Myths have grown up about the success or failure of IBM graduates after they leave the alma mater. One school of thought says that the IBM graduate is helpless outside IBM, that he was an automaton inside, never given responsibility for strategy; therefore (they reason) he is unable to think for himself successfully in companies that are less splendidly organized. This glittering generalization is just as untrue as the one that says the only solution to major problems in a computer-related company is to hire in a team of the whiz kids from IBM to put things right.

The reasons people leave IBM fall broadly into two categories: one built into the structure of IBM, and the other a characteristic of the men IBM hires. The company is hierarchical; the men are ambitious. At fairly predictable points in IBM careers, the men become more aware of outside opportunities, or begin to notice concave sides to the pyramid of their IBM success.

One pervasive reason people leave IBM is simply the reverse side of the reason they joined it. IBM has a depth of management that is unsurpassed. This reservoir of talent, particularly management talent, has been built up from inside, like the company itself. Becoming a part of it is a primary attraction to a young man; being a part of it can be a primary frustration as he approaches 40. IBM takes capabilities for granted that most companies would appreciate more noisily.

Two eminent graduates, both self-employed, met one afternoon and discovered that they both left IBM on the same day, in offices a hundred miles apart. It's like a big bucket,' said one of them. 'Put your arm in, all the way to the elbow, and pull it out again. The time it took the water to fill the space where your arm was is just how long it took them to fill our places.'

This 'leaky bucket' brings mixed reactions inside. Because loyalty was such a strong part of the Old Man's creed, and 'belonging' to the IBM community such an important benefit to its members, the ultimate penalty was always to be forced to leave — and the ultimate sin was to choose to leave. The few men who departed in the fities and early sixties were seldom mentioned among their former friends; associating with them after defection was *not* encouraged, and the few who did so were secretive about it, for fear of acquiring a kind of guilt by association.

By 1968, Domestic's record year, the computer industry was full of new competitors who believed their key to success was headhunting from IBM. IBM at the same time had too many people — and each IBMer had too many good peers and superiors. (One graduate stressed that IBM didn't have too many good people; 'just more than any other corporation in the world'.)

When the defections began to increase in the later sixties, one result was a tightening of internal security, cutting down the amount of important confidential information a manager was given, because of the potential damage the company believed defectors might be able to do. However, IBM underestimated their built-in loyalty, making the mistaken assumption that it all evaporated once a man was disloyal enough to leave. It also overestimated the commercial value of its little secrets; the real secret was the culture, and that only worked inside. This new compartmentalizing of information simply reinforced the outflow of managers. They began to say to themselves: 'If IBM doesn't think I'm important enough to know about this or that, then I might as well look for a job somewhere else where they'll appreciate me a little more.' Thus the security cure made the morale illness, and thus the departure rate, even worse.

Plotting age versus departure rate, IBM personnel researchers found two distinct peaks along the chart. Behavioural scientist Warren Bennis,[4] who did some of the earliest studies of this phenomenon, referred to such peaks as the Identity Crisis and the Destination Crisis. He also pointed out that they seem to occur in most large corporations.

The Identity Crisis shows up on the chart as a peak around the age of 25, when the young employee asks himself: 'Who am I?' Sometimes he decides he is not the obedient, presentable, well-trained young man on his way up that he believes IBM would like him to be. It happens relatively soon after the employee has joined the corporation, so the investment in his training and development is rather small and his job is seldom a crucial one.

The Destination Crisis — 'Where am I going?' — makes a somewhat smaller numerical peak on the age chart, right around the 40 mark, but the men involved are more important to IBM. By the time he reaches 40 a man has typically been with IBM for ten to twenty years. His span of rapid promotion is reaching a close, unless he is one of the few crown princes. He can look ahead to 20 or 25 more years of his working life He can look over his shoulder and see an impressive group of younger men, all eager for more responsibility, some of them equipped with more current skills than his own. He knows that if he waits until he is 45 or 50, his opportunities outside IBM will be more limited.

When he departs each man leaves behind a hole, one that can turn into a learning experience for some other young man on the way up. Although IBM will still go to almost religious lengths to redeem a sinner, it now worries less about those who fall by the wayside. IBM's recent experience reveals that many become valued customers. Most of them retain a strong nostalgia for the alma mater.

This raises an interesting dichotomy in the company, which is now more than 60 years old. Its managers are promoted from within, and a large percentage of IBM people have never worked anywhere else. They spend their entire careers inside this single culture. On the other hand, it is an exceptionally young company. The average age in most European countries in 1970 was just over 30. The youthful optimism, the enthusiasm (what Tom Junior called 'the tone') is constantly renewed as the new young men come into IBM's bloodstream. The older ones are not fired; but beyond a certain point, if they have not been marked for the top they are not likely to get there, and they know it. Yet they have been programmed for all those years to strive for the top. IBM encourages these older people to stay with retirement benefits, stock purchase plans, awards for merit, and ongoing prizes for production or sales achievement. All of these emphasize 'membership' and are administered similarly in every country. One graduate called them 'the golden handcuffs — the things you have to swallow the guff in order to get.' The decision to leave entails financial as well as cultural excommunication.

Bob McGrath, who publishes a thriving *IBM alumni directory*,[5] once received this letter from an IBM employee:

> Unfortunately I still find myself in the same position as when we last worked together with no prospect for improvement, yet too chicken to quit and face the world after all these years with IBM.

McGrath's directory by 1973 had more than 1,500 names — and those were only collected on a hobby basis from friends or announcements in the trade press. He estimated that about 2,000 people leave IBM by their own choice every year. Where do these people go? The directory itself gives strong indications.

By far the largest number stay in DP, either in computer-related companies or in other industries that use the machines. One-third of the people in McGrath's list are chairmen, presidents or vice-presidents. Some of their companies are huge corporations; sometimes one gets the impression that the company consists of the chairman and his dog; others are small specialist firms. The success rate seems fairly high.

For those graduates with no business experience outside IBM, the difference in corporate cultures came as a shock. Most of them agree that it can take a year or two to adapt to the different environment, even when it is the environment of another large, advanced, well-managed company. For those who went to small companies or started their own, the shock was even greater. Some had simply assumed that to be an executive meant one must have an important office and a good address. Some of the new ventures died in their infancy from too rich a diet of carpets, copiers and executive secretaries. One graduate who competes with IBM had several difficult experiences with other graduates, and now simply won't hire them until they have worked somewhere else for at least a year.

The growing number of graduates has its effect on IBM internally. Country organizations experience a certain relief. Each departure means it takes less energy to resolve the stress between required manpower cuts and the sacred full-employment policy. Each man who leaves creates a hole, and sets up a new wave of fluidity in his former organization as another man can be moved in to replace him, creating yet another hole. Thus people keep moving. In the older country organizations the departures can be a revitalizing elixir to stir the corporate bloodstream and keep the organizational arteries from hardening. In the newer countries, especially in the third world, each departure is still a wound, one that takes time to heal because the bloodstream of qualified nationals is still thin. In those countries the company's problem is developing salesmen and managers, not what to do with all those who are already overdeveloped.

From the company's viewpoint, both the moving around and the rising departure rates are blessings in disguise. Those that leave look back fondly on their IBM years and keep their 'THINK' signs. Those presentable people who stay in IBM are intensely devoted to the company, and extraordinarily well treated. But what advice could one offer a young person considering a a career with IBM?

One mother who knows the company well stated her viewpoint clearly; 'I would be delighted if my daughter decided to work for IBM. It is a gentler place than most, and she would enjoy working with capable people in that ambiance. But she has not been brought up to nurture any deep concern about a 'career'. For my son, on the other hand, I would not be so happy. I would hate to see his iconoclastic streak submerged in that unified culture — and

I don't think the culture does much to nurture fledgling wild ducks, no matter how gentle it may be with them once they are well-formed. Perhaps in his thirties, when he has had time to develop more internal certainty, he would enjoy a chance to exercise his skills in this splendid environment, where there is so much room for achievement and so little petty politics or bureaucracy. But I wouldn't want him to go to IBM right out of school.'

9
Control by fear

Fear is more effective than force in controlling a creature as large and powerful as IBM. And to some extent IBM must be controlled, to make sure that its size and power continue to be pointed in directions that are good for society as well as for IBM. The company has a healthy fear of its employees and large customers — a fear both groups have learned to exploit. It also has an inordinate fear of governments, unions, and the press (in roughly that order). This means that a clear comprehension of the fear and how it operates can help outsiders maintain healthy pressures on this healthy company, so it will voluntarily take the right steps.

I would *not* like to see IBM's almost neurotic fear of governments, unions and the press, cured. I would particularly not like these neuroses to be cured in the classic way — by having IBM actually experience what it fears. I would not like to see IBM broken up by the anti-trust people, for example. But I want the anti-trust pressures to continue. The company's fear of being broken up is animal-like, a powerful thing that keeps it relatively well behaved and cooperative, encouraging greater centralization on a voluntary basis. The world doesn't understand IBM's regenerative powers; a broken-up IBM would easily turn into two, five or seven small tigers, afraid of nothing once the ultimate threat had been exercised — able to pounce with invincible ferocity on hapless new market sectors. Most of the competitors are aware of this; very few want IBM to be broken up.

For the same reason, I would not like to see IBM unionized, but I want the company to retain its fear of unions, not only for the benefit of IBM's own employees but also for other companies — and perhaps unions themselves — who can learn from IBM's excellent examples in industrial relations. Nor would I like to see IBM's public image get any more tiger-like and distorted; once this happened the powerful constraint of IBM's self-image would be erased, and the public would be not only less well-informed but also less protected from corporate aggression.

These fears deserve careful exploration; they are the only real control we have over IBM.

'Some of our best friends are governments'

Anthony Sampson[1] suggested that ITT, 'too big and too cunning for any country to control,' is the forerunner of a new kind of industrial animal. One important characteristic (among many) that differentiates IBM from ITT — and can prevent such a prediction from coming true — is IBM's awe of governments.

The Old Man loved — and feared — kings and governments. So does IBM. A fairly healthy awe of political power and respect for governing institutions led IBM very early to take an austere, hands-off policy towards politics itself, but to operate actively in the realms of industrial diplomacy and public service. The Old Man also made an early policy decision to keep ownership of overseas companies completely in IBM hands as much as possible. The overall view reflects the Watsonian ideal of World Peace Through World Trade, even though the corporate entity that pursued it remained American-owned.

Despite a statesmanlike, far-sighted approach to its dealings with governments, IBM has run into difficulties in recent years. Computers in many countries are considered a matter of national ego as well as national industrial health. Governments which sponsor indigenous computer companies frown upon this giant intruder, no matter how much IBM behaves as a good citizen. The stresses are increasing and it is only IBM's built-in skills at diplomacy which have kept the company relatively unregulated into its seventh decade.

The two specifics IBM fears most could be over-simplified as anti-trust controls at home and economic nationalism abroad. As 1973 approached it became clear that the widely reported anti-trust suits in the United States were helping fuel a domestic increase in economic nationalism. Multinationals were big and able to move factories from country to country. Unions worried that the big companies like IBM were exporting jobs that should belong to American workers. New legislation was proposed, and IBM's hopes of a relatively quiet settlement of the anti-trust suit filed by the US government in 1969 were dashed by the growing isolationist sentiment, and then the Watergate scandals, which involved other companies (including ITT) trying to buy government favours. IBM shareholders were urged to write to their Congressmen in defense of multinationals, and Maisonrouge testified capably before a UN group investigating the subject.

IBM had not tried to buy government favours; the large Watson contributions to both parties — Dick's to Nixon and Tom Junior's to Muskie — had been made through the normal channels with no attempt to influence the course of justice or the Justice Department. Even so, Tom Junior's contribution earned him a place on the famous list of 201 White House 'enemies' and a special income-tax audit. (Cary was among Nixon's 200 business guests honoured to meet Brezhnev the week the enemies list was published.)

One technique IBM has always used to deal with foreign governments is protective colouration. The wolf in sheep's clothing actually believes it is a sheep, even though the host governments like Britain or France with sheep of their own to protect tend to see the fierce American feet sticking out underneath the British or French sheepskins. The local managers, employees and salesmen in Britain are impeccably British, with the right degrees from the right universities, and the right old school ties. But no matter how French IBM seemed in France, no matter that 99½ percent of its employees or machines were tri-colour to the core, no matter how easily de Waldner chatted to de Gaulle, no matter how elegant the laboratory de Waldner and de Gaulle wrung out of the Watsons for La Gaude, the French were not impressed. As far as they were concerned, IBM remained American.

The American government itself could be obstructive on occasion. When de Gaulle was developing his atomic striking force, neither IBM France nor Control Data Corporation was allowed to sell to the French the large computers they wanted for simulating nuclear explosions. Thus the French, clearly and visibly deprived of computers they wanted, developed even more wary attitudes about 'le défi Americain', and increased their commitment to a French computer industry that could build the large machines, even though this was not a particularly profitable end of the market as time passed.

IBM has a strict policy towards taxes — one that is sometimes irritating to other companies. It pays them in full. IBM never uses tax havens. The taxes can sometimes be *deferred*, but never dodged. This gives the company a fine reputation when it wants to enter a new country, but it often causes governments to ask of other companies: 'If IBM makes so much money, why don't you?' This was another legacy from the Old Man. He had, and passed on, utter confidence in his ability to build a great, everlasting company. Thus, he reasoned, why fool around with short-term tax fiddles that could endanger IBM's eternal growth? This basic premise helps every IBM company behave as a good corporate citizen in its host country. Both the IBM people and the governments believe that IBM is paying its fair share of taxes — because it is true.

When it comes to moving money around the face of the earth, IBM is similarly law-abiding but less open about the mechanisms. Generally these boil down to royalty and license fees paid by country organizations to headquarters, and the transfer prices charged by one country to another. The UK organization normally pays IBM 10 percent of its revenues as a combined royalty and license fee for the technical and management benefits it gets from the corporation. This is computed separately from the reported profits, so it becomes part of IBM's revenues and profits, but is charged as an expense to the UK company (which, like IBM companies in France, Germany and several other countries, must publish certain results locally). Adjusting these fees by a percentage point one way or the other allows the corporation to plough back more cash into a country, or less, according to local conditions and reserves. The goal is usually to keep the overall trends steady and upwards, and to maintain a balance between imports and exports in the major countries where these draw political attention.

Certain countries cause frequent difficulties. In Nigeria, for example, there are severe restrictions on 'repatriation of currency'. Similar situations exist in Ghana and Zaïre. Most of these operations in Africa are reasonably profitable, albeit small in IBM terms. However, getting the money out is another question; a former

manager of the area noted that IBM hasn't really extracted from
Africa the cash it put in. 'Sometimes you can't do anything about
it, so a surplus builds up. This encourages you to own or put up
buildings rather than renting them, and so on.' One of several ways
these stresses can be alleviated is to move people around instead of
money. If a man on the IBM Nigeria payroll goes on assignment to
a European country for several years his pay continues to come
from his home country, even though the work he does is helping
some other part of the organization. This 'free ride' helps ease the
surplus and it also returns to Nigeria a man with up-to-date
training in some new and useful part of the business.

In its early years IBM was welcomed as a good corporate citizen
almost everywhere. But as nationalism increased the company's
firm stand, especially on the issue of local ownership, sometimes
led it into delicate negotiations. At a 1963 ceremony in Nigeria,
Dick was lunching between several top Nigerian ministers when
one of them asked: 'Why can't Nigerians own some of the IBM
company in Nigeria?' Dick responded with practised smoothness
that most companies in most countries found the centralized
arrangement to be best. He pointed out that a major factor in
IBM's success over the years was the high percentage of its retained
earnings it could put into R&D. Because very few shareholders
outside the United States were sophisticated enough to
appreciate that fact, IBM found it best to retain 100 percent
ownership of its companies in other countries. He also referred
to the corporation's ability to run at a loss for years if necessary
to build up the level of skill in places like Nigeria. Even so,
Nigeria kept pushing IBM to form a company there, though most
of the other African countries allowed branch offices to be set up
without a corporate framework. IBM stood firm. In 1972 more
Nigerian difficulties arose as the government began to demand
the 'Nigerianization' of foreign-held companies, with at least 40
percent local shareholding.

The issue recurred in Japan a number of times. Each delicate
renegotiation of IBM's unique place in Japan was a separate drama
in itself, and each one could settle the matter for only a few years.
IBM has been for many years the only 100 percent foreign-held
company in Japan. It speaks for IBM diplomacy that Japan is
today one of IBM's five largest and most profitable national
markets — and IBM is Japan's largest computer manufacturer,
for the time being. On the other hand, IBM's skilful and tough
negotiations in Japan are often given credit for Japan's insistence

on a native computer industry — an industry that is beginning to impact *all* computer manufacturers in the United States, including IBM.

Stress remains, quite naturally. The Japanese government would like IBM Japan to be a net exporter, while IBM with its global manufacturing strategy would prefer each major country organization to maintain a rough balance between its imports and exports. (It is Maisonrouge who pointed out, often, that it is of course impossible for every country to have a positive trade balance.)

IBM Japan started in the mid-twenties, when the Old Man sent his emissaries out to register IBM as a corporate entity in countries all over the world. During World War II it was taken over by the Japanese government, but reopened in 1949 as an IBM-owned enterprise. The company built up a long history of low-profile good citizenship, but it remained mainly a marketing company (and thus an importer) until the early sixties. Then the government clamped down formally on the import of American-built computers, refusing import licenses whenever Japanese companies could make comparable equipment. Then the government demanded that the wholly owned IBM subsidiary be converted to a joint venture with Japanese holding a majority. They threatened even stronger sanctions if IBM did not agree. In addition, IBM Japan was having labour union problems at the time — a matter taken very seriously at Armonk. From the corporate viewpoint there was never any question of giving in on the joint venture. IBM either remained 100 percent owned by the American parent company, or it left Japan entirely.

The company mounted a three-month task force to survey the problem. Could the Japanese manufacturers make comparable machines? And would the Japanese customers remain with IBM despite government restrictions? Once he knew the customers would continue to deal with IBM no matter what their government did or said, Gordon Williamson got the backing of Jones and both Watsons to take a hard line with the government negotiators, telling them (most regretfully and politely) that IBM would have to close down its operations rather than yield on the ownership issue. During the survey phase the customers had not only been canvassed about their loyalty, but once that was assured they had been encouraged (like the US shareholders in 1973) to bring to the government's attention the dangers to the Japanese economy if IBM should leave.

With its industry support evaporating rapidly, the government asked Williamson to have the IBM board review his decision. When he refused in a final dramatic meeting, the government gracefully withdrew its demands. IBM just as gracefully increased its manufacturing and education facilities in Japan, and continues to do so whenever the stress levels on the issue seem to be rising. In 1972 a 22-storey IBM building was opened in Tokyo. Though it had 8,800 Japanese employees by mid-73, IBM politely maintains a low profile in Japan, with less than half the market — albeit a profitable 30 percent.

Most governments are made aware that IBM does not make deals. However, 'not making deals' is not quite as important as 'not letting foreigners own half of your company'. In the Bahamas government policy had been to demand a controlling local share in any venture, but the time came when the government needed some computer equipment. IBM sent in some Canadians (who are more acceptable in former British colonies than American IBMers). The government waived the local-partner rule, and IBM was in. Because there was no local manufacturer to protect, there was no need to keep a particularly low profile, so IBM's market share around Nassau is well over 50 percent.

Governments are aware that large multinational companies like IBM have the ability to make internal decisions that affect national or local employment as well as trade balances. IBM goes to great lengths to avoid such confrontations; only once has there been a widely reported conflict between national and corporate goals. IBM proposed in 1970 to build a new component factory in Hannover, Germany. The factory would have provided about 1,000 jobs at first, scaling up towards 5,000 later. The decision to site it at Hannover was heralded as an honour to the city. However, the site the city proposed for the factory was a racetrack — and thus roused considerable local opposition from racetrack-ecologists. Nonetheless, IBM bought the land and the city demolished the ancient monument to make way for the factory.

At that point someone in Armonk discovered one of IBM's greatest planning errors. All the projections for semiconductor components had been based on fairly conservative 'yield' estimates — the percentage of components which would emerge from the process successfully. But the IBM plants in France and the United States had made some production innovations and yields were getting much higher. The planning figures and the production figures didn't come together on one desk for several months. When they finally met, the discrepancy revealed that new components factories would be an expensive and unnecessary luxury. Furthermore, World Trade was under a hiring freeze and needed *less* manufacturing people, not a few thousand more. Domestic was consolidating some plants already. IBM reacted with its usual dispatch. Swallowing hard, the company *paid* the Germans to take back their former racetrack site.

This underscores one of IBM's primary reasons for keeping all shares of foreign subsidiaries owned by the parent. If there had been independent IBM Germany shareholders, they might have been able to interfere with the business decision, if they believed it conflicted with the national or community interest.

Although IBM can be tough when it is threatened — as in the Japanese negotiations — it still holds government and supra-government bodies in the same deep respect the Old Man demonstrated. Maisonrouge said in a 1973 speech: *'Political power is stronger than economic power when the two collide.'* Few governments seem aware of this reverence (which sometimes approaches awe), but it is probably the single factor most responsible for IBM's good behaviour as a guest in about 130 countries. Thus IBM diplomacy is carried out with all the professional panache of a major government — but more emphasis on the velvet glove than the iron economic fist. IBM is more scared of governments than they are of it.

The ultimate threat from IBM is to pull out of a country. The ultimate threat from the country is to take over the IBM company. At one point this occurred in Burma, where a new dictator made threatening noises towards the tiny IBM company there. This political stimulus naturally brought a World Trade executive (Gordon Williamson, who had negotiated in Tokyo) into Rangoon on the next plane. After appropriate heel-cooling, he entered the chief's chambers.

'I'm going to nationalize your company,' the dictator said firmly.

'Go ahead,' Williamson responded just as firmly. 'But don't forget what happened to Castro when he did that.' (IBM had made it known throughout its diplomatic circles that Castro would get no more spare parts when the Cuban company was taken over.)

Williamson's bravery was rewarded in the Burma case. As the IBM man started to stalk out of the room, the dictator responded: 'Come back. Let's talk about it a little more.'

The IBM ambassadors are extremely varied. IBM's board of directors, for example, included Dick Watson, Nicholas Katzenbach (former US Attorney General), Keith Funston (former head of the New York Stock Exchange) and William Scranton (former governor of Pennsylvania). Lord Cromer, who became Britain's ambassador to the United States in 1970, was (and is again) chairman of IBM UK. Politically, Democrats predominated, so the IBM population went up when the Republicans came to power in 1968. In addition to Katzenbach from Lyndon Johnson's reign, there was Dr Eugene Fubini, former Assistant Secretary of Defense for R&D, and Burke Marshall, former Assistant Attorney General.

There are IBM 'government specialists' in most major countries, and the corporation has its own 'ambassadors' to such revered bodies as the EEC and OECD. Their job is somewhat akin to those of the press officers — to limit the flow of information as nicely as possible, and at the same time to carry out the necessary 'education' tasks. Like journalists, civil servants are not a particularly manageable breed. Imagine the plight of the IBM ambassador to Brussels who has been given by EEC commissioners a list of financial, commercial and political questions to answer — charming intimacies such as 'How much does IBM spend on R&D in the United States? In Europe?' The poor man quickly discovers that the corporation's only response to the detailed list is likely to be a high-flown document full of statements condemning sin and approving motherhood, to the effect that standardization is a Very Good Thing, which IBM has been trying to promote for years. Like all ambassadors everywhere, the circumloquacious IBM diplomat in Brussels weaves around this bit of corporate fluff as much importance as possible, tries to maintain 'control' of the ensuing interview, and departs with as much dignity as possible. The usual result of such an interview is more information for IBM about EEC policy than vice versa.

Relations with host governments are often enhanced by IBM's pleasant tendancy to buy parts locally whenever this is practical. Sometimes, as in Australia in 1973, a foreign government can nudge IBM into local manufacture for parts used all over the world. However, the high IBM standards for even simple components are not always interesting to local businessmen. As one manager in a developing country put it: 'I have corporate permission to manufacture some parts for typewriters locally, but even though the country needs foreign currency the various little companies here can get richer by making junk for the local market. The plastics company down the road would rather see a 70 percent return from making buckets which don't take any skills or fancy machinery than the 30 percent return he'd get supplying me with fine parts. In his shoes I would do the same thing.'

160

One important part of the IBM culture is the edict that IBM
is apolitical. The company resolutely keeps its hands off party
politics, with good reason. Today's 'opposition' may be tomorrow's
customer. 'Some of our best friends are governments,' said Dick
Wight, an old hand at corporate communications.

This independence of the IBMer from political involvement
once took a wry twist. In 1961 Tom Junior gave the sales force
a thumbnail sketch of the new Kennedy adminstration as he
saw it. 'It was not a political talk,' he later reflected. 'I urged no
views on them. It was an optimistic assessment, nothing more.'
Some of the IBMers complained. They would listen to whatever
he wanted to say about business, but didn't want to hear about
the new government in a company meeting. Tom was surprised
at first. 'I was a bit annoyed at having been misunderstood,'
he said. 'But when I thought about it, I was pleased, for they
had made it quite clear that they wore no man's collar and
they weren't at all hesitant to tell me so.' So the cultural edict
is not 'no politics', but 'your politics are your own' — an edict
that Tom Junior and Dick themselves demonstrate by supporting
different parties. Like their father, they seem more interested
in the structural phenomenon of government than the ideological
colour of its skin.

The changes in IBM World Trade since 1971 have been quiet but
important, in government dealings as well as decentralization.*
The countries now have more autonomy in their announcement
dates; the people in Maisonrouge's Paris headquarters can now
make some kinds of business decisions that affect all of Europe
without having to refer to World Trade headquarters or Armonk.

Governments don't quite realize that they, too, could have
access to corporate decision-makers through the Open Door. But
IBM's organization is so opaque that governments seldom know
where to go beyond their local IBM people. Taking the Old Man's
example, it does no harm to start at the top.

'Will the President support us in public over Eastern Europe?'

IBM's Eastern European dealings give an interesting glimpse into
the corporation's attitudes towards governments. The company

*However the 1974 re-organization that brought Maisonrouge back to Paris
also, in effect, replaced a French corporation with a Delaware corporation
whose Board is dominated by men from Armonk.

there were more tabulating machines in Vienna than all the rest
of Europe. The Russians, however, had historically shown an
irritating tendency to copy IBM products. In 1928, for example,
the first IBM punches and verifiers were installed in Moscow.
In 1929 Russia began to manufacture its own punches and
verifiers. At a 1934 Leningrad fair IBM exhibited sorters and
numerical accounting machines; in 1935 Russia produced its
first sorters and numerical accounting machines.

After the war the Russians swooped up every IBM or Remington-
Rand machine they could. Relations started up on a 'business as
usual' basis with many of the Eastern European countries, but the
beginning of the cold war in the late forties and early fifties
effectively cut off these activities.

During the fifties it had become uncomfortably fashionable
for the Eastern European countries to jail IBM men as spies. Baron
Niki ('Nick') Hauser, for example, had been manager of IBM
Rumania. He was jailed for four years in Bucharest. A contemporary
said: 'Dick finally managed to trade some machine parts for Hauser
and brought him out to Paris.' In Hungary there was Gyula ('Julius')
Sandorfi to extract. When the cold war set in Sandorfi was
imprisoned. Released during the 1956 uprising, he immediately
dashed to his office and cabled Dick that IBM Hungary had 36
installations and was open for business again. Three days later
a young girl arrived in Sandorfi's office and said: 'Bring your
family and come with me.' As contemporaries tell it, the family
went through the countryside with nothing but the clothes they
were wearing, crawling through forests until they reached the
border. There George Daubek (himself a veteran of a 1948 escape
from Czechoslovakia) waited in his limousine to whisk them to
safety.

Only in the last few years have business activities resumed, in
response to a thaw in the US government's attitudes, though
IBM has been pushing for greater trade for some years behind the
scenes. In Czechoslovakia, for example, the government in 1949
appointed an administrator over the IBM properties throughout
the country. In 1967, after sitting by in competitive agonies while
the Czechs bought British or Univac computers, the IBM people
in Vienna finally managed to break through the Iron Curtain
with an approved order for two old 7040 computers. The East
German market, new after the war, manufactured a few of its
own computers, but the political situation never made it appropriate
for IBM to look for business there until the early seventies.

One of the most dedicated groups in all IBM was IBM Hungary, typified by Sandorfi. Even though the government took over the company very early, a faint theme-song continued: 'There'll always be an IBM Hungary. IBM continued to supply the Hungarians with spare parts for the old machines they had. Even during the war IBM Hungary had managed to get money out to the parent corporation, and in the later troubles they usually managed somehow to pay their bills to IBM in hard currencies, though IBM also had blocked currencies within the country. In the early sixties a World Trade executive made a rare visit to the state-owned little company — and they turned out for a classic Family Dinner in his honour! Later in the sixties another executive visited Budapest on an exploratory trip, and talked to most of the 15 to 20 former IBM people there. 'They still consider themselves IBMers,' he commented. 'There's a building there about four storeys high, with the sign 'IBM' 20 feet wide up near the top of the building. Every IBMer I met there pointed it out to me proudly.'

Yugoslavia was a slightly different case, ever since the war years when IBM's manager Milan Stefanovic worked closely with Tito. He was supplanted in 1960 by Zvonko Cebasek, but Stefanovic remained special representative for government activities. In the same year the government's statistical office installed a French-made IBM 705 computer. But by 1964 the stresses of politics demanded that the IBM operations be closed and the government turned to British computers to some extent. Yugoslavia is still a friendlier market than the others for IBM, and is handled separately within IBM's Eastern Europe operations by selling at the border to a Yugoslav agency.

By the mid-sixties Armonk realized that there were potential customers behind the Iron Curtain who, like the IBM customers in Japan, would be quite willing to help convince their own governments to ease restrictions, if similar easing could take place outside. (Most of the potential customers were government bodies, of course.) At that time any sale of technical equipment to an Eastern European country had to go through a barrage of approvals, including the US Export Control Office and the CoCom (Coordinating Committee) machinery of the NATO alliance.

IBM had always been cautious about Eastern Europe because of its own unfortunate experiences with copied equipment, blocked currencies and nationalized companies. Added to this was the Old Man's patriotism, filtered or amplified through his sons and their subordinates. In his 1962 speeches Tom Junior made references to 'our enemies'. Later there was public relations 'exposure risk' to worry about.

By the mid-sixties, though, the market demand was strong, and IBM was getting quiet but active encouragement from the US State Department. So in 1965, as a form of 'doing its homework', IBM sent a hard-working Eastern Europe veteran named Ralph Stafford to set up what they called the Austria Control Centre in Vienna. This small office for 'market research' was known internally as 'that cloak-and-dagger operation in Vienna'. Stafford settled in to learn about the Eastern Europeans. Evidently they studied him with equal interest. He once told a colleague: 'Prague is OK, but it's a nuisance being shadowed and bugged all the time.'

Contact between IBM diplomats and Eastern Europeans began to increase. A 1440 computer was shown by the US Commerce Department in Budapest in late 1965. Then an IBM team was sent to a Czech trade show in June 1966 with a 1410 computer (much to the discomfiture of British exhibitors). These first emissaries came back with the recommendation that the time was ripe for a 'name' IBM person to go to Eastern Europe. The best 'name' around was Watson, and Dick was the logical choice. With Jones and a few others in early 1968 Dick swept through the Eastern European countries like a potentate, wined and dined at every stop. Heads of state turned out to greet IBM's chief ambassador, and each country gave him a welcome back that was surprisingly warm and sincere. After 20 years of IBM's absence from most of those countries, the greeting was not just because this was Dick but because people remembered his father, and still felt a sense of identity with the company.

During this period Armonk's key committees began discussing in earnest the question of whether they could do business again behind the Iron Curtain. The government and public relations aspects were still delicate. The Young Americans for Freedom began picketing IBM sales offices in the United States in 1967 when word of IBM's forays behind the Iron Curtain leaked out. The press coverage of these happenings was uncomfortable. While the government was making encouraging noises in private about IBM's involvement, it was not rushing to make public statements.

Tom Junior assigned Bob Hubner to head an élite task force to look into the matter for three months. A meeting date was finally set with the MRC. That morning Tom Junior had about 20 people around the horseshoe-shaped table in the MRC room — everybody who might have inputs. Hubner set up his easel at the bottom of the horseshoe and cleared his throat.

Tom Junior looked up from his place at the head of the horseshoe, glanced at the summary chart, and before Hubner could say a word Tom Junior asked coolly: 'Will the President support us *in public* if we get in trouble?'

Hubner looked nonplussed for a moment, so Tom re-phrased his question. 'What is the adminstration's attitude? Is the President offering to let us sell 360s?'

Hubner talked for about five seconds and his boss interrupted: 'We will sell in the Eastern Bloc if the President will stand up and support us publicly if we get in trouble.' He turned to his brother, sitting in his usual place two seats to the left: 'Dick, you go to Washington and talk to Dean Rusk.'

So ended the meeting. The task force had spent hundreds of man-months getting ready for its unheard presentation. But Tom Junior knew they would have every 't' crossed and every 'i' dotted. He asked the one crucial question; how strong was the government's commitment? Obviously IBM did begin to do business with Eastern Europe, so Rusk and the President must have given the necessary reassurances.

At this point Stafford's operation in Vienna became ROECE (pronounced ro-see — it stands for Regional Office Europe Central and East), incorporated in Delaware as a separate subsidiary. Thus it became part of Tom Junior's empire rather than Dick's, though it depended upon IBM Austria for housekeeping and administration. Stafford was given what amounted to a blank cheque in tightly controlled IBM terms. There was no question of the traditional 'balanced growth', building slowly on the results of previous sales. Penetrating the Eastern Europe markets, with their ideal combination of a scarcity of computers and a surprisingly high level of computer competence, was going to take a lot of time and money. Stafford built the operation into a 300-man organization, one of Europe's top ten groups in terms of sales, albeit less impressive in profit with all the training, paper-shuffling and sales people it took to do business across the Iron Curtain.

ROECE is no longer a cloak-and-dagger operation. Housed in a portion of IBM's new Vienna building (on the Danube canal site where Strauss's 'Blue Danube' waltz had its premiere performance), it is a typical bustling IBM operation, with only

the standard smiling doorman for security. If there is any appreciable difference from other IBM operations it is a degree of
enthusiasm and openness, not secrecy — perhaps because this
corner of IBM is still pioneering, and pioneering is exhilarating.

Contrary to popular belief, IBM does not barter its equipment
directly for salt or handicrafts. 'If necessary we involve a non-IBM
Western trading company,' commented one ROECE executive.
'We don't want to sell cars or tomatoes.'

According to *Datamation*,[2] the system works something like
this. The Polish Ministry of Machinery is buying two 360/50
computers and a 360/40. They have Polski Fiat cars, but no
dollars. While the US and CoCom negotiations for the licence get
under way, the Polish foreign trade ministry gets its trading
agency, Pol-Mot, into the act. Meanwhile IBM finds an English
agent, Geoma Impex, and 'introduces' the two. Geoma Impex
arranges for the sale of 500 Polski Fiat cars to a firm in Nigeria
called Midmotors. Though the Nigerians are not as prompt as all
the other parties might like in paying, neither are the negotiators
at US Export Control and CoCom. Eventually Midmotors pays
Geoma Impex, which remits to IBM when the computers are
delivered, returning the change (minus fees) to Pol-Mot.

Once ROECE was staffed up, business in Eastern Europe began
to increase, but the first IBM licence for Russia wasn't granted
until mid-1972. However, a graduate estimated that about 50 IBM
computers had slipped into Russia through various 'back doors'.
Purchased machines from Sweden and other places have conveniently 'disappeared', no longer available for maintenance or
making demands for any other kind of support. IBM tended to
encounter this situation less often than other computer
manufacturers. One former IBM executive said: 'To my knowledge,
IBM World Trade never knowingly sold anything without full
government approval.'

Trade shows are a common back door to Eastern Europe for
most computer companies. The traditional pattern is for the
exhibitor (who is there, after all, to increase trade in certain
products) to get US and CoCom permission for 'temporary'
export, with a tacit understanding that the machine will be sold
at the show and left behind, with rapid rubber-stamping of the
license when this happens. IBM has been the single exception to
this rule. At a Moscow Trade Fair in the late fifties the Russians
kept asking IBM to take the covers off a 305 Ramac system, so
they could explore the electronics inside. 'We wouldn't do it,'

a graduate later commented. 'We had a marine from the embassy sleeping next to the Ramac.' It went home again with IBM, still unseen inside.

Nor does the company accept questionable orders and then try to pressure the various licensing bodies to approve them. As Maisonrouge described the process: 'Generally, when we accept an order it is when we have a reasonable hope for delivery. We are very careful in following the guidelines.'

The debate over doing business with Russia continued, partly because Jones was reluctant to take on the inevitable problems in currency, patents, licences and copyrights, and Learson simply didn't want to 'do business with Mother Russia'. Then in the autumn of 1970 (several years after Dick's trip) Tom Junior headed an executive team that travelled to Moscow (by Soviet invitation) to explore mutual possibilities 'in frank and friendly discussions'.[3] Returning to scenes of his wartime independence and valour, he was delighted at the opportunity. 'Obviously Russia would offer a vast potential market if conditions ever changed,' he said. Privately, he invited the Russians to visit IBM as soon as possible — a visit they returned in 1972. When he came home he described a market with potential for $20 or $30 million a year sales for IBM.

As relations improved the Russians proposed various kinds of cooperation with IBM. A joint venture factory to build IBM-type computer components met with only lukewarm reactions in US government and CoCom circles and no interest at all in IBM circles. They were warmer about an 'exchange of technology'. In IBM language, this meant sending a couple of capable technical people for extended visits to Russia. This met with the blessings of all the authorities, and in 1972 the technology began to exchange itself, very quietly. Order levels remained low. Although IBM was insisting on a guarantee of 15 orders if it were to go into the Russian market, the Russians traditionally order one or two items at a time, exploring relationships and building them up slowly. The $1.5 billion wheat purchase in 1972 also limited the hard currency available to the Russians. Nonetheless, IBM's Russian order book began to grow, steadily if slowly. By the time President Nixon visited Russia and China, IBM was all ready to take advantage of the relaxed relations.

IBM is now fairly open about its trade across the dissolving Iron Curtain. In 1972 Maisonrouge said:[4] 'We think the Eastern European countries are an important market because they have great needs. Today they recognize the importance of computers in

solving management problems — or challenges. So they will
certainly need more computers . . . It will not be a big boom.
It will take time. It's very hard to know the market in countries
even where you have all the market data available. It's even
harder without the data. But there's one rule of thumb. If
Russia has one half the US GNP they could have one half the
number of computers. I'm sure they have a market for at
least 25,000 computers there.'

When it comes to China, IBM's reticence is similar to the
shroud of silence that used to hang over the company's Eastern
Europe intentions. In the same 1972 discussion Maisonrouge
dismissed China somewhat coyly: 'The Chinese? They don't
need labour-saving devices.' A nice point, perhaps, except that
IBM for some years has been making the point that computers
are not labour-saving, but information-giving. As early as 1967
IBM veterans in Tokyo knew the corporation was interested
in the Chinese market, and in 1972 discussions were held
between IBM and Chinese representatives at a Canadian trade
show. In 1973 Maisonrouge himself spent a week in China, as
did Dick. There have been reports of one or two strange IBM
orders — 'as if a Malaysian garage were buying a 370'.

'Armonk gets pretty worried about union situations'

The only thing IBM is more scared of than governments is unions.
All of IBM's personnel policies carry between the lines a breath of
concern that if IBM doesn't do it first, a union might get in and
bite into the company's control of its own destiny. Yet no
production worker has ever lost an hour's time in strikes at IBM,
in spite of general unrest and the major growth of unions
elsewhere. The pay and full employment policies give employees
a sense of belonging. Several authors[5] compare IBM in this respect
to Japanese companies, which have very high employee identification. Even so, a 60-year-old paternalistic policy is not enough to
keep unions at bay forever. Or is it? IBM's fear of unions hides
under a cool, almost superior, exterior. Company executives are
not blatantly anti-union — but they say unions would be a serious
detriment to IBM. Customers value the history of continuous
service, never interrupted by strikes. Citing the excellent pay
scales and personnel policies, they simply adopt the attitude that
'third parties' are unnecessary — an IBM euphemism that implies
even the word 'union' is unwelcome.

Underneath the layer of ideology, there lurks a near-hysteria, characterized by crisis reactions to the slightest threat, and a belief throughout the company that one way to get fired is to have a part of the organization under your management unionized. No one was ever actually fired on this basis because no part of IBM (Domestic) was ever unionized — but the idea lives on in IBM's management mythology.

You *can* get fired for trying to organize a union, or even an employee group. In 1971 George King in Mobile, Alabama, tried to form an employee group (or 'company union') called the '101 Percenters'. He is no longer with IBM, though his efforts to form the group continued. According to *Datamation*[6] another man named Brian Cunningham in San Jose tried to form a group called the 'IBM Norcal Employees Association'. One of the aims stated in his first circular was to 'assure that employees who voluntarily leave IBM receive at least normal severance pay'. Another was to 'establish a totally new grievance procedure as a viable substitute to the Open Door (it leads to the street) or Speak-Up! (and be put down) programmes.' With the dual crimes on his head of attacking sacred institutions and proposing a union-like organization, it was little wonder that he rapidly resigned (voluntarily of course — 'to pursue other interests' the company said.

The corporation has a labour relations department in New York, headed by a former labour relations consultant who goes around advising IBM managers how to cope with potential 'situations'. As one European expressed it: 'The basic position taken by our labour people, no matter what question you raise with them, is to tell you not to do it. They sound like lawyers or doctors. "Don't", they say. "You can't!" "Impossible!" "Illegal!" Most of the experienced managers pin them down about the shades of grey and the specifics and then make their own decisions.'

The headquarters labour relations people get very uncomfortable whenever European personnel people put out a questionnaire with union-related questions; some of the European questionnaires (notably in the UK) have been very direct, to an extent that might be construed as a 'union election' under the stringent American laws.

The laws differ *drastically* from country to country. In the United States it is almost a binary situation — you either negotiate with unions or you don't. Companies could negotiate voluntarily, but nobody ever does, so there is a very clear yes-or-no answer to the question 'Are we to have a union?' Only where such a clear-cut system exists can one say 'IBM is not organized' — as indeed it is not in the United States. On the other hand, in Sweden, whether IBM is 'organized' or not, about 25 percent of the employees belong to unions. ('Belonging to unions in Sweden is like belonging to the Republican Party in Westchester County,' said one graduate.) Even the CEs in Sweden have a 'club'. Many workers in Germany, France or Italy belong to unions, but the unions seldom bargain directly with IBM; instead they bargain collectively, with all the companies in an industry; then the individual companies can pay more, but not less, than the agreed rate. In those countries IBM often pays exactly the agreed rate to most employees.

IBM is a strong company and in most places unions are un-likely to give it problems. It could afford to ignore these industry-wide agreements, to which it is seldom a signatory. But it does not. In Germany, for example, when the metal trades association (the employer group to which IBM belongs) called a lockout during one set of union negotiations in 1968. IBM closed entirely for one day, then reopened its doors to essential maintenance people and pressed the other employers (most of them customers) for a rapid settlement. To the relief of Paris and Armonk, the lockout was over in less than three days. IBM's action strengthened the union position; this didn't bother IBM much — a fear of unions is not necessarily a hatred of unions. The important thing to the company was its image with its own employees.

The British situation has been intriguing. 'It's remarkable that IBM could avoid unions at Greenock,' commented Charley Smith, who observed some of the crises at Greenock when he worked with Jones in the sixties. Encouraged by the government the Old Man picked a location in the heart of Scotland's 'red Clydeside', one of the parts of the UK most troubled by industrial unrest. With skilled unemployment high, he reasoned that it is easier to have noticeable success if you start with abject failure. Yet Honeywell's factories at Newhouse, Bellshill and Uddington, in more serene parts of Scotland, suffered several months of strikes in the summer of 1972 in an uproar that eventually cost the company £7 per week per employee, the loss of 12 weeks' production and customers who didn't want to take chances with labour problems interfering with their delivery or service. ICL has also had strikes in the UK. Why not IBM?

The Greenock plant had a history of crises, but they came at opportune times. Greenock was making keypunch equipment (and feeling unimportant in the IBM technology hierarchy) well into the computer era; IBM had Greenock under serious consideration for shutdown for quite a while in the sixties. But the man running the plant at the time was a charismatic Scot (albeit an American Scot, like the Old Man), and beloved by most of his employees. He won for his plant the right to make the first 650 computers in Europe. When he died IBM had the sense to replace him with another Scot. 'It was just a series of happy accidents that we weren't unionized at Greenock,' said one IBM UK man.

There is another factor that differentiates IBM from all the other computer companies who have suffered labour unrest in the UK. The other companies didn't have IBM's personnel policies, or managers who knew how to make them work.

The IBM UK organization is still non-union, and the IBM UK company keeps its ear very close to the ground, surveying opinions more often than some other countries, task-forcing any potential problem, correlating on its computers the answers to those uncomfortable union-related questions. It also spends far more on external affairs than most IBM companies. In 1973 Clive Jenkins, fiery leader of the Association of Scientific, Technical and Managerial Staffs (ASTMS), made a speech referring to IBM as a 'friendly, affectionate organization which is about to be organized.' He continued: 'IBM is no longer an island surrounded by a cordon sanitaire.' The corporation hardly winked an eye. 'Company policy in the UK is that membership in a union is a purely personal matter,' said a serene voice from the press office. 'IBM's stance is based on respect for the individual; we neither encourage nor discourage our employees to take up union membership.'

Jenkins had claimed that the computer industry was 'utterly vulnerable' to trade unions — and demonstrated by organizing 1,100 NCR CEs a month later. But IBM's 'vulnerability' consisted of less than ten union members among the 2,000 employees at Greenock; not one of them turned out for an ASTMS organizing meeting called soon after Jenkins's speech.

One graduate with experience in a number of countries saw three reasons for IBM's relatively union-free situation. First, IBM pays well. Second, it takes great pains to have a well-publicized and adequate grievance procedure. The third reason the insider sees is IBM's management: 'You can't get away with being an autocratic sonofabitch in IBM. You'd be fired in microseconds. The company has a fundamentally decent management.' Another

World Trade graduate had his own ranking of the reasons for IBM's union-free position. Like his colleague he cited the good pay. Then he said: 'Don't forget that IBM has almost always had a huge backlog of orders. The result? No layoffs. And IBM's retirement, health and other benefits are not only superior but free. In Maslow's terms, unions exist to provide their members with safety, security and justice. IBM has filled these needs for years. So what does a union organizer have left to offer IBM employees?

The unions in such countries as Germany are strong, and IBM treats them with great respect. In France the IBM magazine is published in connection with the comité d'entreprise, a form of works council. During the general industrial uproar of May 1968, IBM France's manufacturing employees rejected a strike proposal. Even so, the company increased its watchfulness by creating a personnel manager, Manufacturing, at IBM Europe's Paris head-quarters to keep an eye on the labour situation and 'monitor employee morale, utilization and full employment'.

The only country where IBM was ever subjected to an individual strike (as opposed to an industry-wide strike) was Japan. There the company had done an excellent job of bridging an enormous cultural gap between American and Japanese ways (although Antony Jay and Drucker say Japan's values such as loyalty and the view of the paternal company are quite similar to IBM's own internal values). From the start IBM observed the customs of each country. Japan was highly unionized. There was a constant striving to bring salesmen and middle managers into the unions. When IBM suffered its strike there it was a direct result of cultural conflict. An American was sent over as sales manager, without too much experience outside Domestic. When he arrived he was aghast to find that the IBM Japan salesmen were not being paid on the standard commission basis — one of the Old Man's most sacred precepts for motivating salesmen. There were cultural reasons for the difference, but the new manager in Japan referred to them as 'nonsense' and insisted on changing the pay basis immediately. Not too surprisingly, there was an immediate strike. Not too surprisingly, the shock troops from World Trade headquarters were on the next plane to Tokyo. All the salesmen were back at work the next day. The man had to change his mind and his policy, thus 'losing face' publicly. He was packed off to the United States rapidly. As one veteran expressed it: 'A gradual change is OK out there, but if you're proposing an overnight change you'd better think again.'

The Philippines situation proved very delicate. 'It's easy to understand that Japan is different from New York or California,' said another graduate. 'It *looks* different. But the Philippines are more difficult. The place seems so American. When you drive around Manila, unless you get into the barrios, it looks like Los Angeles. But the Filipinos are *not* Americans. The American overlay is only skin deep. Under that you find a feudal Spanish pattern. Beneath that layer is yet another — the Malay and Chinese ways of doing things. Beneath those you find a primitive tribal culture. The country is over-populated, under-developed, and yet it is over-educated. It has one of the world's largest universities, which means there is an enormous number of graduates with no place to go.'

Philippine labour law is, at least on the surface, similar to that of the United States, with similar provisions for union elections. One day in the early sixties, IBM suddenly heard that more than 30 percent of its Filipino employees had signed a request for a union election. Tom Junior was understandably upset, and assigned a personnel professional by the name of Walter Pedicord to the task.

The Philippine company at that point had about 200 employees, clustered in a 'compadre system' of intertwining groups related to the regions or villages of the workers. A fellow-villager already employed puts in the good word to get his friend a job, and thus creates a bottomless obligation; as the process continues a network of such obligations grows up. 'The compadre system is the most powerful thing I've ever come across,' commented a man who was there in the late sixties. 'You couldn't keep secrets, not even salaries. On payday people gathered in groups of five or ten and all gave their paycheques to one member to take them to the bank. It is impossible to build a management structure on the basis of confidential information in this environment.'

When Pedicord arrived in Manila he decided the best course was to hold in-depth interviews with every employee — a huge job, but the only way to establish the real reasons for the seemingly superficial grievances. Management/employee communications were obviously at a low ebb, so he did the interviews himself.

One factor that had led to the trouble, as it turned out, was a fine new office across the street from the plant, to which José Arguelles, the president, had recently moved. 'Joe was kind of like a father figure to everybody,' said the American. 'He used to walk up and down and call everybody by their first names. When he moved with his staff across the street people felt cut off from him.' Then there was the problem of pay. The employees *felt* under-paid, whether they were or not, because they had adopted the standards of the rich parent company and tended to compare themselves to the Americans rather than fellow Filipinos. They were also demanding fringe benefits they already had! In other words, once communications were cut off between the managers and the workers, the highly political cliques began to buzz with conflicting rumours, some of the most agitated or agitating types called the union in, and the employees were promised (or promising themselves) the moon.

Pedicord believed that the majority of employees did not want a union, but the political situation was so intense and security so lax that he did all his real communication with New York from his hotel room rather than the IBM offices. Then he did two things to improve communications. First he had a Filipino appointed personnel manager, and gave top priority to a simple brochure that told the employees what their benefits already were. Then, making use of the lax security system and grapevine that characterized the operation, he wrote a memo to Arguelles, outlining what IBM planned to do to rectify the problems if the union lost the election. The memo was straight-forward, stating IBM's intention to encourage a free election. Arguelles would spend more time with his people. It also mentioned across-the-board rises for the (not quite underpaid) workforce, improvements in benefits, and much stricter adherence to the IBM personnel policies that had kept unions out every-where else.

The memo hadn't been on Arguelles's desk for more than half a day before the word spread through all the compadre groups. When the union election was held shortly thereafter, the union lost. Pedicord stayed to make sure the IBM promises became fact, then went back to New York 'covered with glory'. As one observer commented: 'When you mention Pedicord's name in the Philippines now it's as if you were talking about God. They were overjoyed when he was appointed personnel director for World Trade.' (He was later the first personnel professional to hold the corporate post of vice president, Personnel. All his predecessors in the position had come up through sales.)

The Philippines remained a hotbed of personnel problems. At one time a manager's life was threatened by an unhappy and 'not-too-stable' employee who had been promised some management training. When the tea-break hours were changed there were troubles. Whenever a breath of union involvement cropped up again the task forces flew in, surveying and memoing each other. When Americans arrived with too-rapid changes, local managers would threaten noisy resignations or Dear-Tom letters.

The problems in Europe now come from national differences inside IBM more than union organizers outside. 'The fear of unions, like the paternalism, is a little out of date now,' said one of the company's personnel managers in Europe. 'Europeans are not as afraid of unions as the Americans; unions are different here.' Times are changing. Whether or not IBM has kept up with them in Europe, there are signs of greater openness about unions. At Blaricum, for example, a Dutch union leader now goes in regularly to talk to IBM managers during their four-week training sessions. Most of them think that the fact he is invited to do so marks a more more open attitude in Paris, if not Armonk.

Another European went to a personnel gathering in New York. 'One executive lectured to us about unions, making it clear that in his view they were bad,' he later commented angrily. 'We looked at each other, shocked. It was as if we were in the Congo and he was dishing out advice suited to Eskimos.'

Scandinavia, for example, has had unions for many years. 'Many American managers regard the presence of the union as a failure of management,' said a Swedish IBM man. 'In Sweden it is not. In most Swedish companies 95 percent of the blue collar workers and 60 percent of the white collar workers belong to unions. In IBM Sweden our percentages are 25 and 20 respectively.' This kind of situation puts pressure on the general manager and personnel managers, squeezed between the IBM culture and the national culture, forced to translate all the US policies and expectations to the local companies where there are unions. One Scandinavian graduate said: 'You always had the feeling that once you had 'let' the union into your IBM company, the boys from Paris would come swooping in at every little flurry. You were guilty unless proven innocent.'

'My introduction to IBM was a month at World Trade head-quarters in New York,' a Swedish personnel man said. 'I had already read about the personnel policies, and I still remember those main points as we heard them in New York: respect for the individual, justice in promotions, good working conditions, good communications, good opportunities. All those words really meant something to me. They coincided with my own viewpoint and the Swedish pattern I already knew. I was enthusiastic at the idea of really putting the sound and valuable personnel policies of IBM into practice to a greater extent. However, very soon I found out my real job was to translate the New York and Paris intentions into the Swedish pattern — but dealing with unions was a natural way of doing business in Sweden. The CEs are even unionized, under the white collar union. Just before I arrived IBM had had some trouble with a union which interfered with the tough, hard IBM management style. When I joined I was already a marked man among the other personnel people because they knew we had unions and union troubles . . . Why didn't they use Sweden as a pilot country to implement participation in depth and learn how to work *with* unions?' They did not, and he eventually went to a company that did.

IBM's cooperation with the unions finally improved when IBM entered the Swedish Employers' Association in 1970, an act which came about after a certain amount of public and government pressure. But Swedish unions were still treated as an 'issue' with task forces and MRC discussions well into the seventies. One possible rationale for IBM's aversion to working with the union in a country like Sweden is the fear that unions in other countries might use the Swedish case as an argument for their own advancement. 'Yes, Armonk is *that* sensitive to unions,' commented an American.

Under the serene 'It's the employee's own business' exterior, IBM continued to take a hard line about union membership wherever it could. One European personnel manager complained: 'I often had trouble explaining the IBM policy, with its heavy US emphasis, compared to our own pattern. Again and again a CE or plant worker would come into my office asking: "What's wrong with being a member of the union? All my colleagues in other companies are members; why can't I join?" The way we handled it, under US instructions, was to maintain a separate list of the union people. They had no promotions. The men in New York told us that our policy must be to manage the company so people wouldn't go into the unions.'

Just as the fear of being broken up keeps IBM's monopolistic tendencies under control better than any breakup the US anti-trust troops could devise, so the fear of being unionized seems to have a profound effect on the company's personnel policies — a greater effect than any union could actually bring about within the company. This means, of course, that IBM's non-union employees in most countries are benefiting from the dues that union members in other companies pay. On the other hand, the examples IBM sets to other companies in personnel may help offset this 'free ride'.

'IBM doesn't have to talk to anybody'

IBM's press corps has sometimes been called the corporation's 'internal CIA'. According to Tom Junior, IBM's reticence in dealing with the press stems from 1966, when *Fortune* published two articles about the 360 gamble and the internal debates that surrounded it. For the preceding ten years IBM had been shy but not opaque. But when these articles appeared, with quotes like 'We called it "You bet your company" ' and ' . . . blood all over the floor' Tom Junior's temper flared up. 'And when the chairman sneezes, the office out in Dallas or somewhere tends to explode,' he said wryly a few years later. Whatever the cause, IBM began to build up an almost impenetrable wall around the company, whose press corps serve as the infantry platoon guarding it, and do it so tactfully that the hordes of journalists outside don't usually realize the wall exists.

This is one of the curious anomalies about IBM — that one of the world's most successful and ethical corporations, with one of the finest internal communication systems, should be so paranoid about the press. The press corps is literally the tip of the communications iceberg. In IBM UK, for example, there are 50 people in the various parts of the communications department; only five of them are in the press office. IBM Netherlands has a similar ratio at 30 to 3. So do most other country organizations. Yet these few press officers have the monumental task of controlling all information that flows outside. In the United States the press officers have to handle a new inquiry on average every ten minutes of every working day. The amount of behind-the-scenes research and top-level task-forcing that goes into a minor response is awesome. In smaller countries press officers receive fewer inquiries, but the lines to headquarters are longer, so the workload is still overwhelming.

IBM publishes a demure guide for its employees, making it clear that journalists are *not* welcome inside the wall. 'The handbook doesn't say half of it,' a former press officer commented. 'It's all toned down in case the handbook itself leaked to the press. Communications actually maintains an iron grip over the rest of the company, with severe penalties for stepping out of line.'

IBM seems to believe that a well-documented trickle of technical information is all that it owes the outside world. However, this limited 'cooperation' is not sufficient to keep the more intrusive questions (or questioners) at bay. At one point the handbook admits: '. . . we usually make news when we want to, occasionally when we don't want to, and often whether we want to or not.' The company's philosophy about the press is politely summed up: 'We try to cooperate with the press, but we place the interests of the company above their interests.'

IBM has both cultural and practical reasons for this reticence. One that carries great weight inside is 'risk of exposure' — simply the worry that one of the quarter-million employees will inadvertently tell the press too much about what is going on inside, or that something will raise levels outside curiosity. Men who are known to be outspoken are not always permitted to attend symposia or conferences where they might meet the press, and delicate negotiations are carried out over every article that is published with an IBM by-line. The worries about risk of exposure have been particularly strong since the onset of anti-trust lawsuits in late 1968.

The Old Man once said to a press officer: 'If you tell the truth you never have to remember what you said.' But the press man read into this a further silent comment: 'That didn't mean you had to tell *all* the truth.' The press handbook includes another guideline: 'We believe in the principles of a free press, but we also believe we are not always obligated to respond to the press and are free to remain silent.' The company's preference for opaqueness was most succinctly expressed by a senior communications man named Dick Wight when an Armonk group was discussing an earlier book about the company:[7] 'IBM doesn't have to talk to *anybody*,' he decided firmly.

The influence of the two Thomas Watsons is still strong in IBM public relations. After the Old Man's NCR exposure to press criticism, he believed that reputation was everything. This was expressed during his era in the neatness he demanded from his presentable men, the well-publicized grand gestures or good deeds, and the gush of internal and external publicity from IBM. Much of the publicity centred on himself. No speech went unrecorded for posterity, at least in IBM journals or books. No award or honour went unphotographed. His anger at slighting comments in the press could be awesome, and journalists who incurred his wrath became non-people.

After the Old Man died in 1956 Tom Junior quietly clamped

down on the IBM machinery for turning out lavish copy to the outside world. *Think* became less a Watson organ and more a journal of think-pieces: articles about executive intuition or Peter Drucker's views on education replaced the Watson speeches and flag-waving editorials of the earlier days. *World Trade News* quickly toned down on old-fashioned typography as well as Watson photos and speeches, but kept up its steady flow of news about IBM sports, Hundred Percent Clubs, promotions and achievements. After 1957 it was no longer sent outside the company. Tom Junior started his tenure with a low-profile approach to the press. Dick Watson followed suit, and IBM's stance has remained that way ever since, amplified since the mid-sixties into an attitude approaching benign paranoia.

Adding to the cultural factors was the growing concern about government regulation. As IBM shares doubled, split and doubled again, it became a very popular stock on Wall Street. IBM became more important as computers became more important. Its announcements were major events in the financial community. The US Securities and Exchange Commission has very strict rules about publicity or 'insider trading' in publicly held shares. Thus the role of the press corps became even more CIA-like — to prevent any leak to the press or to investors before products were ready to be announced.

IBM has another practical reason for its reticence with the press: simple embarrassment. Tom Junior was embarrassed, I believe, at his father's sometimes overflowery and over-publicized announcements and pronouncements. So the son adopted a quieter attitude to publicity — the same low profile that characterized his architecture.

Top management reticence to talk to the press is even more understandable. The IBM executive contract filed with the US Securities and Exchange Commission in 1968 includes the following statement:

> Item 9 (c): The executive shall not, without prior written authorization from the company, disclose to any person outside the employ of the company any of the confidential affairs, policies or operations of the company or its subsidiaries, including confidential matters relating to the inventions and engineering, production, financial, purchasing, and sales development work of the company or its subsidiaries.

Every executive who goes on the bonus plan signs this contract.

Each of them also understands that 'confidential' applies to most matters at IBM. Industrial espionage is fairly common in the computer industry, and 'trade secrets' are usually considered to be technical. But IBM's real trade secrets are the means by which it motivates its sales organizations and builds its products profitability — concepts no competitor has yet managed to copy even though IBM is often happy to talk about them.

The close attitudes of the executives could do nothing to stop what *Business Week* called 'the greatest breach of security ever to occur in US industry.' During the 1973 trial of the lawsuit filed against IBM by Telex, the judge decided that 40,000 pages of internal IBM documents should become a matter of public record.[8] These papers included not only the technical plans for existing and proposed products, but also the minutes of the top level MRC and the MC. Whether Hubner, Hume, Cary or Jones chose to speak to the outside or not, their inside discussions were suddenly visible to outsiders. The press naturally had a field day with the material.

Individual employees are also embarrassed to be mentioned in the press. Being quoted is *not* a good thing. As one veteran said: 'If an article makes you a hero, you are anything but a hero in the eyes of your associates, who really did the majority of the work. Articles tend to put credit or blame on one person.'

'Blame' is another concept that keeps IBM people quiet. For every slip of the corporate tongue, a scapegoat is found. Often the slip is on the part of the journalist, not the interviewee. Nonetheless, somebody has failed in the task of educating the journalist properly or speaking in a manner that cannot be misunderstood. Thus IBM people are often grateful for IBM's tendency to shepherd them through every interview. In most foreign countries, the IBM general managers, no matter how eminent, seldom give interviews to the press without the watchful attendance of their shepherds.

It is intriguing to watch IBM tidying up after what it considers to be a faux pas in the press. In 1960, for instance, *Life* magazine did a cheerful little piece called 'Oasis for a Top Salesman', which showed an IBM salesman after a tough and fruitful tour of duty in Central Africa, enjoying an outing in Paris. Most of the photos dealt with his work but one showed him at the Lido Club with dancing girls in the background; the article stated his boss was footing the bill for the outing. An American schoolteacher who was on holiday in Paris saw the article and complained to Tom

Junior. Though IBM seldom responds publicly to even the most damning press comments, the next issue of *Life* carried a letter from IBM denying that the boss paid for the night-life.

An even more curious example occurred in 1972, when *Fortune* ran a major article about the pay scales for black employees of American companies in South Africa. IBM not only came out on top of the pay-scale charts, but the article also showed that IBM paid its black employees almost twice the average rates of most US companies. The article was illustrated with several photos of black and white IBM people working together, but had only one nondescript quotation from Maurice Cowley, managing director of IBM South Africa. In terms of world opinion, the article was deservedly 'good press'. Yet the next issue of *Fortune* carried a letter from Learson himself. IBM's chairman first corrected the journal's estimate that IBM was paying all _ blacks 'over $200' a month, pointing out that a few had salaries between $170 and $180 (still above the poverty line and the other companies surveyed). Then the Learson letter carefully clarified that one secretary who had been identified in a caption as having two bosses (one white and one black) was actually working only for the white man, but she handled both his secretarial assignments and those of his black subordinate. For a company with IBM's equal opportunity policies this careful re-wording seemed strange, until viewed in the context of South African business. Clearly IBM would be in trouble with the national government there if both the wage leadership and the situation of a white woman working for a black man were allowed to go unchallenged, no matter how well they fit the corporate ethics. Therefore, IBM business took precedence over good press.

Then there are letters — from employees, shareholders, or members of the public. 'We never ignore letters,' said one top communications man. 'We answer letters most companies would throw away.'

In addition to all their other activities the press officers must keep track of non-words. At one time, for example, Corporate Communications decided that the term 'information utility' no longer existed in the IBM vocabulary — because utilities in the United States are regulated. The wires around the IBM world hummed with messages, and every press officer had to convey to every internal author or speaker word about the non-word. Every article and speech that an IBM man makes outside is checked by a communications expert, not only for non-words but for ambiguities, and to make sure the corporate low profile is intact.

For most authors the situation is simple: go through the approval process, speak anonymously, or both! Gellerman's 1963 best-seller *Motivation and Productivity* doesn't even have an index entry for IBM.

The press officers keep close track of every mention in the press, not only of IBM but any other issue or company related to the computer industry. In one country the press office keeps a monthly score card of the number of references to each company in the industry, graded as to content. Thus in one November IBM had 149 favourables, 167 neutrals and 42 unfavourables, while in the same month Honeywell had 51 favourables, 40 neutrals and 2 unfavourables. So the press officers must read every paper every day, anticipate any future inquiry that might stem from any of the articles, and prepare answers just in case the inquiry is made.

If this description of their tasks makes the IBM press officers sound like overworked ogres, guarding some corporate treasure, that is only true in the general sense. Individually they are pleasant, intelligent, tactful people who are trying to be helpful to the greatest extent possible — within the corporation's impossible limits. One of the most impressive things about their work (usually invisible to the press) is the amount of homework they put into each inquiry or event. Like the press office relationship to the communications group, this is the other nine-tenths of an iceberg. At one time, for example, a member of the UK communications group wrote a speech for a senior executive to present to an out-side body — the usual impassioned plea for the multinational company, carefully tailored for the individual audience. Then another man in the press office was assigned to anticipate any possible hostile comment from the popular national press. His response was written as though it were a *Daily Mail* leader. The speech was then denuded of all the items he had used as 'pegs' for the dummy hostile editorial.

The word from the watchdogs is 'don't phone us, we'll phone you.' The press handbook for employees is clear about the IBM employee's role in press relations. In almost every case the instruction is to notify the press office rather than answer even the simplest question directly. The handbook warns: 'Unless you are sure you are completely within your area of authority and certain of your facts, either limit your comments or don't comment at all, explaining it would be inappropriate to do so. It is perfectly acceptable to get the reporter's name, paper, and his deadline and promise him he will be called. In fact *buying time* [my italics] in this manner is usually the wisest course.' The employee understands the implicit message: 'If you are quoted, it's your neck!' For those exposed to interview situations, there are nine additional 'tips' for dealing with the press:

1. Deny firmly (or say you don't know, but someone who does will call back).

2. Deny as quickly as possible.

3. Don't gossip.

4. Treat 'no comment' gingerly. (They prefer 'It is our policy not to discuss things of this nature.')

5. Watch colourful language.

6. Watch for questions starting 'I have heard . . . ' (Don't confirm reporters' guesses.)

7. Don't comment on competitors.

8. Don't speak for others. (The correct answer is 'You'll have to ask him that question.')

9. Don't tell a reporter to phone someone else in the company. (Instead tell the reporter you'll have someone else phone him.)

The preparations the press officer puts into an interview are monumental. From the reporter's point of view, the press officer has set up the time and place, meets him at the door or takes him to the location if it is out of town, and introduces him to the chosen people, then sits quietly through the interview, buys the reporter a drink afterwards, and goes home. The truth is quite different. From the first inquiry a file begins to build up. Do we want to talk about the subject? If so is this the right journal or journalist? If so, to whom should we expose the outsider? Then the press officer goes through delicate negotiations (often so casual and friendly that the journalist does not realize he is being interviewed himself). What specific questions do you want to ask? (Vague answers make IBM press officers perspire.) Could we have an outline of the ground you want to cover, so we can get together all the background information you will need? That is the important question. Their definition of 'all the information' is a maximum; the journalist usually thinks it is a minimum. From all this they make up a 'Q&A', a question and answer sheet, including all the questions the journalist is likely to ask (including the devilish ones they can infer or dream up from the subject matter as well as those he has revealed). The Q&A lists the right answers to any that might require delicate handling. If he has given them a detailed list, then any deviation can be handled simply by saying 'Oh, we weren't prepared for that. We'll get back to you tomorrow.' If he has been vague, it is harder, because the company tries to preserve the image of openness (the innocent 'I don't know' rather than the ominous 'no comment').

Once the Q&A has been prepared (and checked by other members of the press corps and management), the interviewee usually memorizes it. Often the answers to certain touchy questions must be worded exactly, for maximum privacy, yet these answers must be delivered with a casual openness as if they just popped to the IBM man's tongue. His limits have been discussed with his superiors and the press office watchdogs, and certain un-touchy areas (sometimes quite newsworthy) will have been prepared as diversions. The open, candid, relaxed manner of the ensuing well-rehearsed interview is usually a joy to behold.   .

'Control' and 'delay' are the keywords in IBM's public relations. Even so, in its dealings with journals the company is absolutely ethical and above-board. The response may be silence or a 'don't know', but they don't tell lies. They understand and respect deadlines, and go out of their way to be helpful when they can. Direct complaints to superiors or pressures on journalists through use of IBM's large advertising budgets are rare — much more so than in sales! However, the press officers *do* have one weapon: a sad, almost wifely expression clearly translatable as How-could-you-do-this-to-me? when they encounter their counterparts in the fourth estate after a particularly devastating article.

Mutual respect exists between the two groups. IBM sometimes 'plants' an article written by a 'tame' journalist. Most editors don't mind these because they are relatively free of puff, and guaranteed to be accurate and informative once they reach the editor's desk. The other side of the planted article is the quiet knowledge among technical journalists that if one loses one's job IBM will be along rapidly with lunch and at least some sympathetic noise about the possibility of freelance assignments writing such articles — a friendly kind of social security for an insecure profession. Its fair and impartial administration over the years shows this to be a gentle and charitable practice rather than an attempt to control what is written by the journalists while they are fortunate enough to be employed.

While the press officers are impeccable in resisting the temptation to exert influence on the journalists, one can occasionally catch a glimpse of top-level chats that may have influenced editorial policy. In the April 1973 *Fortune*, for example, an article about the soaring legal costs for American corporations carried photos of a number of leading corporate lawyers — but nowhere in their number could one find Nicholas Katzenbach, the former US Attorney General who leads IBM's legal troops. Nor was there any reference to IBM's legal expenses (sometimes estimated around $200 million a year), though one anonymous company in the *Fortune* top 1,300 survey was said to spend more than $10 million a year for in-house lawyers. This oversight seemed particularly strange at a time when IBM's legal budget was being debated by a US Senate subcommittee on multinational activities, where one witness had testified that IBM spent more on lawyers than the US Justice Department itself. Another 'oversight' occurred several months later when *Fortune* ran a major story about multinationals, listing the foreign trade balances of more than 100 international corporations; included on the list were Honeywell and Remington Rand — but IBM was strangely missing.

When the lights in the IBM buildings burn late, they are often the lights in the press offices. A Sunday article sends every press officer scurrying into conference, so the Monday papers have IBM's denial or clarification, and every involved executive knows by heart the answers to the inevitable questions.

The crises themselves sometimes have a funny IBM-ish complexion. One Friday, several years before IBM went into the copier business, the shares of Xerox Corporation plunged sharply due to rumours that IBM was going to enter the copier field. An alert press officer, realizing that many innocent Xerox shareholders would sell and lose money for no good reason, got on the phone and managed to find Tom Junior, who was in the Maine woods over the weekend. The press man explained the situation and got Tom Junior's consent to a story denying the rumours. This was fed to the press in time for Monday morning's papers. Xerox stock promptly recovered and the potential damage was minimized.

The question of how IBM *should* deal with the press is not easily resolved; any lessening of control or opening of outside information channels will take place slowly and gradually. The real exposure IBM suffered in the Telex trial may have ameliorated the fear of 'risk of exposure' somewhat; experiencing the thing one fears is one way to bring excessive anxiety within more normal bounds. But press policy is a legitimate problem. IBM is a successful company, always in the public eye. Every time it deals with a journalist it is exposing itself. There is always more danger than benefit to the company in a press situation. As one executive put it: 'We have to decide how far we are going to open the kimono.'

The all-encompassing kimono is closed tight over some perfectly respectable portions of the IBM anatomy. Time after time as I did research for this book I found policies, systems or practices that were ahead of their times. Invariably those who had created the systems or set up the procedures were sorry that their achievements had not been recognized by their professional colleagues outside IBM. The hardest things to find out about were those which any other company would brag about — the Good Deeds. This degree of modesty seems unnecessary. The bad news gets out anyway; every time a small group of employees is disgruntled enough about something, some journal stands by to take up their case. But this is one of the few companies that could *afford* to stand up under close scrutiny, to live in a glass house.

10
IBM's future

Long before it was fashionable to talk about
corporate responsibility, the Old Man extended the normal view
and talked about a firm's responsibility to its employees and
customers as well as its shareholders. Then in the McKinsey lectures
in 1962[1] Tom Junior added a fourth element — the company's
responsibilities to the public or national interest.

Bigness itself is a relatively new phenomenon in our society.
Even if nothing else had changed, the vast concentrations of
power in our society would demand that businessmen reconsider
their responsibilities for the broader public welfare. I believe we're
going to have to ask ourselves a little more seriously if what we
are planning to do in our business decisions is as good for the
employees as it is for the stockholders — and as good for the
country as it is for both these groups.
Business is subject not only to existing law — but to the tolerance
of the public. Lawful or not, if business does things which the
public regards as wrong and abusive, that public has the power
to demand new laws with which business will have to comply.

Using the example of anti-trust laws, he went on to give a
practical rationale for public involvement. In essence, he said that

more businesses fail because they are *behind* their times than those who have been ahead of them. But business was still his prime concern: 'If the businessman fails at business, then all his other concerns will mean nothing, for he will have lost the power to do anything about them.'

'Doing well by doing good . . .'

IBM views 'Social Responsibility' as a simple business necessity. Every IBM employee knows that he can devote up to 10 percent of his working time to community projects, so long as his manager approves. To disapprove, an IBM manager would have to be able to show his superiors that the work in hand had over-riding importance (a difficult point to make in IBM's culture) or that the suggested project was not actually helpful in the community, in which case useful ideas might be put forward to improve it. The employees can also apply for IBM grants for $100 to $1,000 in the United States for projects in which they are personally involved. In its first six months in 1972–3 this Fund for Community Service was used for 650 projects in 260 communities.

The good works were originally paternalistic, in keeping with the Old Man's own style, and his experience with the Dayton flood. Tom Junior shifted from his father's more flamboyant posture of public involvement to his own low-profile approach that emphasized the need for skills as much as for money in public affairs. Leaves of absence were given for full-time positions in federal, state and local government agencies as well as charities, with guaranteed re-entry and continuous service credit for up to two years — sometimes four if the project were a Really Good Thing. Peace Corps or VISTA service was accorded the same blessing. Domestic often made up the difference between a low salary in such a public service appointment and the more municifent sum the involved IBMer was accustomed to, just as it did for military service. World Trade companies were encouraged to follow similar policies in their own countries. The leaves also eased the manpower stresses, so the MRC explored ways to make them more attractive in 1972.

IBM was one of the first employers to think about disabled employees. In 1943 the company's programme for handicapped workers was headed by a blind man; IBM was hailed in 1952, when it had 746 handicapped workers, for hiring 'on the basis of ability rather than disability'. In the sixties IBM was among the first US

corporations to use mentally retarded workers for the repetitive
assembly jobs which they enjoy and do well.

IBM's experience in community relations goes back a long way
to the days when the company constituted an overwhelming part
of the Poughkeepsie/Endicott area in New York. There is a
corporate policy that the IBM population should be a small proportion of any one community, to avoid the kind of dependence
that Seattle had, for example, on the Boeing Corporation. As a
result IBM tends to cluster in areas, but not specific towns. Once
Armonk and Westchester County in New York were close to this
saturation point, World Trade planned its new headquarters in
Mount Pleasant, a few miles farther out. IBM also had land in
Connecticut for further expansion. Hampshire in England is a
major IBM area, with the Hursley laboratories and the Havant
plant, but the IBM population spreads over a 30-mile area. In
Germany's twin towns of Sindelfingen and Boeblingen the IBM
people are dispersed among overshadowing hordes of Mercedes
employees.

Even little things — such as babies — can be IBM Good Deeds.
In 1972 when the black market price for white babies for
adoption in the New York area had soared to as much as $25,000
IBM changed its personnel policies so that all IBMers (male as
well as female) were entitled to adoption assistance in the United
States, on a level equal to IBM's maternity benefits (reimbursing
80 percent of the expenses up to a ceiling of $800). Around the
same time IBM was also proposing to help authorities set up
a national databank of parents and babies, so shortages like New
York's could be offset by surplus babies elsewhere. These socially
creative adoption ideas exemplify IBM's normal attitude to
personnel benefits — to lead, not follow. The cost of the adoption
assistance was estimated to be about $25,000 in the first year —
the cost of training one salesman. Yet that small investment would
ensure the devotion and loyalty of more than 30 IBM families.

Management contributions cover a wide span of activities,
unrelated to computers in most cases. Britain tends to lead the
corporation in its external affairs activities, partly due to the
commitment and energy of a dedicated IBMer named John
Hargreaves, supported staunchly by Parry Rogers and UK
general manager Eddie Nixon. Hargreaves set up a separate external
affairs group as early as 1966, and began to use *IBM UK News* to
encourage community participation. IBM UK was always an
outspoken, maverick member of the World Trade family, and led

the rest with its 10 percent rule-of-thumb for outside participation of employees. Some UK employees would like to see IBM, which spends 5 or 6 percent of its turnover on R&D, divert 1 or 2 percent to external affairs. That would be an overwhelming $100 to $200 million every year. Tom Junior has suggested that 1 or 2 percent of *profit* (still a healthy $30 to $60 million) could do a great deal of good. Already most country organizations in World Trade officially set aside about 0.5 percent of turnover for public affairs.

'Will success spoil IBM?'

We have explored the culture of IBM, the history of the highly motivated man who created the company and his sons who were brought up to carry on the culture and the company, and the behaviour patterns that are the secrets of IBM's success. One further enigma remains. As an irreverent graduate put it: 'If IBM is so super, why don't people love it?'

IBM is an emotive subject. Competitors 'talk to their shrinks about it', as one admitted. The graduate suggested some reasons that this huge company which tries to be good and Do Good is disliked more often than it is loved (except for self-love inside the walls). 'We don't love people who are terribly successful, nor those who are virtuous. Therefore we don't love IBM — rather like we don't love the Swiss. IBM has a lot of power, and it has an air of superiority which makes it hard to love, too. This isn't the sort of strident chauvinism you get from a couple of other computer companies. It's more like the quietly assumed superiority of the British in India, saying to themselves ". . . it isn't their fault they're not British".' Like the civilians in India, IBMers are intelligent and fairly civilized people. Similarly, they are noticeably incorruptible. It indoctrinates its people, but the doctrines it instils are good ones. Even so, more people object to the *fact* of indoctrination than to the content.

National government is an old concept. The power of nations was originally established by the land they held. Power today is much more related to information technology. The modern multinationals like IBM have mastered this technology more rapidly than most governments. They represent a new institution, able to carry information and money across national boundaries with ease — yet they behave according to centuries-old patterns.

In the past few years IBM has grown into an extreme example of an organization with an identity quite separate from those of its members. Thus one hears that 'IBM thinks this . . .' or 'IBM says that . . .' We seem to be moving towards a situation in which not even the Armonk clique really determines what IBM thinks, or what 'its' views are. As the Watsons become figures in IBM's history (or mythology), and as the poly-centric World Trade overtakes Domestic, 'it' takes on a life of its own. It begins to seem that *no one* controls IBM.

The few men in Armonk's interlocking committees are getting older. These men — the nearest one can find to a personification of 'IBM' — set the strategies. In recent years these have been reactions to outside forces far more than they have been initiating action for internal reasons. The men who are taking over from Tom Junior are gifted managers, powerful men, responsible citizens — but as products of IBM they tend to be organization men rather than innovators. The primary questions about IBM's future revolve around whether they can be encouraged to bring in young men and young ideas to their own meeting rooms, or to push down more of their functions onto younger shoulders at lower levels in the company. IBM needs a new flock of wild ducks.

My own prognosis about their ability to do so is not optimistic. I started my research reading a thousand pages of *World Trade News* from the fifties; they seemed cut off from reality. I finished it with a thousand pages of MRC and MC minutes from the seventies; they, too, seemed cut off from reality. The minutes are sterile, brief résumés of what actually takes place around the horseshoe tables of Armonk. Even so, they bring to life the nerve centre of IBM.

In MRC meetings of 1971 and 1972 there were flashes of humanity, notably when Tom Junior was there. Many of the discussions naturally centred on the problems of keeping the profit line going up at IBM's normal steady rate while doing business in the increasingly saturated computer market. But the MRC still found time to discuss the fate of 26 IBM employees in Bulgaria, or how the salesmen would feel if their Hundred Percent Club were cancelled.*

It was one step down, in the (now defunct) MC, that I felt uneasy. For hundreds of pages I read humourless summaries of current issues, yet something seemed to be missing, some sense of the life within IBM. These men seemed out of touch. In one 1971 meeting, for

*'But that's got a *lot* to do with profit!', exclaimed an irreverent graduate.

example, the MC heard that IBM's executives who were students at Sands Point had expressed concern that IBM managers seemed less committed to the corporation than ever before. The minutes said in classic IBMese:[2]

> Broadly, they concluded that while commitment is a personal thing, it could be defined as dedication to IBM's beliefs and principles as well as a willingness to pay a personal price for the benefit of the corporation. They think the prime causes for the decrease in commitment are:
>
> (a) Concern over credibility and fallibility
> (b) Bureaucracy and over-control
> (c) Environmental changes with resultant impact on growth potential.

The Sands Point students seemed to have encapsulated IBM's most serious concerns quite well. Yet the czar-like reaction of the MC members was less realistic. They said it was 'helpful' to hear this, but they felt that many of the concerns were based on 'naïveté or emotionalism'. Executive Dean McKay was assigned to give pep-talks (calling for 'more realistic communications') to the people who give presentations at Sands Point. This cosmetic brainwashing seemed to me to be begging the real issues. Rather than asking themselves whether they might indeed *be* overcontrolling, or too closed with respect to mistakes or future prospects, they reacted as if a teach-the-teachers technique would solve the 'problem'. Several months later one member of the MC complained that the quality of IBM's executive students at Sands Point was dropping.

As I see it, IBM faces three major problems in future years. They are *not* anti-trust, unions and economic nationalism. The more important and long-lasting problems will be:

* learning to live in the no-growth environment
* finding something useful to do with all that money, and
* fighting off bureaucracy with *real* reorganization

The first two will be problems for a long time, but IBM's superb problem-solving machinery should be able to cope with them. The minutes indicate that they have been task-forced since 1971, and sensible actions are already being taken on both fronts. The third problem — over-control from the centre — seems to become worse every time they do something about the first two. Yet this will be the crucial one. Yet why should they change a system that has worked so effectively in the past?

'Maturation equals saturation' one World Trade sales manager commented when he was pondering IBM's future. He thought that real saturation of the computer market could be delayed at least until after the year 2000. The Domestic market for IBM actually began to shrink in the late sixties. IBM's income and revenues kept rising, but the MRC noted that the growth came from selling more expensive systems to existing users. The company's percentage of new systems actually fell. IBM was losing market share. This is traditionally a terrible fear for executives. It may not be so terrible when it happens to an IBM under anti-trust pressure. If the company can accept the need to have a smaller market share, to keep from being broken up arbitrarily by outsiders, and still maintain a profit picture that is appealing to its investors, it might be healthier and more autonomous in the long term. It can also choose where to lose market share — in the least profitable sectors. In the UK, for example, one of the two countries in the world where IBM is not always the industry leader, IBM nonetheless dominates the most profitable sector: medium to large-scale commercial computing.

The market itself is changing. 'Computers are dead; you sell *systems* now,' said a graduate who designs systems for a competitor. 'We say "controller" instead of "computer" now, and we build our controllers into instruments or systems to do complete jobs. With the cost of computers dropping the way it is, they won't be very important in a few more years.' IBM recognizes this more diffuse market. All the recent plans that went through the MRC and MC emphasized three over-riding goals. The first was always to maintain IBM's role as a *total systems supplier*.* The second was to provide for continued growth; the third to redeploy excess resources (people and money).

These three goals are inter-related. As technology changes, IBM's decision in the sixties to become a manufacturing company turns inside out. Advances in the company's own research make it possible to manufacture more circuits with less people at lower cost,

*'An important part of the IBM sales policy,' commented the graduate. 'Especially because the individual boxes are so expensive compared to the competition.'

and the company shifts back from manufacturing to the 'total systems' posture, stressing service to the customer. The shift from manufacturing raises the question of how to resolve the Old Man's full-employment policy with the need to divert thousands of manufacturing people to other jobs.

Tom Junior focused on the no-growth problem in an MRC meeting on 23 April 1971. He insisted that IBM must 'swallow whatever financial pills are required now and get ready for the future'. He told the MRC: 'We can't have ourselves mesmerized by the balance sheet. Irrespective of financial considerations of one or two years, we must return this business to a growth posture and operate accordingly.'

'Growth is absolutely necessary'

With less of the market, less fluidity inside the company, and a sense of crisis at Armonk, there is a natural tendency to over-control from the centre. A system as huge and complex as IBM behaves like other complex systems — a living cell, the human anatomy, or the world's economic systems. A small change in one part can have unexpected and large effects in other parts of the system. The most important effect may be a fear-based tendency to revert from the posture of participation to one of autocratic management, all the way down the line. Although an autocratic stance may be the right short-term reaction, to assure IBM's normal unified and energetic response, it is unlikely to be best in the long term. The effects on morale were already noticeable in the 1972 attitude survey. People perceived their managers as more autocratic, more interested in enforcing the letter of the law than its spirit. More of them were apathetic about IBM. IBM takes its attitude surveys seriously, but some of the 'fixes' seemed more cosmetic than serious. Redesign of jobs, filling openings from inside, expanding the retraining — these all helped. But they did not change the structure or the culture. 'This happens with any growth company,' one expert commented. 'It has to stop growing or it becomes the whole world. When the growth slows down you begin to hold different kinds of people — those who are happy in a stable, non-growth environment.'

IBM itself doesn't necessarily accept the inevitability of a no-growth situation. The beliefs are still strong. Rather than stabilize permanently, it will go on looking for new growth. As Maisonrouge wrote in 1973:[3]

> This company has still the goal that it has always had: we want
> to grow. Growth is absolutely necessary. We are not satisfied
> with our present anticipated growth rates and we are working
> to make them higher. It's easier to manage a growing company
> than a company that stands still.

IBM's Midas touch gives it a lot of ready money with which to
explore diversification paths. But this richness has its drawbacks too.
As one American said: 'When that kind of company gets rolling, it
is unstoppable, and probably a natural monopoly. In the United
States, such companies are usually regulated or broken up.' Yet
like most well-to-do people, IBM is close-mouthed about its wealth
and very careful about the disposition of its pennies. Yet in 1972
IBM had more than $3,000 million in cash or near-cash, stashed
away in negotiable securities or reserve accounts for every possible
contingency. A 1973 article in a US trade journal said:[4]

> In 1972, IBM's cash and marketable securities increased by
> almost $1 billion, to a total of about $3.3 billion.
> If IBM were a bank, it would rank as one of the country's
> largest.
> But like a feudal baron in his sumptuous castle, under siege by
> his enemies, there is little IBM can do to employ its riches
> profitably. IBM has $3 billion in trapped riches.

This really was an embarrassment of riches — too much money
and too few places where the company could put it to work with
its customary skill. Some of it had to be kept in reserve in case the
anti-trust suits resulted in large fines, of course. But IBM is used to
a 25 or 30 percent pre-tax return in its traditional business. The
1972 interest income $191 million return on $2,900 million
investments) was only 6.6 percent. Finding places to sequester
the money profitably without drawing more attention from the
US anti-trust troops or foreign governments is one of the
challenges of the seventies. At the problem-solving level IBM
will probably succeed brilliantly; strategically, though, it may be
more important to accept a no-growth environment and learn
to live with it. Whatever growth there is will be outside the United
States which may be why they picked the president of IBM Europe,

Frank Cummiskey, to head the top level task force to explore diversification strategies.

As one eminent graduate said: 'The company's strength has been that it was never diversified. It had total concentration in terms of marketing. But that very strength can turn into a limitation. Now they have no basis or direction to diversify.' Thus, some of the ideas they came up with for diversification seemed slightly silly or out of scale. There was the TV maintenance venture, for instance, discussed by the MC in mid-1972. They looked carefully at the market for home typewriters, too, and even considered making electronic wrist-watches.

Maisonrouge proposed to the MRC that World Trade combine its 300-man real estate team with a financial institution like Lazard Frères in Europe to invest in existing or projected IBM facilities, for a 10 to 18 percent after-tax return and a chance to sidle into non-IBM property opportunities. The MRC turned down the plan because it worried about conflict of interest with the partner if IBM decided to terminate a lease. It also worried about minority ownership problems (IBM would always rather be in charge) and questioned the general attractiveness of real estate as an investment.

Acquisitions began to be considered seriously, even though the company prided itself on having done all its growth from within. The only acquisition it ever made was a technical publishing house called Science Research Associates. That was made almost by accident when one key executive, very much in vogue at the time, put all his energy behind the proposal when IBM had a lot of surplus cash at the end of the 1400 computer cycle. However, they could never expand the business because of anti-trust worries from other companies in the *publishing* business.

The fields in which serious diversification was most likely were telecommunications, office equipment, and such industry-specific applications as retail, hospitals, insurance and banking, with large requirements for special terminals. The competitors would less often be computer-makers. The growing emphasis on World Trade as a not-yet-saturated market as well as a test bed for these new markets brought more World Trade involvement in new products, and new World Trade attention to competitors.

'World Peace Through World Trade'

Economic nationalism is more important as an internal IBM stress than an external problem, though there are few signs that the men in Armonk recognize the fact. In mid-1971 the MC perceived the European general managers as a cohesive group — but thought they looked at New York and Armonk decisions as being in the interest of the United States. How to change the perception was again the MC's focus, not whether the perception was correct. Many of the stresses I found in talking to past and present IBM people revolved around this question of country organizations growing up and wanting greater autonomy, while the parents at Armonk put off as long as possible whatever emancipation was necessary.

IBM's greatest need is not for diversification or even continued growth, but for real reorganization. If it is to continue genuine growth the company must do this for itself, not as a brilliant strategy to cope with outside pressures like anti-trust or economic nationalism, but as a sincere response to internal needs for autonomy and involvement. One blueprint for such change comes from behavioural scientist Warren Bennis:[5]

> Perhaps there are forms of organic populism which can take place within the big corporations like GE or IBM. I think that it will be virtually necessary, if the companies want to attract the brightest and most creative of our young. There may be ways for the companies to provide cultural pluralism within their present framework. To set up mini-companies and economic boutiques which will have their own unique environments and goals within the framework of the parent company.

The stresses are not confined to the foreigners who want more national autonomy. Within a single company like IBM UK Ltd there are groups that complain they have too much control from Chiswick. One of the company's greatest strengths since the days of the Old Man has been the position of the branch manager. If the Catholic Church was the first multinational organization, it has always been one whose roots were in each village. In IBM the branch manager has always been the local priest. 'Five or ten years ago a branch manager was really something,' said one of the graduates. 'He had his fingerprints all over his organization. He doesn't have nearly the status or thrust now, and the situation is spreading to World Trade too. Somehow they need to restructure the organization so people can have fun again — restore the sense of involvement, the sense of importance.'

Yet in 1972, both in World Trade and Domestic, IBM was closing some branches and lumping others together, rather than pushing out more autonomy to the smallest possible unit. The short-term economies will cost far more than they saved. Keeping many small branches or even starting new ones may seem less efficient, but it is a necessary step. 'Less efficient' assembly groups have already shown their benefits in many IBM factories.

Most of all, society must find some way to turn IBM's magnificent machinery to its own ends. It would be a shame to see these strong, efficient mechanisms slow down, freeze up, and slowly (albeit richly) rust away. IBM is in no danger of failing. Technically it has already proved that it can no longer make major 'mistakes'. The sun will not set on the IBM empire in the foreseeable future. But the erosion that can set in along with bureaucracy would be more loss to society than to IBM's shareholders and employees.

The multinational corporations with their superb techniques are not answerable to the public. There is still a need for the less efficient but more accountable machinery of government. Now is the time for the public to begin putting the multinationals to use.

While governments keep their pressures on IBM for more national or local autonomy, gentler competitive practices, more cooperation in standard-setting, and continuation of its excellent personnel practices, they might consider broader policies too. If there were concerted action among European governments, for example, IBM in its present reactive state would probably go further towards a relatively autonomous IBM Europe with European shareholdings. Even a few shares in IBM Europe (rather than the parent corporation) held by outsiders would bring greater response from IBM's top men to European issues. (And Europe literally could not *afford* a majority offering all at one time.) Once there were shareholders it would be possible to erode IBM's traditional closed attitude towards the outside world in R&D, personnel, social responsibility, and publication of financial results (something IBM can afford to do more that most multinationals). This has already been discussed in the MRC, and IBMers like Maisonrouge have put their weight behind the concept internally, no matter how negative their outside postures. A little more pressure from outsiders (of course) would probably bring gradual concessions.

Somehow IBM's natural inclination to be a good corporate citizen in the Old Man's pattern should be encouraged in a positive way by all the countries which could benefit from IBM's administrative and management skills. The positive encouragement IBM understands best is profit. Small contracts to subsidize IBM people involved in community and education projects, for example, would bring a rapid and positive reaction from the company.

IBM understands that it cannot move too far away from the computer business, but it has administrative and management skills that would be a great addition to any major project. These skills are not the same qualities it takes to decide whether a school should be built, for example, or what it should teach the students. These matters belong in the public domain. But if government bodies specified them, IBM might be an excellent 'facilities management' or 'turnkey' contractor to oversee the building of the school, the detailed development of the curriculum, the recruiting and training of the teachers, and even the day-to-day management of the resulting institution.

If I have been pessimistic about the ability of the men in Armonk to pay attention to the internal needs, I am optimistic about their ability to respond to external demands. Civil servants, legislators, citizens, shareholders, supra-national bodies, academics and the press should keep the heat on IBM, so it will do for society what it also needs to be doing for itself.

It is important to emphasize that this exploration of IBM's history, strengths, successes and problems pertains only to a single corporation. Compared to most large companies IBM is superb in every respect — including the ability to respond to internal needs. I simply hope external attention will help to amplify them. Most important, I know of no other company that has the unique strength of IBM's Basic Beliefs, which are still reverently observed.

One of IBM's secrets of success was the wall between Domestic and World Trade. That wall has almost evaporated as the Watson brothers have left their respective halves of the company. What IBM needs now is some new walls, lots of them, low ones, breaking up the increasingly monolithic company into the small, exciting, manageable units that gave it early strength. Given the power of the IBM culture, its people could then turn more of their energies to young ideas and goals that matched the ideas and goals of society today.

Appendix:
The financial
pictures

'IBM's secret of success is semi-log paper,' said one of the graduates when he was discussing IBM's financial performance. This is the kind of graph paper marked out by tens, then hundreds, then thousands or millions. IBM's smooth lines of the financial graphs sometimes do get unmanageable without it, especially if one begins at the beginning and attempts to plot the growth of the company since the Old Man took over in 1914. Separating the Domestic and World Trade results, though, puts some of the bumps back into the graphs; on semi-log paper it is much easier to see a flattening of the curve or a downturn. The charts, notably figures 1 and 2 which describe IBM's revenue and profit histories, show several things about IBM. First, the speed with which downturns are met, recognized, and reacted to; second, that the time of sharpest growth came *after* the Old Man's two sons had taken over the company's two halves.

IBM's growth patterns have become classic in business circles. In any industry, a company doubling its revenues or profits every three or four years tends to say: 'Look, we are growing as fast as IBM! In seven more years . . .' Although this rate of growth is easier the smaller a firm is, this leaves the impression that the unique product or service will do for that company's shareholders what IBM has done — Today Widgets, Tomorrow the World.

The semi-log paper graphs give a clear picture of the 'maturing' process. Figures 1 and 2 show a downturn during the war years, when the Old Man imposed limits on IBM's profits as well as his own. The only other dip occurred in Domestic from 1969 to 1971 during the economic recession — another sign of a maturing market. The graphs give substance to the idea that Dick, who set the patterns for the less organized little international company, actually created the blueprint for IBM's continued success in the later years of this century.

The intriguing thing these figures reveal, when one splits the OP activity from Domestic DP, is that World Trade surpassed Domestic DP in revenue as well as profits in 1972. IBM would prefer to play down this aspect of the change. For several years preceding the crossover, although World Trade brought in more of the profit than Domestic, Domestic people had been able to retort that their overseas brethren had certain benefits in delayed product cycles, with easier 'learning curves' and thus a 'free ride' on some of the R&D costs for IBM products. The projections for 1976, showing Domestic DP around $600 million profit while World Trade soars up to $1,065 million, make it quite clear IBM knows that its future lies overseas.

The numbers are necessarily sketchy, but the picture is clear. IBM publishes as little information as possible, and in a form that does *not* encourage comparison between the two 'halves' of the company. Although competition between the two halves is still an important factor in the motivation of IBM people, this is truly one of the company's 'secrets' of success.

Figure 3 explains why IBM can continue to show a relatively steady overall growth line, even though its largest group suffered such severe ups and downs since 1968. The number of employees is clearly dropping — still — and the employment chart *never* followed the steeper ups and downs on the revenue or profits graphs. This smoother line is also an expression of IBM's 'full employment' policy; in times of growth, IBM people simply work harder.

One of the questions many people have about multinational corporations is how they move money around. Figure 4, a summary of IBM's long-term debt, gives some indications. World Trade was a relatively insignificant portion until the mid-sixties, when debt went up to match the build-up of installations — just as Domestic's portion of the debt was dropping and more of the growth was being financed from within. Domestic's interest rate dropped too; it ran around 3·8 percent in the late fifties, but has held steady at 3·5 percent since Tom paid off a large debt in 1964 to the Prudential Insurance Company of America.

World Trade's loans (and interest rates) continued to rise steadily until 1972, when the company negotiated a $300 million medium-term Eurodollar loan in Japan and was able to pay off $91 million owing in German marks, which were rising in value compared to the dollar. The best description of IBM's borrowing activity ('the most important thing they do these days,' as one graduate said) comes from a demure little list in the 1972 annual report:

Table 1   Long-term debt

Currency	31 Dec. 1973	31 Dec. 1972	31 Dec. 1971
US dollars, due 1974 to 1987	$364,266,640	$393,595,782	$179,020,589
French francs, due 1974 to 1991	65,785,065	88,256,849	73,547,311
Swiss francs, due 1974	—	66,814,198	83,319,218
Canadian dollars, due 1974 to 1991	22,504,000	24,258,351	31,774,236
Netherlands guilders, due 1974 to 1981	17,617,174	17,771,685	17,919,003
German marks	—	—	91,690,478
Belgian francs, due 1975 to 1983	19,001,500	1,300,000	—
Other currencies, due 1974 to 1991	29,811,969	36,935,909	44,125,870
TOTAL	$518,986,348	$628,932,774	$521,396,705

In context of IBM's total cash and marketable securities on hand at the end of 1972, the total of World Trade's borrowings is pretty small, a mere $629 million, compared to $3,300 million on hand back at Armonk. One graduate pointed out that this negative gearing means IBM is going to have to increase its dividend payout even if it must eventually borrow to do so.

The remaining figures are necessarily vague, based on recent annual reports and a certain amount of educated guesstimating. Figure 5 shows the functional sources of IBM's gross revenues — Domestic and World Trade DP and OP results, plus US military work (3 percent) and interest (a surprisingly large 2 percent).

Figure 6 relates to the company's profits, which are a little easier to derive on a country-by-country basis than the revenues, recalling that almost every penny of IBM's 'export' business in any country is really incestuous transaction with sibling companies.

On the profit scale, Germany and France are almost equal, with Germany a little ahead, both hovering around the 7 percent mark. The UK share at 6 percent is much larger than its contribution to revenues. Britain has historically been World Trade's most profitable company on a percentage basis; even though ICL sometimes seems to have a larger share of the market, IBM UK jealously guards the more lucrative segments. Figure 6 also shows the relative shares for IBM's four future elements: Europe, Latin America, Asia/Pacific and Domestic. These are becoming more important, while World Trade headquarters takes a lower-profile posture. If the company succeeds in creating more walls but lower ones, one might expect to see some of 'Europe' put into the Asia/Pacific area, and Domestic shrinking (relatively) as Latin America continues to grow, until they are more equal 'quarters' of the company.

Figure 7 shows where all the money goes. The largest slice of the pie — about 53 percent — covers the cost of sales and operations, including the cost of leasing the almost 80 percent of IBM machines that remain the property of the manufacturer. These machines also depreciate, which explains the next-largest slice of the outgoings. World-wide taxes are only about 12 percent of revenues.

The numbers seem enormous — interest at less than 1 percent was still $80 million in 1972, and legal expenses were close to $200 million. But IBM's revenues and profits are enormous. The best way to keep this huge money-making machine in perspective is to look at the preliminary judgment against IBM in the anti-trust suit filed by Telex. Judge Christensen's 1973 fine of $352 million was more than five times Telex's entire revenues for the preceding year — yet it was less than a single quarter's profit for IBM.

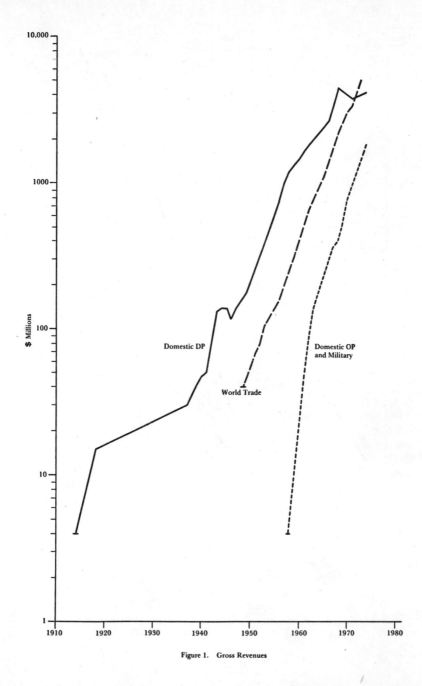

Figure 1. Gross Revenues

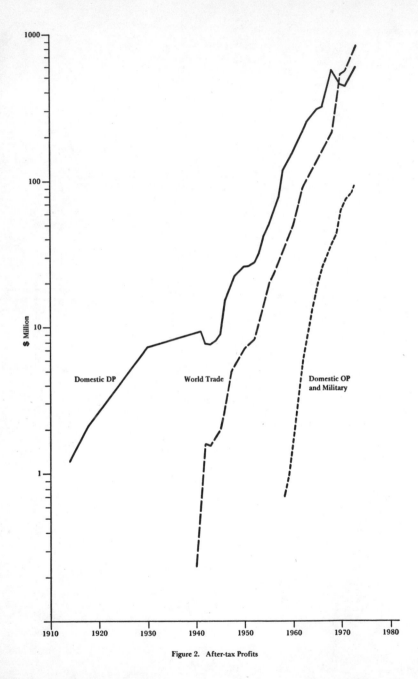

Figure 2. After-tax Profits

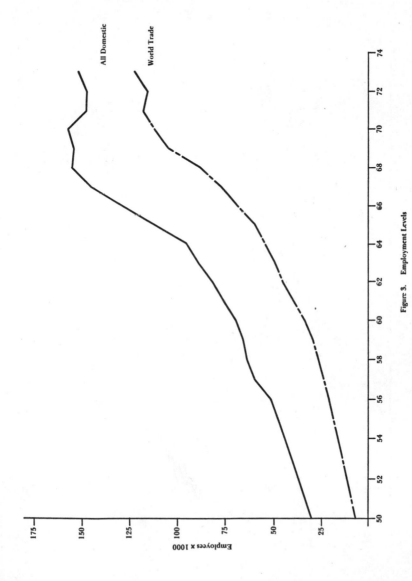

Figure 3. Employment Levels

Employees x 1000

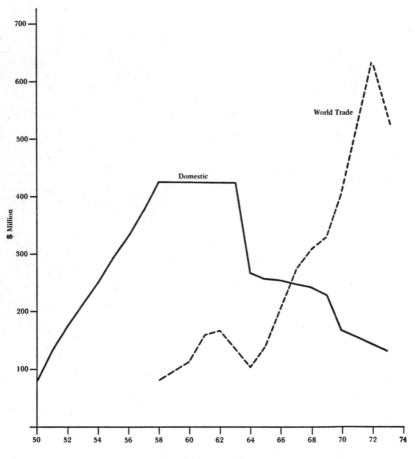

Figure 4. Long-term Debt

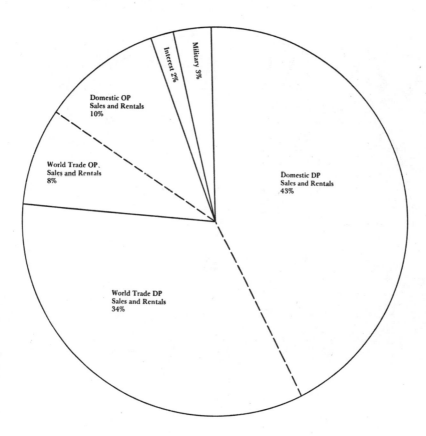

Military 3%

Interest 2%

Domestic OP
Sales and Rentals
10%

World Trade OP
Sales and Rentals
8%

Domestic DP
Sales and Rentals
43%

World Trade DP
Sales and Rentals
34%

Figure 5.   Sources of Revenue
*(Source: 1973 IBM Annual Report
and author estimates)*

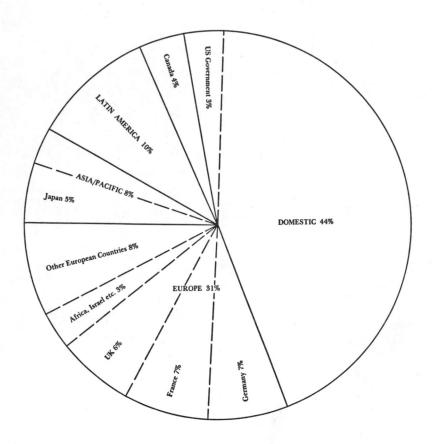

Figure 6.   Sources of IBM Profits
(Source: annual reports and author estimates)

Labels within the chart:

US Government 3%
Canada 4%
LATIN AMERICA 10%
ASIA/PACIFIC 8%
Japan 5%
Other European Countries 8%
Africa, Israel etc. 3%
UK 6%
France 7%
Germany 7%
EUROPE 31%
DOMESTIC 44%

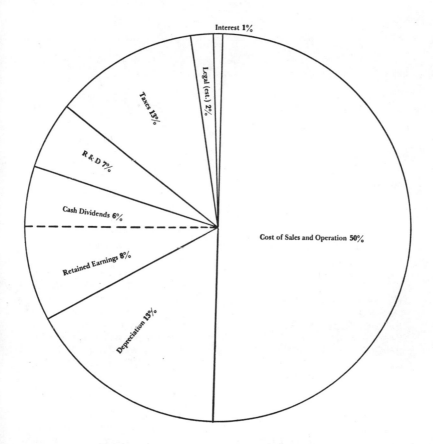

Interest 1%

Legal (est.) 2%

Taxes 13%

R & D 7%

Cash Dividends 6%

Retained Earnings 8%

Depreciation 13%

Cost of Sales and Operation 50%

Figure 7. Where the money goes
(Source: annual reports and author estimates)

Notes

Preface

1. Ways, Max, 'Business needs to do a better job of explaining itself', *Fortune*, September 1972.
2. Rodgers, William, *Think: a biography of the Watsons and IBM*, Weidenfeld & Nicholson, London, 1969.
3. Belden, Thomas and Marva, *The lengthening shadow*, Little, Brown & Company, New York, 1962.

Chapter 2

1. Belden, op. cit. Much of the factual material in this chapter about Watson's early life comes from Belden, and William Rodgers, op. cit. The interpretations of the facts are entirely my own.
2. Engelberg, Saul, *International Business Machines: a business history*, Doctoral dissertation, 1954. Available on microfilm at the New York Public Library
3. Watson, Thomas J., *Men, minutes and money*, IBM, 1934. A collection of Watson's speeches from 1915 on.
4. Watson, Thomas J. Jr., *A business and its Beliefs: the ideas that helped build IBM*, McGraw-Hill, New York, 1963.
5. Connolly, James, *History of computing in Europe*, published (then restricted) by IBM World Trade Corp., 1967. This book furnished many of the details of the war years. It also includes an excellent chronology of European computing events (with a strong IBM flavour) from the early tab. machine days through 1967.
6. Engelberg, op. cit.
7. Watson, Sr., op. cit.
8. Watson, Jr., op. cit.
9. Watson, Jr., op. cit.

10. Sheehan, Robert, 'Q. What grows faster than IBM? A. IBM abroad', *Fortune*, November 1960.

Chapter 4
1. Watson, Jr., op. cit.
2. Watson, Jr., op. cit.
3. Beman, Lewis, 'IBM's travails in Lilliput', *Fortune*, November 1973.
4. Maisonrouge interview with Angeline Pantages, August 1972.
5. Watson, Jr., op. cit.
6. Smid, Allan M., 'Blaricum: training tomorrow's top management', *Think International*, January/February 1972.
7. 'How IBM World Trade gives foreign students a fresh perspective on US business', *Business Abroad*, 2 October 1967.

Chapter 5
1. Foy, Nancy, 'A blow at the factory automaton', *The Times*, London, 5 March 1973. I am grateful to Richard Spiegelberg, Management Editor, for permission to use some of that material in this chapter.
2. Sirota, David and Alan D. Wolfson, 'Job enrichment: what are the obstacles?', *Personnel*, May/June 1972.

Chapter 6
1. Vincendon, Daniel, 'A mini-think-tank in World Trade', *Computing*, 29 March 1973.
2. Foy, Nancy, 'Human beings make better computers', *New Scientist*, 14 June 1973. I am indebted to Deputy Editor Nick Valery for permission to

use material from that article in this chapter.
3. Wise, T. A., 'IBM's $5,000,000,000 gamble', *Fortune*, September and October 1966.

Chapter 7
1. Watson, Jr., op. cit.
2. Gellerman, Saul, 'Passivity, paranoia, and "Pakikisama" ', *Columbia Journal of World Business*, September/October 1967.
3. Pantages, Angeline, 'IBM abroad', *Datamation*, December 1972.
4. Hinrichs, J. R., 'What employees are thinking', *Dialogue-3*, IBM World Trade Corp., July 1973.
5. Watson, Jr., op. cit.
6. Sirota, David and J. Michael Greenwood, 'Understanding your overseas work force', *Harvard Business Review*, January/February 1971.

Sirota, David and Diana Coryell, 'Letting the first-line manager know where he stands', *Personnel Administration*, May/June 1972.

Sirota, David and Alan D. Wolfson, 'Work measurement and worker morale', *Business Horizons*, August 1972.

Hofstede, Geert H., 'The colors of collars — are all workers alike?', *Columbia Journal of World Business*, September/October 1972.

Sadler, P. J., and Geert H. Hofstede, 'Leadership styles — preferences and perceptions of employees of an international company in different countries', *Mens en Ondernemig* (Leiden, Holland), January 1972.

212

7. Sirota, David and J. Michael Greenwood, op. cit.
8. Hofstede, Geert H., op. cit.
9. Hofstede, Geert H., 'Employee surveys, a tool for participation', *European Business*, Autumn 1973.
10. Hinrichs, J. R., op. cit.

Chapter 8
1. Watson, Jr., op. cit.
2. Whittemore, Hank, 'IBM's low profile in Westchester county', *New York*, May 1972.
3. 'Assignment international', *Dialogue-3*, IBM World Trade Corp., July 1973.
4. Bennis, Warren and Philip Slater, *The temporary society*, Harper & Row, New York, 1968.
5. McGrath, R. W., *IBM alumni directory*, compiled and published quarterly by R. W. McGrath & Associates, 7034 Dartbrook Drive, Dallas, Texas 75240.

Chapter 9
1. Sampson, Anthony, *Sovereign state: secret history of ITT*, Hodder, London, 1973.

2. 'Look ahead', *Datamation*, May 1972.
3. 'The Russians were here', *Think International*, May/June 1972.
4. Maisonrouge/Pantages interview, op. cit.
5. Jay, Anthony, *Corporation man*, Jonathan Cape, 1972.

Drucker, Peter, *Management*, Heinemann, 1974.
6. 'IBM employee group seemingly headless', *Datamation*, May 1972.
7. Rodgers, William, op. cit.
8. These papers from the Telex trial have been copied and indexed by the Computer Industry Association, Encino, California.

Chapter 10
1. Watson, Jr., op. cit.
2. IBM papers from the Telex trial, op. cit.
3. 'A conversation with the president', *Dialogue-1*, IBM World Trade Corp., January 1973.
4. Warren, George, 'What is IBM going to do with its "trapped riches"?', *Computerworld*, 8 August 1973.
5. Bennis, Warren, 'How to survive in a revolution', *Innovation two*, June 1969.

Index